FINAL CURTAIN

THE LAST GILBERT AND SULLIVAN OPERAS

John Wolfson

FINAL CURTAIN

THE LAST GILBERT AND SULLIVAN OPERAS

*Including the unpublished
rehearsal librettos and twenty
unpublished Gilbert lyrics*

CHAPPELL & COMPANY

in Association with

ANDRÉ DEUTSCH

Chappell & Company Limited
50 New Bond Street, London W1A 2BR

London Amsterdam Brussels Hamburg
Johannesburg Madrid Milan Paris
Stockholm Sydney Toronto Wellington
Zurich New York

First published 1976
© John Wolfson 1976

Set in Monotype Walbaum

Printed in Great Britain by
William Clowes & Sons, Limited
London, Beccles and Colchester

ISBN 0 903443 12 0

For Reginald Allen

Contents

List of Illustrations

Foreword

In the 80s Gilbert and Sullivan couldn't do anything wrong. In the 90s they couldn't do anything right.

From 1875 to 1889 they wrote eleven operas, all of which have remained in the popular repertoire. Between 1891 and 1896 they wrote two more operas, *Utopia, Limited* and *The Grand Duke*, neither of which has achieved lasting popularity.

When Gilbert first read the story of *Utopia, Limited* to Sullivan on the Riviera in January of 1893, Sullivan declared it to be the best plot that Gilbert had ever done! When Gilbert read him the outline of *The Grand Duke* in London in August, 1895, Sullivan wrote a few days later, 'I . . . like it even more than when I heard it first on Thursday. It comes out as clear and as bright as possible.' If Gilbert and Sullivan both had a high regard for these operas when they started to work on them, something must have gone very wrong during their production to account for their initial failure. Gilbert and Sullivan's judgement had never been so wrong before.

The difficulty was that both *Utopia, Limited* and *The Grand Duke* were written in the aftermath of the famous *carpet quarrel* of 1890. After Gilbert and Sullivan had faced each other in the law courts, it was very difficult for them to face each other in the theatre. Once Gilbert became convinced that Sullivan had wanted to dispense with his services as a librettist during their quarrels, it became impossible for him to tell the composer any of the things that were bothering him about their ongoing relationship. And when Gilbert was no longer able to tell Sullivan *to his face* what was bothering him, he attempted to tell him *in his librettos* – in the librettos specifically of *Utopia, Limited* and *The Grand Duke*!

Gilbert filled these two operas with a new 'dark humour' not understood in its day, not known in any of his previous works, and borne out of the librettist's long years of frustration in his dealings with Sullivan, D'Oyly Carte and the British system of monarchy.

Utopia, Limited and *The Grand Duke* are both political satires – as of course are *Iolanthe* and *The Gondoliers*. But Gilbert's late librettos abound with a bitterness and cynicism which his audiences at the Savoy were quite unprepared for in 1893. Gilbert had taught his audience over the years how to laugh at the foibles of their society. But he had not taught them to squirm uncomfortably as much of his new dark humour required them to do.

The London audiences of the 90s were not interested in this new aspect of Gilbert's wit, and they refused to accept it. The last two Gilbert and Sullivan operas failed to amuse them. They stopped buying tickets; and the operas closed so quickly that subsequent generations have relegated them to an obscurity which they do not deserve.

The two final Gilbert and Sullivan operas are far more interesting today when looked at with some knowledge of the intimate circumstances surrounding their composition, for the story of *Utopia, Limited* and *The Grand Duke* is the story of the Gilbert and Sullivan collaboration in its final phase, in the 1890s, in the years when the partnership wasn't working.

Failure was not an easy thing for Gilbert and Sullivan to achieve, for once having gained the public's support for their works, it required a very determined effort by both of them to lose it. The history of the great collaborators' closing years together has a universality that seems to attach itself to all great men, institutions and even nations which, having once achieved greatness, enter upon a period of decline. The story of how the Savoy partnership declined is told in the chapters that follow.

Acknowledgements

THE material in this book derives from no less than five major archives of Gilbert and Sullivan history. To these famous collections and to their respective owners and curators, I am deeply indebted and grateful.

I would like to thank Dame Bridget D'Oyly Carte for permission to consult the cutting books of her famous grandfather, in which all of the contemporary press accounts of the Gilbert and Sullivan partnership are preserved.

I am further indebted to Frederic Lloyd of the D'Oyly Carte Opera Trust for his interest in my little project, and to Albert Truelove for his constant attention while I was in London.

One of the most comprehensive repositories of Gilbert and Sullivan material is located at the Pierpont Morgan Library in New York City. To this collection I am indebted for the use of early editions of librettos, further press cuttings, and contemporary letters. I am most grateful to its wise and able curator, Mr Reginald Allen for his continued advice and assistance.

Gilbert's papers have been deposited at the British Library. Illustrations from the Gilbert Papers and from the Lord Chamberlain's collection are reproduced by permission of the British Library Board.

Grateful thanks are extended to the Royal General Theatrical Fund Association, as owner of the subsisting copyright in Sir William S. Gilbert's unpublished writings, for permission to publish in this book writings still in copyright.

I am personally grateful to Colin Prestige, Trustee for the Royal General Theatrical Fund, for his kindness in reading an early draft of this book and his assistance in the elimination of a great number of errors.

Sir Arthur Sullivan's personal diaries are owned by the Beinecke Rare Book and Manuscript Library at Yale University. Passages which have been included from the Sullivan diaries have been quoted by permission of the Beinecke Library. I am indebted to Dr Herman W. Liebert who first granted me permission to read the diaries several years ago, and to Miss Marjorie Wynne who has given me permission to quote from them.

The earliest known printed texts of *Utopia, Limited* and *The Grand Duke* are the Copyright Deposit copies now located at the Library of Congress, Washington, D.C. I am grateful to Mr William C. Lichtenwanger who made these librettos available to me some time ago.

All drawings and cartoons from contemporary newspapers and periodicals were provided by the Newspaper Library (Colindale) of the British Library.

Finally, in the complex and frequently baffling process of accumulating the diverse materials reproduced in the pages that follow, I must acknowledge gratitude to Mr I. de Keyser, my oldest friend in London, for his wisdom, insight, humour, patience, and letters.

PART ONE

The Writing of *Utopia, Limited* and *The Grand Duke*

1

The Carpet Quarrel

THE story of *Utopia, Limited*, which opened at the Savoy Theatre in 1893, really began ten years earlier.

Sullivan had been trying to free himself from the confines of the Savoy for a long time. He had first expressed the desire to leave the world of comic opera after the opening of *Patience* in 1881. He claimed that he wanted to write serious music, specifically grand opera, and oratorio. But year after year, opera after opera, Gilbert and Carte had managed to lure him back to the less glamorous reaches of the Savoy – each time only increasing his determination to break away.

In 1888, after the opening of *The Yeomen of the Guard*, the 'five-year agreement', by which Gilbert and Sullivan had bound themselves to write and produce a comic opera for the Savoy on six months' notice, finally expired. Sullivan refused to renew it, and Carte realized that he no longer had any control over his composer.

Sullivan was now determined to write grand opera. He could not be talked out of it. And Carte finally, in order not to lose his connection with Sullivan altogether, agreed to produce Sullivan's opera as soon as it was written. Carte was building a large new theatre in Shaftesbury Avenue that would be ready in a year or so. He would finish it as an opera house and Sullivan's masterpiece could open there. Only one condition would attach itself to Sullivan under this arrangement: he would have to agree to write *one more* opera for the Savoy. The result of this fateful agreement was *The Gondoliers* which opened in December of 1889.

After this, Sullivan and Carte turned all of their energies to their production of the grand opera, *Ivanhoe*. That was when the trouble began.

Gilbert, Sullivan and Carte had been equal partners in the management of the Savoy Theatre. Gilbert had no objections to Sullivan and Carte producing an opera without him. What concerned Gilbert was the fact that his partners' new project might prejudice their responsibility to the Savoy. And Gilbert's instinct proved to be correct.

After the opening of *The Gondoliers*, Gilbert went to India for a long holiday. When he returned to London, he received his first royalty cheque from the Savoy. This was payable the first week in April. *The Gondoliers* had been playing to very good houses for three months and Gilbert thought the amount of his cheque was unusually low. He demanded to see the account books. When Carte produced them, Gilbert challenged many of the expenditures which had been charged against his royalties. Carte justified the expenses by saying that all money spent on the production of *The Gondoliers* had been spent at Gilbert's insistence – an explanation which only heightened Gilbert's anger.

What annoyed Gilbert most, of course, was the expenditure of £140 for a carpet for the theatre lobby. Carte had charged it against the three partners' profits. Gilbert thought that it should have been paid for out of Carte's operating allowance. Gilbert was furious.

He and Carte had quarrelled before, but never at a time when Carte had Sullivan firmly under his control – as he did now that he was building him an opera house.

Gilbert enlisted Sullivan's aid, but as Carte was about to produce his grand opera, Sullivan was forced to take a position *against* Gilbert, whether he wanted to or not.

Gilbert understood how the sides were shaping up. Beneath his bellicose exterior Gilbert was a deeply sensitive human being, and friendships and loyalties were extremely important to him. He felt that he was being cast aside by his former associates. He confessed to his friend and fellow playwright, Brandon Thomas, that he believed Sullivan and Carte, having joined forces to produce a grand opera, had made their decision to work without him, and had purposely taken sides against him in the carpet quarrel in the hope that he would pull out of the Savoy partnership voluntarily. This is what hurt Gilbert most of all. It was a deep hurt, and not one which would be easily forgotten.

Gilbert was in no position to accuse Sullivan and Carte of trying to harass him out of the Savoy Theatre. But he was in a position to prove that the posture which his two partners had taken with regard to the royalty statements was wrong. Gilbert insisted on a re-rendering of the accounts, and Carte (with Sullivan firmly in his control) refused to co-operate.

Carte said that if Gilbert were dissatisfied with the way things stood he could take his work elsewhere.

Gilbert replied that if *that* was the way things stood he would write no more for the Savoy.

Carte accepted Gilbert's ultimatum, confirming Gilbert's fears that his partners wanted to be done with him.

Gilbert thereupon withdrew the right from Carte to produce any of his operas in London. After the closing of *The Gondoliers* there would be no more Gilbert and Sullivan at the Savoy.*

Carte's reply to this was to withhold £2000 from Gilbert's royalty cheque in July. Relations were going from bad to worse.

Gilbert appealed to Sullivan, but Sullivan, by virtue of his forthcoming production of his new grand opera, was forced to side with Carte on the question of royalties. Carte claimed to have 'legal justification' for withholding them.

Gilbert had no choice but to take Carte to court to recover his impounded royalties. Gilbert was a barrister-at-law and used his legal knowledge for forty years almost exclusively in his own behalf.

When the newspapers learned that Gilbert was suing Sullivan and Carte in court, there was no end of publicity, and none of it was good. Victorian England was not pleased to learn that its idols were airing their dirty linen in public.

If Gilbert had been deeply hurt before at the thought that his old partners were ganging up on him, Sullivan and Carte were just as hurt now that Gilbert had chosen to give such public voice to what was, after all, a very private quarrel. To make matters worse, Carte and Sullivan were, at that precise moment, trying to characterize themselves as artistic philanthropists in the launching of the Royal English Opera. They therefore found the lawsuit doubly embarrassing. But they had in fact brought the quarrel with Gilbert upon themselves, and with it, all the attendant publicity which their outspoken librettist attracted whenever he spoke out.

On 3 September 1890, *Gilbert* v. *Carte and Sullivan* was argued

* The provincial rights to the operas had all been leased to Carte for five years and Gilbert could not withhold them.

before Mr Justice Lawrence. It was an open and shut case and discharged summarily in favour of Gilbert. Gilbert may have won his suit but he had lost his friends. When he wrote to Mrs Carte a few days later to propose a reconciliation, Sullivan and Mr Carte were much too shaken by their recent humiliation in the law courts to want to sit down with him and shake hands.

When *Ivanhoe* opened in January of 1891, however, Sullivan, by way of peace-making, offered Gilbert a pair of stalls. Gilbert knew that his presence in Sullivan's opera house on the opening night would be a signal to the public that the great quarrel between them had ended; and Gilbert wanted desperately to go.

Unfortunately, by this time, Gilbert, whose perfect memory and meticulous legal mind got him in trouble all his life, had had the chance to go over the transcripts to *Gilbert* v. *Carte and Sullivan*. He took great offence that Sullivan, in his affidavit, had testified that Carte had impounded Gilbert's royalties *as a reserve against an 'outstanding' lawsuit* which had been brought against the partnership by Lillian Russell in 1884* and disposed of later that year. The lawsuit was not *outstanding* at all – and Sullivan most certainly should have known that at the time that he made his affidavit.

Gilbert could not bear the thought that his old friend Sullivan had purposely given false evidence against him in court, and he asked Sullivan to admit that he had *not knowingly lied* on the affidavit, but rather had testified *on the basis of incorrect information supplied to him by Carte*. It was a fine point that Gilbert wanted conceded, but it was important enough to make the difference between Gilbert's being able or unable to forgive Sullivan. Gilbert was scrupulously honest in his dealings with others, and expected others to be so with him.

Sullivan, however, refused to give Gilbert the satisfaction he required.

Gilbert did not go to the opening of *Ivanhoe*.

The bitterness between him and Sullivan persisted.

And when *The Gondoliers* closed in June of 1891, no Gilbert and Sullivan work, old or new, replaced it. Gilbert continued to withhold from Carte the right to produce his old operas at the Savoy. And as to his new operas, well, there were not to be any for a while.

* Lillian Russell was to have starred in *Princess Ida*. When Gilbert 'released' her from her contract for missing a rehearsal she sued.

During the spring of 1891 both Gilbert and Sullivan were in London. Neither of them was working on a production. And neither of them tried to contact the other.

A year later Gilbert would say that he had been ready to collaborate on a new opera, and that he was waiting for Sullivan to call him. A year later Sullivan would claim that he too was ready to collaborate on a new opera and had been waiting for Gilbert to call him.

But two more years were to go by before the two partners would work together again.

In the meantime *Ivanhoe* closed after playing a little over four months. It was a long run for an opera, but a short run for an opera house. Both had failed. Carte had lost a fortune. Sullivan had lost his dream, his reputation, his relationship with Gilbert, and in the following year he was to lose his health. For the summer he went to the spas in Switzerland.

In his absence Gilbert arranged to produce a new opera, *The Mountebanks*, at another theatre with another composer. Sullivan had already read the story of *The Mountebanks* and had refused to collaborate on it – so eventually Gilbert would have *had* to give it to another composer. In his own way Gilbert was still waiting for Sullivan.

When Sullivan returned to London in the autumn of 1891, Tom Chappell, the music publisher, tried to effect a reconciliation between him and Gilbert. As Chappell published the scores and librettos to the Gilbert and Sullivan operas, he was losing as much as anyone when Gilbert and Sullivan were not working together.

Once Chappell had entered the picture as mediator, it took him only two weeks to bring about a reconciliation. The two men had been in fact most anxious to work together – but once more pride intervened. It was now October 1891. Gilbert was about to open *The Mountebanks*, his new opera, *without* Sullivan. He would be available to begin work *with* Sullivan in January of 1892.

But Sullivan felt that if Gilbert was doing an opera without him, *he* had to do one without Gilbert – *Ivanhoe* apparently didn't count. Sullivan said that he would write his *next* opera with Gilbert. Shortly *after* that message was delivered, Sullivan agreed to set a libretto by Sydney Grundy called *Haddon Hall* for the Savoy.

Haddon Hall should have opened in the spring of 1892 – with a new opera by Gilbert and Sullivan to follow – but it didn't. It was postponed until the autumn of 1892, because Sullivan finally had his long-feared physical collapse, the result of the overwork, tension, and failure of *Ivanhoe* the year before.

Sullivan's incapacity lasted fully six months. He was very ill. At one point he was not expected to live. When he finally did recover it was only slowly, very slowly, that he began to be able to work again.

And when he did, Gilbert was still waiting for him. Gilbert's loyalty expressed itself in strange ways. And so did his animosity.

2

The Writing of
Utopia, Limited

Haddon Hall opened on 24 September 1892. The music which Sullivan composed for it was magnificent. Musically, it was the finest opera that he wrote without Gilbert. The libretto, however, was generally condemned (unjustly so) because, although it was effective in its sentimental moments, its humour was obviously inferior to Gilbert's.

Two weeks after the opening of *Haddon Hall*, Sullivan conducted the Triennial Music Festival at Leeds. When he returned to London the week following, he received a letter from Gilbert inquiring about their next opera.

There remained, however, a difficult series of negotiations which had to be concluded before the collaboration could continue. Gilbert and Sullivan and D'Oyly Carte had traditionally split the profits of the Savoy Theatre in thirds. But since the closing of *The Gondoliers*, no Gilbert and Sullivan operas had been presented there, and the traditional three-way division of the profits was no longer in effect. With the production of a new Gilbert and Sullivan opera, a new financial agreement would have to be made.

Since the quarrel of 1890 had resulted from cost accounting, Gilbert could obviously no longer agree to a one-third share of the *net* profits as in the past. He would want instead an equivalent share of the gross. Precisely *what* percentage of the gross equalled one third of the net was the matter that then fell under discussion.

Gilbert wrote Sullivan a few letters on the subject, but Sullivan wanted absolutely no part of any negotiation with Gilbert on the subject of money. One can well understand. Sullivan wisely pleaded ill-health and beat a hasty retreat to the Riviera, leaving the problems of the contract to D'Oyly Carte who spent the month of January arguing over percentages. Gilbert was asking for eleven per cent of the gross! Gilbert was also asking for a clause which stated in writing that no gags could be interpolated into the opera by the performers. Once the opera opened, the stage manager was to enforce this – with recourse to Gilbert if any performer failed to heed a reprimand. Gilbert further required to be consulted on every change of cast, with the understanding that he could object to the hiring of any player who did not please him.

How wise Sullivan had been not to have been a party to these negotiations. Instead, he preferred to wait patiently in France, having extended an invitation to Gilbert to come down and visit him *after* the contract had been settled.

I have been in hourly and anxious expectation of a telegram from you or Carte saying that all details about the new agreement were settled and that I might expect you down here at any moment. Don't misunderstand my silence. I have purposely refrained from writing until now; so that I could not by any word or phrase, accidentally used, prejudice the understanding we are striving to arrive at.*

Eventually Gilbert and Carte came to an agreement and Sullivan was delighted because, the contract having been signed, he and Gilbert were *still* on the best of terms.

You will of course come *here* and make this your home, to do exactly what you like from morning to night, and I want to feel that – the agreement being signed – there is not a single question to be discussed between us except how we shall make a brilliant opera . . .

In their entire collaboration Gilbert and Sullivan never approached a new work with a greater degree of earnestness and enthusiasm than they did *Utopia, Limited*. It had been over three years since either of them had had a success, and they both realized that in all probability neither of them would ever be successful without the other. Their new spirit of co-operation would make for great courtesy, many accommodations, and surprisingly little friction during the writing and rehearsing of *Utopia, Limited. The Mikado* and *The Yeomen of the Guard*, however, had been written during periods when the two collaborators were far less cordial to each other.

Gilbert and Carte did not finalize their agreement until the end of January. When it was settled, Gilbert set out upon his long delayed

* Letter from Sullivan, dated 7 January 1893, Pierpont Morgan Library.

visit to Sullivan for a mid-winter script conference on the Riviera.

'Long pow-wow with Gilbert about past works,' Sullivan wrote in his diary on 27 January. 'Think things can be arranged on a satisfactory basis.' After lunch, Gilbert read a sketch plot of a new libretto, which would eventually be titled *Utopia, Limited* to Sullivan and his other house-guest, Sir George Grove. 'The reading went off *most successfully*,' Gilbert wrote to his wife later that day, 'both Sullivan and Grove enthusiastic – declaring it's the best plot I've done.'*

One of Gilbert's early plot sketches for *Utopia, Limited* begins as follows:

Utopia is ruled by an Autocratic Monarch whose lightest word is absolute law. It is death to dispute his will or even to show the slightest want of alacrity in obeying it. He is supplied with immeasurable palaces sumptuously furnished, an abundance of the most beautiful pictures, jewels, wines, horses, carriages – indeed with everything that a luxurious and self-indulgent prince can possibly desire, and his privy purse is practically inexhaustible. His position, magnificent as it is, is nevertheless subject to one important drawback. Every one of his actions is closely scrutinized by two judges and on his first abuse of the despotic power with which he is entrusted, it is their duty to denounce him to the Public Exploder who thereupon has to blow him up with dynamite . . . This form of government – or Despotism tempered with Dynamite – has been found, after many experiments, to provide the most satisfactory form of Monarch – an Autocrat who dares not abuse his autocratic power.†

This plot embodies two elements common in the later Gilbert works: an increasing concern with monarchy, and a milieu that is non-English.

From *Trial by Jury* to *The Yeomen of the Guard*, eight out of ten operas take place in England. Beginning with *The Gondoliers*, Gilbert wrote five operas in a row that take place elsewhere.

The Gondoliers	Venice, Barataria
The Mountebanks	Sicily
Utopia, Limited	'Utopia' (Polynesia)
His Excellency	Denmark
The Grand Duke	Germany

From *Trial by Jury* to *The Yeomen of the Guard* only one opera, *The Mikado*, deals with a head of state. Of the five operas listed above,

* Pearson, p. 169.
† Pierpont Morgan Library.

heads of state appear in four of them. (The one exception, *The Mountebanks*, is based on a plot which Gilbert had developed ten years earlier.)

The Gondoliers	Luiz, King of Barataria
Utopia, Limited	Paramount I, King of Utopia
His Excellency	The Prince Regent of Elsinore
The Grand Duke	Rudolph, Grand Duke of Pfennig Halbpfennig

Gilbert had always been a satirist first and foremost and his earlier operas had abounded with social criticism. And while he (skilfully aided by Sullivan) was able to poke fun at institutions as austere as the British Navy and the House of Peers, the spirit of his satire in the 80s had never been cynical, sardonic or cruel, as it was to become in some of his later pieces. In the 80s in fact, whenever a Gilbert lyric appeared to be controversial, it was tactfully eliminated from the opera, either before the opening, or during the first week of its run. There are numerous examples of lyrics in *The Pirates of Penzance*, *Iolanthe* and *Ruddigore* which Gilbert decided were too racy to be performed.

The 'Hymn to the Nobility' from *The Pirates of Penzance* was only performed once, in the performance given at Paignton, Devonshire, on 30 December 1879, to secure the English copyright. Gilbert and Sullivan were rehearsing the opera in America at the time and word had not reached the English company that the 'hymn' had been cut.

'HYMN TO THE NOBILITY'

Let foreigners look down with scorn
On legislators heaven born.
We know what limpid wisdom runs
From Peers and all their eldest Sons:
Enrapt the true born Briton hears
The wisdom of his House of Peers.

And if a noble lord should die
And leave no nearer progeny,
His twentieth cousin takes his place
And legislates with equal grace.

12

But should a Son or heir survive
Or other nearer relative,
Then twentieth cousins get you hence,
You're persons of no consequence.
When issue male their chances bar
How paltry twentieth cousins are.

How doubly blest that glorious land
Where rank and brains go hand in hand;
Where wisdom pure and virtue hale
Obey the law of strict entail.
No harm can touch a country when
It's ruled by British Noblemen.

The theme of incompetence in high places – especially when resulting from inherited wealth and titles – recurred in many Gilbert works and always brought strong words from his pen. Two songs on the same subject, 'De Belleville' from *Iolanthe*, and 'Henceforth All the Crimes' from *Ruddigore* were actually performed at the Savoy, but eliminated shortly after opening.

Less well-known examples of Gilbert lyrics, which due to their political overtones were *never* sung in performance, include the first 'Sentry Song'* from *Iolanthe*:

'SLEEP ON'

Fear no unlicensed entry,
  Heed no bombastic talk,
While guards the British Sentry
  Pall Mall and Birdcage Walk.
Let European thunders
  Occasion no alarms,
Though diplomatic blunders
  May cause a cry 'To arms!'
   Sleep on, ye pale civilians;
    All thunder-clouds defy:
   On Europe's countless millions
    The Sentry keeps his eye!

Should foreign-born rapscallions
  In London dare to show
Their overgrown battalions,
  Be sure I'll let you know.

* This lyric was published by Gilbert in *Songs of a Savoyard* in 1891.

Should Russians or Norwegians
Pollute our favoured clime
With rough barbaric legions,
I'll mention it in time.
So sleep in peace, civilians,
The Continent defy;
While on its countless millions
The Sentry keeps his eye!

and the Duke's Song from *Patience*:

Though men of rank may useless seem,
They do good in their generation.
They make the wealthy upstart team
With Christian love and self negation.
The bitterest tongue that ever lashed
Man's folly drops with milk and honey,
While Scandal hides her head, abashed,
Brought face to face with Rank and Money!
Yes, Scandal hides her head, abashed,
Brought face to face with Rank and Money!

Society forgets her laws,
And Prudery her affectation,
While Mrs Grundy pleads our cause,
And talks 'wild oats' and toleration;
Archbishops wink at what they think
A downright crime in common shoddy,
Although archbishops shouldn't wink
At anything or anybody,
A good archbishop wouldn't wink
At anything or anybody.

During the 80s then, the bitterest verses from Gilbert's satiric pen became 'cancelled passages' usually during the rehearsal period. During the 90s, however, as will be shown, Gilbert's bitter sentiments and political criticisms formed the central core of his operas – at least the operas that he wrote with Sullivan.

Gilbert wrote four original librettos in the 90s. Two of them, *The Mountebanks* and *His Excellency* were innocuous enough. They were set to music by Alfred Cellier and Osmond Carr. But his other two librettos, *Utopia, Limited* and *The Grand Duke*, abounded with political overtones, undertones, innuendos and frontal attacks upon the English monarchy, Parliament, and the upper classes. It was these librettos that Gilbert gave to Sullivan to set. Given the relationship that existed between the two men in the 90s, the fact that Sullivan was given the 'controversial' librettos can hardly be ascribed to coincidence.

Gilbert's great concern with the excesses of monarchy began to appear in *The Gondoliers*. In songs like 'A Regular Royal Queen' and 'Rising Early in the Morning', the satire is fairly gentle, although the message is clear. Gilbert wrote one not so gentle lyric for *The Gondoliers*, a number curiously entitled the 'Growling Chorus of Gondolieri':

> Republicans we
> And we do not agree
> That under a monarch a man can be free.
> We grunt and we groan
> At the thought of a throne
> We prefer to be free with a will of our own. *

Wisely, it was decided to eliminate it before the opera opened. By the time Gilbert got to *Utopia, Limited* his feelings towards royalty had not changed a bit, and he was somewhat more inclined to express them. In an early draft of his libretto Gilbert wrote his verse to be sung by King Paramount upon his first entrance:

> Why should Royalty be stately?
> King and people widely parted?
> Why should I, jocose innately
> Seem reserved and strong hearted?
>
> Life is what you please to make it.
> Happy all who best employ it.
> Sad are they who wisely take it —
> Let's be foolish and enjoy it.†

These lines could easily have been inspired by Queen Victoria who was indeed 'widely parted' from her people and who, since the death

---

* In British Library MS 49298.
† In British Library MS 49300.

15

of Prince Albert thirty years earlier, had been 'reserved and strong hearted' to say the least.

Another set of verses, also for King Paramount, which Gilbert cancelled before the opera opened, ran as follows:

> Oh, I'm a kind of a King –
>   A sort of a Despot bold –
> An utterly insignificant thing
>   Who does whatever he's told –
> Oh, cruel is my lot,
>   My fate unkind I call –
> For I'm a Kingly Never Mind what –
>   A Royal Nothing at All!*

There is something self-indulgent in these lines. King Paramount is in fact completely controlled by his two ministers Scaphio and Phantis, and can do nothing without their approval; the King's power is only titular. Queen Victoria, while not as self-effacing as King Paramount, was the constitutional head of state; the real power of the government, however, lay with her Prime Minister, such as Gladstone or Disraeli.

A bit of unused dialogue, appearing early in Gilbert's plot-book for *Utopia, Limited*, proves that he definitely had Europe in mind when he placed his satire on monarchy in the South Seas:

SCA.   I want to buy a quantity of government stock.
K.   Well? What am I to do?
SCA.   Declare a war, of course, with your nephew, the Emperor of Samoli. Withdraw your ambassador at once and place your army on a War footing. The thing's obvious.†

'Declare a war, of course, with your nephew, the Emperor of Samoli . . .' Most of the royal families of Europe were interrelated, especially Queen Victoria's. And recent wars had been fought on the Continent (Franco-German) because a king's first minister (Bismarck) had urged them. Gilbert's satire was leading him in a very serious direction.

---

* See p. 145
† In British Library, MS 49289.

Opening Chorus - Gibberish

Enter Official - perhaps Tarara

Expostulation. Utopian forbidden at Court - English only permitted. The King who desire to model Utopia on England, he has sent his oldest daughter to be educated at Girton from which she is to bring the elements which have made England what she is & in the mean time, as a preliminary step, English is the only language permitted at Court. Song. Theres a little &c.

Enter King. Two younger daughters & duenna. King explains about his younger daughters (song) Duenna shows them off. Enter Messenger. Who is this President of this Republic King explains - (song) Messenger has come to say that his eldest daughter, the Princess Zara is on her way & will soon arrive, having completed her education in England & is bringing with her samples of the Flowers of England, Progress. Joy of everybody. Hymn to England. General all to prepare for reception of Princess. Manent King Scaphio & Phantis.

Scene between them in which their power over him & his miserable position are shown. Grand S. & P. To King enter Duenna & Scene between them in which his love for her & her scathing rejection on account of scandalous paragraphs are shown.

Re-enter Court heralding arrival of Zara from England with her Suite.

A page from Gilbert's plot-book of Utopia, Limited. (*British Library.*)

As a writer, Gilbert developed his librettos in a very craftsman-like manner. His procedure seldom varied. First, over a long period of time he would record his ideas and impressions for characters, incidents, and subjects for satire in a 'plot-book'. Over and over ideas, trial scenes, and outlines would be written down, developed and discarded until something like the librettos as we know them began to take final shape.

Then he would write a complete plot outline (with some musical numbers indicated) and at this point stop and wait for the acceptance of Sullivan (or another composer) before developing the libretto further. The next step would be the writing of the indicated lyrics which he would send to his composer as they were completed. The final step was always filling in the dialogue.

Fortunately, Gilbert's plot-books for *Utopia, Limited* and *The Grand Duke* survive, and they can give us a very clear idea of what the librettist's intent was when he *began* to outline these operas.

Gilbert's very first plot sketch for *Utopia, Limited* leaves no doubt that his original intent was a comic opera satire on monarchy:

THE HAPPY VALLEY

The constitution of the land is as follows:

It is governed by an autocratic monarch – whose acts are supervised by a council of Two Sage Men. It is their duty to keep a close watch upon the King's doings. He is permitted two lapses from virtue and propriety, but at the third he is required to permit himself to be blown up with dynamite by the Public Exploder who succeeds him (as a compensation for his unpleasant duties) and is subject to the same restrictions and penalties as his predecessor. Another Public Exploder is selected who succeeds in due course to the throne. The principle of the monarchy is 'Despotism tempered by Dynamite.'*

Corruption in government was to be a major theme in the new opera:

Scaphio and Phantis, the two wise men who are the official censors of the King's conduct, are supposed to be blameless ministers – but they are in fact very deep and unscrupulous schemers. Scaphio is deeply committed to shady speculation on the stock exchange. Phantis is the unacknowledged proprietor of a scandalous Society Paper. These two speculators have entered into a secret agreement with the King that so long as he lends himself to their infamous requirements, so long will they report him blameless . . .

* This and the subsequent excerpts from Gilbert's plot-book of *Utopia, Limited* are from the Gilbert Papers. British Library, MS 49289.

The way out of these difficulties would be found by the introduction of English customs:

The King is betrothed in marriage to the beautiful Princess Sabina who has been sent to Girton to complete her education. There is a general admiration for England in the breasts of all the natives of Abyssinia, and everything English is held to be excellent. Sabina returns to the Happy Valley in Act I, bringing with her certain types of British perfection.

The list of Englishmen included

> a butler as representative of domestic order
> a policeman as representative of the public order
> a lifeguardsman as representative of a secure throne

and

> a curate as typical of moral blamelessness
> an Earl as typical of aristocratic supremacy
> a stockholder as typical of commercial property*

These archetypes of England's institutions (or 'Flowers of Progress' as they were called in the libretto) were to solve the political and social problems of Gilbert's Utopia.

In a very late sketch plot, Gilbert still intended political satire to be the dominant theme of his libretto. The following is Gilbert's outline of an interview between the King and the Princess, now called Zara, showing how English manners look to Utopian eyes.

The King asks what they would do in England if it were discovered that a body of Ministers had sacrificed the welfare of the State to their own private interests? Zara replies that such a state of things would be impossible in England where dishonest and self-seeking patriotism doesn't exist. In that fortunate realm all statesmen are absolutely simple minded and consider no interests except those of their beloved fatherland. 'Bless my heart' says the King. 'What a happy country!' Asked how they would deal with a scurrilous newspaper in which private malignity revenged itself by gross personal defamation, she replies that such a paper is unknown in England – it would be put down at once by the honest execrations of a right-thinking populace.†

Gilbert's first name for King Paramount was Rasselas, presumably after Rastilaus, the ninth-century Prince of Moravia who asked

---

* Gilbert's original First Act Finale included a butler and a detective amongst the 'Flowers of Progress'. See pp. 188, *et seq.*

† From an outline in Gilbert's hand at the Pierpont Morgan Library.

Michael III of Byzantium to send him missionaries capable of teaching Christianity to the Moravians! Gilbert was familiar of course with a novel by Samuel Johnson entitled *Rasselas*, which first appeared in 1768, as well as with a travesty of it entitled *Rasselas, Prince of Abyssinia*, or *The Happy Valley*, an extravaganza by William Brough which was first performed at the Theatre Royal, Haymarket in 1862. The major similarity between these works and Gilbert's libretto, however, was only that they included a character named Princess Nekayah.

Gilbert's first title for *Utopia, Limited* was *The Happy Valley*, presumably derived from a one-act farce entitled *The Happy Land* which he had written in 1873, and in which the similarity to *Utopia, Limited* is much clearer. *The Happy Land* takes place in Fairyland to which Selene, the Fairy Queen, arranges to bring three Members of Parliament!

SELENE. We understand the people of Great Britain are distinguished from the rest of the world by the possession of a certain inestimable blessing called a popular government . . . A blessing which they appreciate and value beyond all price . . . and my object in bringing the three mortals to Fairyland is to ascertain from them, if possible, the principles upon which their system is founded, and to introduce them, if possible, into our Fairyland.

The Happy Land, *The Happy Valley*, Rastislaus and Rasselas were all very much in Gilbert's mind when he wrote the first plot sketches of his new opera, and they developed into a story in which the King of the tropical island of Utopia imports six cultural missionaries from England to reform and modernize his kingdom. Inasmuch as Gilbert's Utopia was susceptible to many of the social and moral problems which were plaguing England in his day, the prospect of English ministers trying to deal with English problems 'in Utopia' promised great fun.

In Gilbert's early design for this opera, the Utopian King learns of the cultural wonders of England under the following remarkable circumstances:

> From yacht that lay in yonder bay
> Ten years ago, or more,
> A stranger, clad in shepherd's plaid,
> Was deftly rowed ashore.

We wished politely to salute
That stranger in the tourist suit,
So spread a meal of bread and fruit,
    And fired of guns a score . . .

He looked around and sternly frowned
    At all our poor display –
Our simple food he quite pooh-poohed,
    To our complete dismay.
At all our ways he sneered aloud.
For O that tourist youth was proud,
And we were all completely cowed
    And didn't know what to say . . .

Then up spoke he as trembled we
    Beneath his lordly ban,
'To show respect, it's quite correct
    To do the best you can.
But your cuisine is coarse and crude –
Your welcome rough – your language rude –
From which remarks you will conclude
    I am an Englishman' . . .

Profoundly stirred by what we heard
    On that eventful day,
'My Lord,' said we, 'we'll guided be
    By all you please to say.'
For England rules from East to West
And when she lifts her warlike crest
(In greeting our disgruntled guest)
    There'll be the deuce to pay.
Let's set to work without relapse;
Who knows but, some fine day perhaps –
When we *our* warlike crest display
There'll also be the deuce to pay!

    If the outline which Gilbert read to Sullivan and George Grove on the French Riviera in January of 1893 presented a story which satirized the British mores and monarchy, it is easy to see how his listeners might have thought it to be 'the best plot' that he had ever done.

Gilbert, unfortunately, did not develop his outline as he had planned.

King Rasselas of Utopia had his name changed (first to Philarion and then to Paramount) and the parallel between the importation of Christianity and English culture to barbaric lands was lost. The King's song about the origins of his Anglomania was cut, and thus the Utopians' passion for English manners appears to be altogether spurious – like so many other plot elements in the final version of this opera. And Gilbert's original satire on monarchy – a king under his ministers' control – was developed so heavy-handedly that any humorous or satiric effect was ultimately lost.

By the time it was completed, *Utopia, Limited* did not develop the ideas presented in *The Happy Valley*. Two things had come between the original whimsical design of Gilbert's Utopia, and the final sardonic result: his still smouldering bitterness against Sullivan and Carte over the way that they had treated him during the production of *Ivanhoe* . . . and a young woman named Nancy McIntosh whom he met early in 1893. Neither of these 'distractions' had been contemplated in the outline which Sullivan and Grove had listened to on the Riviera.

SMOULDERING BITTERNESS

Twenty-four months had passed between Gilbert and Sullivan's confrontation in the law courts and their production of *Utopia, Limited*. During that time Gilbert had made many offers to Sullivan to shake hands. Nobody would have assumed, therefore, that once the collaboration on *Utopia, Limited* had begun, that Gilbert was *still* deeply resentful of the way Carte and Sullivan had treated him two years earlier. But he *was* still resentful and unfortunately much of his resentment crept into his libretto.

Act II of *Utopia, Limited* opens with a song for Captain Fitzbattleaxe, the erstwhile romantic lead, the title of which is 'A Tenor Can't do Himself Justice'. The Captain laments the fact that his voice has become affected by his current romance. The song is a travesty upon tenors, upon musicians in general, and upon romances. At the end of the song, the tenor's amour says to him: 'Why, Arthur, what does it matter?' Why *Arthur* indeed! In twenty-one years of collaboration it had never occurred to Gilbert to call a character *Arthur* before. It is difficult to believe that Gilbert did not have Sullivan in mind in 1893 when he chose to give the name *Arthur* to a character who, as a musician, was no longer able to 'do himself justice' musically.

Another name that Gilbert employed cynically in *Utopia, Limited* was Wilkinson. Mr Wilkinson was a solicitor in a firm which Sullivan employed during the 90s. In *Utopia, Limited* Mr Wilkinson is the name given to an English tenor who performs 'grotesque imitations' of the King at a comic opera house.

In the famous quarrel over the 'carpet' during the run of *The Gondoliers*, the thing which had hurt Gilbert most was the affidavit in which Sullivan had sworn (at Carte's insistence) to false statements justifying the impounding of Gilbert's royalties.

Time after time Gilbert had pleaded with Sullivan privately to admit that he knew the statements in his affidavit were false. Sullivan would never make such an admission to Gilbert and Gilbert continued to brood over it in an early draft of *Utopia, Limited*:

SCAPHIO.   Well – how works the plot? Have you done our bidding? Have you explained to the happy and contented populace the nature of their wrongs, and the desperate consequences that must ensue if they are not rectified?

TARARA.   I have explained nothing. I have done better – I have made an affidavit that what they supposed to be happiness was really unspeakable misery – and they are furious! You know you can't help believing an affidavit.

SCAPHIO.   Of course – an admirable thought!

These are telling points but, as far as the opera was concerned, minor ones, for they had basically little effect upon the plot of the opera as a whole. Where Gilbert did his opera irreparable damage was at the introduction of the character of Mr Goldbury, the company promoter, who proposes to float the island of Utopia as a Limited Company. Much of the libretto is then given over to a kind of 'economic satire' that may have appealed to Bernard Shaw, but in fact had very little place in a comic opera.

There had, in fact, recently been a number of scandals involving misleading prospectuses issued by unscrupulous company promoters. The laws requiring proper disclosure were indeed inadequate and a ripe subject for satire. However, the inspiration for Gilbert's particular digression into economics in the middle of *Utopia, Limited* was probably supplied by a conspicuous advertisement which appeared in the *Financial Times* on 27 July 1892. Richard D'Oyly Carte had recently built himself the biggest white elephant in the West End, the

---

Ad in the Financial Times, *27 July 1892, to float the Royal English Opera House as a Limited Company. Mr Goldbury's song is suggested very strongly.* (Newspaper Library, Colindale.)

Royal English Opera. After the close of *Ivanhoe*, the opera house had stood empty and idle, with mortgage payments accruing month after month. Wasted money was being drained out of Mr D'Oyly Carte's personal bank accounts every day that went by. To get himself off the hook, Carte had interested Augustus Harris (the manager of the Covent Garden Opera House) in renovating the Royal English Opera and re-opening it as a vaudeville theatre. Harris had run the advertisement in the *Financial Times* with the intent of raising the money needed to buy and refurbish the opera house by forming a public corporation.

Gilbert saw it a bit differently: one embarks on a new venture, one begins to lose money on it, and to cut one's losses, one sells one's company to the public. Actually, it was more or less what was happening!

Mr Goldbury explained the procedure in a song called 'Some Seven Men Form an Association', the upshot of which was that 'if you come to grief and creditors are craving . . . you merely file a Winding-Up Petition, and start another Company at once!'

> Though a Rothschild you may be
> In your own capacity
> As a Company you've come to utter sorrow,
> But the liquidators say
> 'Never mind you needn't pay'
> So start another Company tomorrow.

Needless to say there had been Rothschild backing in the financing of the Royal English Opera. In retrospect it becomes disturbingly clear what Gilbert had in mind when he created the character of Mr Goldbury with his plan to introduce the concept of limited liability to the economy of Utopia. In 1893 the subject of 'limited liability' held a great deal of personal significance for W. S. Gilbert. Unfortunately, it did not hold quite so much for the Victorian public.

But the introduction of corporate economics was not the only element which diverted the proper development of Gilbert's libretto.

MISS MCINTOSH

In the spring of 1893 Gilbert was the guest at a party in the home of Georg Henschel.* It was there that he met a young American soprano named Nancy McIntosh who had come to England to study voice. Henschel was her vocal coach.

Gilbert became quickly infatuated with her gifts, undertook to coach her dramatically, and assumed complete responsibility for her career. He totally redesigned the libretto of *Utopia, Limited* with her in mind for the leading role, and unilaterally decided that Sullivan and Carte would agree to engage her for it.

---

* Henschel was an eminent musician, a friend of Sullivan, and a noted singer, conductor and teacher. He spent several years in America as the first conductor of the Boston Symphony Orchestra.

Nancy McIntosh, offstage.

She is rather tall, extremely fair – very nice looking, without being beautiful – good expressive face – no appreciable American twang. Something like a good and ladylike version of Roosevelt.*

Miss McIntosh has sent me some notices. I don't suppose you attach any importance to such things – but they may serve to show you the class of work that she has done.

She sings up to C (whatever that means)† and I am told that she is never out of tune. Miss McIntosh was keenly alive to the advantage of seeing you and she said she would gladly attend any appointment you might make.‡

* Blanche Roosevelt, American soprano who created the role of Mabel in *The Pirates of Penzance* in New York.
† Throughout his entire collaboration with Sullivan, Gilbert pretended complete ignorance of music.
‡ Letters from Gilbert to Sullivan dated 20 and 22 June 1893, Pierpont Morgan Library.

Gilbert did not, however, succeed in infecting Sullivan with his own enthusiasm for his new singing discovery. Sullivan declined to audition Nancy McIntosh privately. He made her wait for the next scheduled audition day at the Savoy (30 June), and then heard her and several other singers on the same morning. 'Disappointed in her voice,' Sullivan recorded in his diary. 'But I don't think she was at her best – however she will do as she is nice, sympathetic, and intelligent.' Sullivan was not about to object to Miss McIntosh. Gilbert was too intent on using her for reasons which were never to be known.

Gilbert, from time to time in the past, had taken a great personal interest in the careers of specific young actresses and singers. In the 70s he had been helpful to Marion Terry at the beginning of her career. In the 80s he had gone to court on behalf of Miss Fortescue, a chorus girl in his company, who had been jilted in marriage by the son of an earl. In 1889 he had championed the début of the seventeen-year-old Decima Moore as Casilda in *The Gondoliers*. But he had never gone so far as to redesign an opera for anyone as he was to now; for W. S. Gilbert was determined to make Nan McIntosh a star.

When he read the sketch plot of *Utopia, Limited* to Sullivan and George Grove in Roquebrune, the title was *The Happy Valley*. Some time later, he changed the title to *Princess Zara*, the name of the character he was designing for Nancy.

In the last outline of the opera in his plot-book, the character who returns from England to Utopia with the 'Flowers of Progress' is 'the beautiful Princess Sabina' who was betrothed in marriage to the King. As the King would inevitably be played by Rutland Barrington (who was hardly a proper counterpart for Gilbert's new discovery), the Princess Sabina, the King's fiancée, became magically transformed into the Princess Zara, the King's daughter, and the opera's new title character.

Once Gilbert became interested in building up the part of Princess Zara, all hope for a sense of focus in the opera went out of the window. A useless character named Captain Fitzbattleaxe was developed as someone for Zara to sing duets with. An irrelevant love interest in the Princess was developed for Scaphio and Phantis. Two songs, irrelevant to the main plot, were introduced because Zara could be featured in them: a duet with Fitzbattleaxe, 'Once Love – on Gallantry Intent' (p. 186) and a quartet with Scaphio, Phantis, and Fitzbattleaxe, 'For Zara is Very Warm Hearted' (p. 196). At one point Gilbert even suggested that the duet 'Sweet and Low' (for soprano and tenor) be rewritten as a solo for Princess Zara. With all this new emphasis on the soprano, Gilbert's original intention to satirize the abuses of monarchy was relegated to second if not third place. The irrelevant songs were eventually deleted; however, the original political thrust of Gilbert's libretto, once Miss McIntosh was thought of as the lead, became hopelessly and irretrievably lost.

Gilbert began work on the libretto of *Utopia, Limited* when he returned to London in late January of 1893. By 4 March he was able to write to Sullivan:

I am working hard at the piece – but I find it very difficult to plot out Act I without being tedious. I have written seven or eight numbers (but some of them are alternatives) and a considerable amount of detatched dialogue. I think the difficulties will all yield to treatment, I would send you a few numbers if you cared to have them, but I expect you would rather wait until Act I is completed.*

Shortly thereafter Gilbert began sending the lyrics over to Sullivan at fairly regular intervals, and the two conferred frequently as work on the libretto progressed:

I will come on Thursday as you suggest by the tram arriving at 12.23 – returning from Weybridge by the 5.47. I assume that you are not averse to standing a bit of bread and cheese and a drop of beer to a pore working man wots bin out of work for some years. Mein fuss is viel besser und ich bin seine deiner niedrig.†

Almost all of the letters that Gilbert wrote to Sullivan during this period complained bitterly of his suffering from gout and sciatica. At times he could barely write; at other times he could barely walk. His health, however, did not interfere with his production of the lyrics.

On 27 May Sullivan met Gilbert in his new 110-acre home at Grim's Dyke. It was the only time that he is known to have visited Gilbert there. In his diary he remarked on how ill Gilbert was looking.

The two collaborators had a final conference on *Utopia, Limited*. A major topic of discussion was the opera's two Finales.

In the First Act Finale the six Flowers of Progress are presented one after the other. In Gilbert's original version (pp. 188 *et seq.*) there

* Pierpont Morgan Library.
† Letter from Gilbert to Sullivan dated 15 April 1893, Pierpont Morgan Library.

Sullivan in the 90s. A very sick man.

was too much metrical similarity in the verses of introduction, and Gilbert agreed to rewrite it.

The Second Act Finale posed other problems for Sullivan. It was too long. It was *very* controversial. And contrary to Savoy tradition, it did not involve a reprise of a number featured earlier in the opera. Sullivan also felt that the metre would not call forth one of his most inspired melodies. Gilbert was *not* anxious to lose this Finale, but agreed to have a second look at it. *

* The original version of Gilbert's Act II Finale appears on p. 34

On 17 June Sullivan moved to his summer home in Weybridge where, two days later, he began writing the score to *Utopia, Limited*.

The next day Gilbert sent him five pages of the First Act Finale, recently rewritten as requested. Two days later he sent Sullivan his 'compromise' version of the Second Act Finale. He had not rewritten it. He merely shortened it by a third (see p. 182).

The following week Sullivan made a trip to London where he listened to several new singers including Miss McIntosh. Of the 'old guard' only Rutland Barrington and Rosina Brandram would be appearing in the new piece. George Grossmith, Jessie Bond and Richard Temple were temporarily out of the Savoy Company, and new blood was very badly needed.

'At 11.30 was at the Savoy Theatre for a seance,' Sullivan recorded in his diary on 30 June. 'Settled upon Passmore, Scott Fishe (perhaps Gridley), Florence Perry and Emmie Owen (the latter a little treasure).'

Sullivan must have had a brief conference with Gilbert about the libretto on the morning of the 30th, for on 1 July he raised his only major objection to *Utopia, Limited*. The character of Lady Sophy, the role that would be played by Rosina Brandram, the leading contralto, did not appeal to him. Sullivan did *not* want one more 'elderly ugly lady' in his new opera.

Gilbert, on the other hand, was not in favour of creating a 'dignified' character for Miss Brandram. Sullivan had had such a character constructed for her in his previous opera, *Haddon Hall*, and Gilbert was very conscious of the fact that the role had created a mediocre impression both dramatically and critically.

Had Gilbert's original plan for Lady Sophy's Second Act appearance been followed, a mediocre impression would definitely *not* have been created:

Lady Sofia, alone, indulges in a recitative in which she confesses that beneath her cold and self-contained exterior there lurks a spirit of wild and passionate devilry. She is compelled for professional and prudential reasons to keep this under the strictest control, but the effort is tremendous and unless she allowed herself now and then to 'break out' she would go mad. As she is alone and unobserved, this is a good opportunity to do so. Thereupon she has a desperate and extravagantly dramatic scena in which she describes, in the wildest terms, her consuming passion for the king, her misery at having to subdue it, and her heartbroken anguish at being compelled to reject the proffered love of a powerful monarch for reasons which really do not sway her at all. This ends in a wildly melodramatic dance.*

This was exactly what displeased Sullivan. 'I thought "Katisha" was to be the last example of the type . . .' he wrote to Gilbert. What Sullivan wanted was perfectly clear.

A dignified, stately, well made-up and well dressed elderly lady is a charming feature in a piece, and can be of real service to the composer, because the music he writes for her is so well contrasted with the youthful bustle of the other elements.**

Sullivan's point of view made a great deal of sense – but not for a libretto which W. S. Gilbert was writing.

In the interests, however, of the great harmony which existed between the partners during the writing of *Utopia, Limited*, Gilbert finally agreed that Lady Sophy would, at all times, conduct herself in a dignified and stately manner. He wrote a sentimental ballad for her in place of the melodramatics he had planned.

Once this was settled there were no more disagreements, and two weeks later, on 17 July, Gilbert was able to write 'I have finished the piece.'

Sullivan too was working efficiently on the score. He had little to distract him that summer. On 21 July he went up to London to play his music for the *new* First Act Finale for Gilbert. 'He thought it the best finale I had done' Sullivan wrote in his diary. After the harrowing quarrels of 1890, the two partners were trying very hard to be accommodating.

Two days later, 23 July, Gilbert wrote to Sullivan:

I have put in a few lines for him (Paramount) to sing in this scene with Zara . . .† he sings an absurd verse (musically in character) out of the burlesque 'King Tuppence' and at the end, overcome with his humiliation, sinks sobbing onto a chair. You will see it in the proofs.‡

The reference to 'proofs' in the last sentence is very important. Rehearsals would begin in September. It was Gilbert's custom to have his librettos set in type by Chappell and Company, his publishers, before the beginning of rehearsals. Printed copies would then be run off and supplied to the cast. Gilbert's letter suggests that by 23 July,

---

* From a plot outline in Gilbert's hand at the Pierpont Morgan Library.
** Pearson, p. 172.
† See p. 145.
‡ Pierpont Morgan Library.

he had already begun to prepare the first printed text of *Utopia, Limited*. He wrote out a clean copy of the complete libretto and sent it over to the typographer at Chappell's. *

Gilbert's health, however, was still a matter of great concern to him. 'I am so afraid of being incapacitated by gout during rehearsals if I don't go and clear it out of my system first,' he wrote to Sullivan.† After his 'final' text had been delivered to the printer, Gilbert left London for a month of medical attention in Hamburg.

During Gilbert's weeks abroad, however, many letters were exchanged between Germany and London as changes continued to be made in the libretto.

Sullivan wanted to omit a 'minstrel' song (see p. 192) which Gilbert had written to precede the King's patter song in Act II. Gilbert agreed.

Sullivan was also unhappy about a sequence in the Second Act (a quartet and a solo, pp. 195 *et seq.*) which Gilbert had recently designed for the benefit of Miss McIntosh. Both numbers, Sullivan felt, impeded the development of the Act.

Gilbert considered the problem. He was generally not averse to cutting his own material when it would obviously benefit the opera. But the case was somewhat different now as the cuts involved material for Miss McIntosh. It took Gilbert two weeks to decide to cut the Second Act quartet, the aria he transplanted to the First Act (p. 144).

In making these changes, Gilbert was bending over backwards to accommodate the requirements of his composer. He was also suffering from a very painful malady.

I think I have discussed all the difficulties you raised (and I see the *raison d'être* of all of them). I am much relieved to find they are not more serious.

I intend to return on Sunday. If three weeks of this place have no effect on me, I am not likely to benefit by four. I am extremely anxious about Act 2, and long to get home to tackle it. At the same time many thanks for suggesting that I should remain – for I know that your difficulties *must* be increased by my absence at such a crucial time. Shall I run down to you on Tuesday?‡

The libretto was almost finished. Two weeks later Gilbert wrote:

Here is a MAGNIFICENT suggestion – before the presentation business and after the King's song, *what do you say to an (unaccompanied?) Old English Quartette?*

* Gilbert's manuscript copy of the libretto, now at the British Library, MS 49300, was probably the copy used.

† Letter dated 17 July 1893, Pierpont Morgan Library.

‡ Letter dated 8 August 1893, Pierpont Morgan Library.

You will have the Tenor, Soprano, Baritone and Contralto on the stage – it seems a pity not to use them.*

It *was* a magnificent suggestion. The quartet, however, quickly became a sextet. It was positioned *after* the Drawing Room Presentations and the full chorus was added. This became the chorale, 'Eagle High'. Sullivan liked it so much that he asked Gilbert to provide him with a second verse.

Once the chorale had been suggested and adopted, the text of the opera was complete.

The chorale was added to the plates being set at Chappell's, and the quartet was deleted. Zara's aria was repositioned, a few other minor alterations were made, and the first printed text of *Utopia, Limited* was proofed and run off the presses in time for the first rehearsal of the opera. This text is reprinted in its entirety, beginning on p. 115.

* Letter dated 21 August 1893, Pierpont Morgan Library.

3

The Production Period

DURING the rewrites and rehearsals of *Utopia, Limited,* Gilbert altered four lyrics at Sullivan's request – in each case in order to allow the music a chance to speak for itself. But each time one of Sullivan's requests was granted, the fundamentally comic or satiric character of Gilbert's libretto was weakened just a little bit. The changes that Sullivan was seeking were not in the best interests of the opera. Had the production of *Utopia, Limited* not followed several years of misunderstanding, Gilbert might well have been less willing to compromise with Sullivan, and may thus have preserved far more of the original satiric thrust of his libretto. Each of the changes which Sullivan influenced took the opera further in the direction of seriousness.

The first number to be altered was the original Second Act Finale, compressed in the interests of efficiency and stripped in the process of its most interesting passages. Here is Gilbert's first draft of the Finale, with the verses cancelled for Sullivan's benefit in brackets.

> There's a little group of isles beyond the wave
>   So tiny you might almost wonder where it is
> Where people are the bravest of the brave
>   And cowards are the rarest of all rarities.
> [Her people all so prosperous have grown
>   The poorest, if they wished it might acquire land –
> Great Britain is the name by which it's known –]
>   To which some add (but others do not) Ireland.
>   Such at least is the tale
>   Which is borne on the gale
>   From the island that dwells in the sea.
>   Let us hope for her sake
>   That she makes no mistake
>   That she's all we believe her to be.

34

[Her constitution's envied near and far –
　　Her Parliament's a model of sincerity;
Her simpleminded Politicians are
　　The source of her remarkable prosperity.]
The proudest nations kneel at her command –
　　She terrifies all foreign born rapscallions –
And holds the fate of Europe in her hand
　　With half a score invincible battalions.
　　　　Such at least, etc.

O may we copy all their methods wise
　　And imitate their virtues and their charities
And may we, by degrees, acclimatize
　　Her Parliamentary peculiarities!
By doing it we shall, in course of time,
　　Regenerate completely our entire land –
Great Britain is that monarchy sublime,
　　[To which some conscientious folk add – Ireland.*
　　　　Such at least is our view,
　　　　If it prove to be true
　　　　　We shall rise to the top of the tree
　　　　But supposing instead
　　　　That we've all been misled –
　　　　　What a kettle of fish there will be!]†

The Second Act duet for Zara and Fitzbattleaxe, 'Sweet and Low',
was another lyric which Gilbert rewrote so that Sullivan could have a
serious musical moment in the score. Unfortunately there was little
serious passion in the scene preceding the duet and consequently
little reason for passion in the duet itself. Gilbert's initial instinct was
correct – a satiric love song.

　　　　　Words of love too loudly spoken
　　　　　　Ring their own untimely knell;
　　　　　Noisy vows are rudely broken,
　　　　　　Soft the song of Philomel.
　　　　　'Tis a truth needs no refutal –
　　　　　　Always whisper when you woo.
　　　　　Sweet and low the ringdoves tootle;
　　　　　　Sweetly let us tootle too.

---

*These references to Ireland may have been a dig at Sullivan's parentage. Another
occurs in *The Grand Duke.*
† Gilbert and Sullivan wrote two other Finales for *Utopia, Limited.* See pp. 202 *et seq.*

Let the conqueror, flushed with glory,
    Bid his noisy clarions bray;
Lovers tell their artless story
    In a whispered virelay.
Let him shout his paean brutal
    Who proclaims a conquest new.
Sweet and low the ringdoves tootle;
    Sweetly let us tootle too.

The relationship between Zara and Captain Fitzbattleaxe is not particularly romantic. And the romantic lyrics, as rewritten by Gilbert and as set by Sullivan seem oddly out of keeping with the rest of the libretto.

Words of love too loudly spoken
    Ring their own untimely knell;
Noisy vows are rudely broken,
    Soft the song of Philomel.
Whisper sweetly, whisper slowly,
    Hour by hour and day by day
Sweet and low as accents holy
    Are the notes of lover's lay.

Let the conqueror, flushed with glory,
    Bid his noisy clarions bray,
Lovers tell their artless story
    In a whispered virelay.
False is he whose vows alluring
    Make the listening echoes ring;
Sweet and low when all-enduring,
    Are the songs that lovers sing!

In his quest for more serious musical moments, Sullivan asked Gilbert to provide him with a second verse to the chorale, 'Eagle High'. Gilbert obliged, but with a satiric lyric which was not exactly what Sullivan needed to extend the mood of the music he had in mind. The second verse, which appears below in brackets, was never used.

Eagle high in cloudland soaring –
    Sparrow twittering on a reed –
Tiger in the jungle roaring –
    Frightened fawn in grassy mead –
Let the eagle, not the sparrow,
Be the object of your arrow –

Fix the tiger with your eye –
Pass the fawn in pity by.
Glory then will crown the day –
Glory, glory, anyway!

[If you hit it, song and story
Shrine you in a glow of glory:
    If you miss it, why bewail?
    For you gloriously fail!
    Hit or miss it as you may,
    Glory still will crown the day!
Leave the sordid and the sorry –
    Fly your thoughts on nobler wings;
Keep your bolt for Royal quarry,
    Fitted for the sport of Kings.

If you hit it, song and story
 Shrine you in a glow of glory:
    If you miss it, why bewail?
    For you gloriously fail!
    Hit or miss it as you may,
    Glory still will crown the day!]

The ballad which Gilbert ultimately agreed to write for Lady Sophy in Act II was already a compromise as far as he was concerned. Sullivan, however, compromised it even further in the direction of seriousness by eliminating two of its stanzas. Here is the original draft of Lady Sophy's song, with the parts Sullivan deleted in brackets:

When but a maid of fifteen year,
    Unsought – unplighted –
Short petticoated – and, I fear,
    Still shorter-sighted –
I made a vow, one early spring,
That only to some spotless king
Who proof of blameless life could bring
    I'd be united.
For I had read, not long before,
Of blameless kings in fairy lore,
And thought the race still flourished here –
    Well, well –
I was a maid of fifteen year!

[But so bad are the best
That absurd is my quest

37

If so stringent a test
  They are tried by –
And I find with remorse
I've adopted a course
Which, though vain, I perforce
  Must abide by!
Too late! Too late
  Another line to choose!
Too late! Too late
  To modify my views!
  And I find with remorse
I've adopted a course
Which, though vain, I perforce
  Must abide by.]

Each morning I pursued my game
  (An early riser);
For spotless monarchs I became
  An advertiser:
But all in vain I searched each land,
So, kingless, to my native strand
Returned, a little older, and
  A good deal wiser!
I learnt that spotless King and Prince
Have disappeared some ages since –
Even Paramount's angelic grace,
  Ah, me!
Is but a mask on Nature's face!

  [For it seems his career's
  Just as bad as his peers'
  And I'm wasting the years
    As they glide by –
  Though the terms of my vow
  Are absurd – anyhow
  To those terms I must bow
    And abide by!
  Too late! Too late
    To break the vow I swore
  Too late! Too late
    It binds me evermore.
  Though the terms of my vow
  Were absurd – anyhow
  To those terms I must bow
    And abide by!]

21

in a woman's eyes! Ah, if we could only make up our minds to invest our stock of youth on commercial principles, old age would be as extinct as the dodo!

Song, Zara.

Youth is a gift of worth
 To one & all allowed
With which all men, at birth,
 Are equally endowed.
But Man is a prodigal
 Who madly lives upon
His little capital
 Till every penny's gone —
And finds himself, at life's concluding stage
With no Youth left to comfort his old age!

Ensemble
Alas — alas —
He finds himself &c.

(coming forward)*
Ah dame, all wrinklefaced,
 If you, in very sooth
In infancy had placed
 Your capital of Youth
At four or five percent
 Prepared, within your breast,
To rub along content
 upon the interest,
You might be still in girlhood's mid-career,
A merry mad-cap maid of four score year!
Ensemble
Alas — alas — you might be still &c.   present together

A page from Gilbert's manuscript copy of Utopia, Limited.
(British Library.)

39

Gilbert in the 90s. Not quite so ill as Sullivan.

Sullivan was struggling desperately to find serious musical moments in Gilbert's libretto. But the text of *Utopia, Limited*, with its satire on capitalism and politics, more than any other Gilbert opera, seemed to defy all attempts at pure musical expression.

Rehearsals for the new opera started at the Savoy on 4 September. Publicity for the piece was begun almost at once. A contemporary drawing was made of Gilbert reading the script to the assembled cast on the first morning of rehearsals.

The recent quarrels, however, were still taking their toll in strange ways. Gilbert's gout was causing him great pain at the beginning of the production, and for a while he had to be wheeled about the stage in a bath chair – an indignity certain not to help his unpredictable temper.

Gilbert's unpredictable temper was of great concern to everyone – especially to Sullivan and Carte who were glad, and somewhat humbled, to have him back. On the morning of the first rehearsal Rutland Barrington, the effective star of the piece, had cabled that he would be late. He had spent the weekend at Ryde and the boat-train was delayed on the return. When Barrington arrived at the theatre where Gilbert and the entire cast had been waiting for thirty minutes for him, both Sullivan and Carte upbraided him furiously for his temerity at keeping Mr Gilbert waiting on the occasion of his first rehearsal. Mr Gilbert on the other hand, was quite cordial and completely undisturbed by the incident.* Sullivan and Carte wanted Gilbert happy at all costs.

And for the most part Gilbert was happy during the rehearsals of *Utopia, Limited*. He may have found it politic to give in to Sullivan when he requested changes that affected the score. But Gilbert was of no mind to listen to Sullivan (or anyone else for that matter) when it came to changes affecting his stage direction. And Gilbert's physical production was promising many surprises.

Gilbert was either having a crisis of confidence during the mounting of *Utopia, Limited* (due to the unfortunate events of the four years since his last Savoy production), or he himself had become, as he began to stage the opera, unsure of the absolute effectiveness of the

* Barrington, p. 94.

41

Contemporary drawing of W. S. Gilbert reading the libretto of
Utopia, Limited *to his company on the first day of rehearsal at
the Savoy.*

opera's diffuse plot. In either event Gilbert compensated for his
insecurities as he rehearsed *Utopia, Limited* by relying upon lavishness
and sheer visual spectacle to a degree never before attempted at the
Savoy.

Hawes Craven, one of Henry Irving's designers, created two
spectacular South Sea Island settings.

The costumes for the Utopians in Act I were wildly primitive. A
strong visual effect was created by the contrast of the Utopian dress
with the stiff uniforms of the Lifeguardsmen who enter in the
middle of Act I. Another sharp visual contrast was created by the
appearance of the Utopians in anglicized costumes in Act II.

But the most lavish of all of Gilbert's effects was the Drawing Room
Scene in Act II in which all of the members of the Utopian Court
are presented to King Paramount in the exact manner of a Court
presentation at Buckingham Palace. A parquet floor was built to
cover the stage of the Savoy for the event. It took five costumiers to
make the dresses worn by the ladies in that scene alone. Gilbert
hired a female teacher of deportment to come to some of the rehearsals and teach the members of the cast how to walk, stand, and bow in

the presence of royalty. Gilbert left no detail unattended in the mounting of this scene, and no expense was spared. The effect was totally visual – no dialogue was spoken in the entire scene.

The preliminary expenses of *Utopia, Limited* came to £7200. This was staggering. The cost of *The Gondoliers*, over which the quarrel had come about, had only been £4500!

THE OPENING WEEK

The week the opera opened there was much rejoicing (although some of it qualified) in the press:

The silver cord at last is bound again, Gilbert and Sullivan are re-united; D'Oyly Carte no longer imagines a vain thing, Savoyards have cast their nighted colour off . . .
Clarion

Mr W. S. Gilbert and Sir Arthur Sullivan and Mr Richard D'Oyly Carte, after a long run of brilliant successes, produced *The Gondoliers* and quarrelled. Who was right and who was wrong nobody knows and nobody cares, had we lived under a paternal autocracy, all three of them would have been soundly birched and kept on bread and water for a fortnight, at the end of which time they would have resolutely set to work to get out a new joint opera . . .
Land and Water

In the Kingdom of the blind, the one-eyed is king. Comic opera as a rule, being an unsavoury compound of ribald buffoonery and sentimental twaddle, we all hailed with delighted surprise the decent and yet humorous exception invented by Mr W. S. Gilbert and Sir Arthur Sullivan and reproduced under superficially varying but fundamentally identical forms in their series of extravaganzas at the Savoy Theatre.
The Speaker

Gilbert and Sullivan's avid following had been responsible for their fame and fortune. The public which had given them so much objected to their not being able to get along with each other. Their quarrels therefore had succeeded in generating a considerable amount of ill will which would have to be overcome.

So Gilbert has presumably promised to be a good boy for the future and has been allowed by Sir Arthur and D'Oyly to come back to the Savoy once more.
Sporting Times

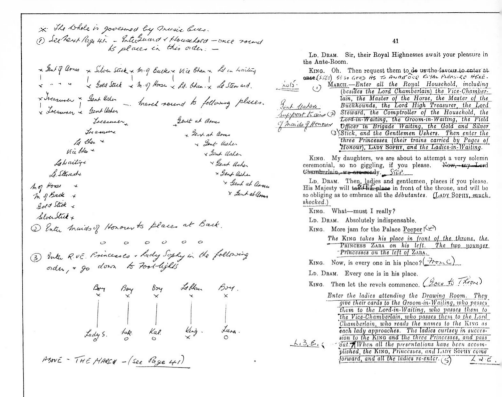

So the good old Savoy brothers, Gilbert and Sullivan have resumed their famous happy reunion of mirth and music at Mr D'Oyly Carte's theatre. Considering that the annual profit to the three of their joint authorship and management was something like £30 000, one wonders that they have been so long in patching up their little difference.

England

It's impossible to say why a serious musician, a Chapel Royal chorister, and student at the Royal Academy of Music, the writer of some beautiful and devotional anthems of so noble, imaginative and musicianly a work as *The Golden Legend* should have been attracted by Gilbert's unique verses.

Musical News

D'Oyly Carte set to counter this by inundating the press with releases covering practically every aspect of the new opera, not the least of which was Nancy McIntosh. She gave any number of interviews to newspapers and magazines during the rehearsal period. And she gave her own account of what it was like to be a starring performer at the Savoy.

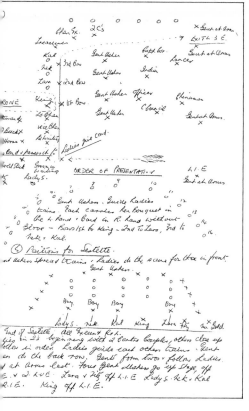

Pages from the prompt copy of Utopia, Limited *showing Gilbert's stage directions for the Drawing Room Scene. (Bridget D'Oyly Carte.)*

Until something like a month ago I had never stepped on a stage in my life; but I have taken very kindly to the boards and, so far from being a weariness, each rehearsal was a pleasant experience. But that, I must confess, was greatly owing to Mr Gilbert who is the most delightful and painstaking stage-manager possible. I never knew so patient a man. After you have done a thing wrong twenty times, he will put you right on the twenty-first as amiably as if he were telling you quite a new thing.*

Other performers have formed other opinions of Gilbert's directorial technique!

One thing was clear, however. The publicity left no doubt that the new Savoy opera would involve a début as well as a première.

By the time the opening day rolled around, practically every newspaper had informed its readers of the plot of *Utopia, Limited*. Even the *New York Herald* picked up some of the releases.

In the endeavor to reconstitute the social and political organization of the nation upon an English basis, it may be taken for granted that Mr Gilbert will find plenty of opportunities for satire at the expense of English manners and customs.

* Quoted by Percy Fitzgerald, p. 231.

45

The Drawing Room Scene was publicized in advance, in the hope that it would prove to be a selling point.

The attempt of the uncivilized monarch to hold a drawing room according to ideas brought back by his daughter from the English court ought to be particularly provocative of fun.

In fact there was practically no aspect of the production that was not ultimately publicized from one point of view or another.

Do not think I need say very much about *Utopia* at the Savoy. I have never known any modern production on the stage so exhaustively treated by the press.

Land and Water

One innovation at the Savoy that was made for the première of *Utopia, Limited* was a public dress rehearsal – or rather an invitational preview – for members of the press and invited guests on the after-noon before the official opening.

Many critics had previously complained that one hearing did not allow them sufficient time to judge a new opera properly, nor did one evening allow them enough time to review it. Openings at the Savoy, and Henry Irving's Lyceum were *the* events on the Victorian theatrical (and social) calendar, and the productions were written up by the press very thoroughly. Considering the recent bad publicity that Gilbert and Sullivan had to overcome, it was a good idea on Gilbert's part to give his reviewers a private backstage glimpse of the Savoy.

The public dress rehearsal took place on the afternoon of 6 October. The house was completely open to the invited public, with the exception of several rows of front stalls which were roped off for staff. The first *event* of the afternoon was the 'arranging of the orchestra pit' conducted by Sir Arthur Sullivan and François Cellier. They took fully thirty minutes in positioning the players to their satisfaction. During this procedure Sullivan quipped that for the next opera he'd write all the string music *pizzicato* so as to save the room taken up by the violin bows.

The arranging of players in the orchestra pit could have taken place at any of the earlier band rehearsals, had not Gilbert felt that this would be a good opportunity for the reviewers to see the composer at work, and a good way of warming up the audience.

The dress rehearsal was apparently conducted with a certain amount of informality. When the orchestra was properly arranged, Mr Harris, the stage manager, called 'Stop the Gallery lights,' and the performance began. The orchestra laughed so heartily at times that they could not play. This lapse of professional discipline was no doubt anticipated by the author and composer, and allowed to occur for the benefit of the audience.

For the most part, the performance went smoothly, and was only occasionally interrupted. Sullivan had his moment at the beginning of the evening. After the performance began, it was Gilbert's turn to get into the act.

'You, miss, you in yellow, and you, miss, next to her, will you put your arms round one another's neck – if you're on good terms' called the author, and turning round said, 'they aren't always, you know.' Still, he was not satisfied. 'You two at the back incorporate yourselves – I mean embrace one another. Sullivan, may I put one right at the back on the mound; will the voice be right?' 'Certainly, Gilbert.' . . . 'You know, I've told that girl about it before. Tell a thing once to a man and he never forgets it. Tell it to a woman, and – well, they're thinking all the time about the question how they and their neighbours look. One rehearsal went almost to pieces till I thought of making them all take off their bonnets and then they did attend me. Oh, that won't do.' '. . . I have never had pleasanter rehearsing – no jars or unpleasantness at all. It's going beautifully, but of course they'll all lose their heads later on, they always do . . . Hi, miss, you in green on the left – I can't tell which now they've got their wings – lie down at once on your face – I've told you about it before.'*

The rehearsal began at 11.30 in the morning and finished at half past five. 'You can't sing the Finale today,' said Sir Arthur, 'for a new one is to be written.' Gilbert and Sullivan did cut things close.

Before the reviewers left, Mr Gilbert stood up in the front of the stalls and addressed the full company who were all assembled upon the stage. Gilbert expressed the great pleasure that he had had once more in working at the Savoy Theatre and declared his conviction that every part in the new opera would be played as well as it deserved, if not better. He added a personal word of praise for Charles Harris, his stage manager, and three hearty cheers were given Mr Gilbert by the company.

Sir Arthur then expressed his gratitude. The afternoon was formally ended, and the critics in the audience went home to make notes on what they had seen and heard, and prepared to return on the following night when the formality of the audience and the atmosphere of the performance would provide a strong contrast to that of the public rehearsal. A Gilbert and Sullivan première was an 'event'. A dress rehearsal was not.

* Quoted by *Westminster Gazette*, 6 October 1893.

4

The Opening of
Utopia, Limited

ON opening day the attention of the English speaking world seemed to be on the Savoy Theatre.

For many years past no event connected with the English lyric drama has excited so much interest as the rejunction of Gilbert and Sullivan in the production of another comic opera for Mr D'Oyly Carte at the Savoy Theatre.

Bow Bells

The seats in all parts, except the pit and the gallery were allotted long ago and a struggle to get into the unreserved part of the house was tremendous. Four women took up positions outside the pit doors at ten in the morning with the prospect of a ten hour wait.

Chicago Herald

The four women, and those who later joined them, passed the greater part of the afternoon in singing songs from earlier operas.

Eventually the evening came. The four hearty women, and a few lucky others gained coveted admittance to the gallery where they shared the hall with some very distinguished company.

The audience on the opening night of *Utopia, Limited* included the Marchioness of Ormonde, Jessie Bond, Mr and Mrs George Grossmith, the Marquis of Granby, Mrs Crutchley, Alec Yorke, the Brazilian Minister, Mrs Ronalds, Mrs Jack Leslie, sister of Lady Randolph Churchill, Nellie Melba and Lady Brooke.

Mr D'Oyly Carte has always an exceptional audience and a distinct following numbering amongst it many who are not regular playgoers, but who make an absolute duty of witnessing each new Savoy production.

Reynolds

Opening night programme to Utopia, Limited.

When Sullivan walked into the orchestra pit that evening at 8.15 Mr D'Oyly Carte's 'distinct following' gave him an ovation that lasted fully sixty-five seconds. He was shockingly nervous according to his diary and perhaps he should have been. He had had two non-successes, one lawsuit and much illness since his last première with Gilbert. His entire future as a composer depended on the success of this evening and, encouragingly, the length of his entrance applause was sufficient to give him badly needed confidence at the beginning of the performance. The very fact, however, that he found it necessary to time his ovation in the first place suggests that this most popular of English composers, for all his successes at the Savoy, still had deep-seated insecurities which would never be compensated no matter how brilliantly *Utopia, Limited* might succeed.

The production began with a thin musical prelude* and according

---

* The 'Overture' to *Utopia, Limited* has been the subject of much conjecture since it was not printed in the vocal score. The critic from the *Sunday Times*, however, reported 'We recognize the familiar style . . . in the graceful measure of the prelude (founded on the gavotte used later in the drawing-room scene).'

Sullivan's diary entry for 7 October 1893, the opening of Utopia,
Limited. (*Beinecke Rare Book and Manuscript Library.*)

to Sullivan's diary went 'wonderfully well – not a hitch of any kind.'
The First Act ran one hour and forty-five minutes (!) and several
reviewers suggested that it should be shortened. 'The Second Act,'
according to the *Globe* 'gave universal satisfaction.'

Eight numbers were encored the first night:

> 'Of Every Mental Lore' (Scaphio and Phantis)
> 'Although of Native Maids the Cream' (Nekaya and Kalyba)
> 'Bold-faced Ranger' (Lady Sophy)
> 'I'm Captain Corcoran, K.C.B.' (Captain Corcoran)
> 'Some Seven Men Form an Association' (Mr Goldbury)
> 'Society Has Quite Forsaken' (King Paramount)
> 'A Wonderful Joy Our Eyes to Bless' (Mr Goldbury)
> The Tarantella

Of the above, two were show-stoppers. The first was the short solo
(in the First Act Finale) of Captain Corcoran, welcomed back as a
bass, with a musical excerpt from *HMS Pinafore* (sung a semitone
lower) to the words 'We never run a ship ashore.' This was a reference to the sinking of the British warship HMS *Victoria* on naval
manœuvres a few weeks earlier (a reference which some reviewers
thought to be in poor taste).

The other show-stopping number was the patter song for King Paramount in Act II in which the happy results of anglicizing Utopia are recited. Gilbert staged the number like a minstrel show and Sullivan set it to a mock banjo accompaniment augmented by tambourines and bones. Inasmuch as the British Empire had recently expanded its territories by the annexation of a willing Fiji and Tonga, it is easy to see how Gilbert saw the Cabinet Meeting of a South Sea Parliament as a minstrel show. The Victorian audience understood it very well and it was one piece of satire which worked.

Another Gilbert device which impressed if it did not amuse, was the Drawing Room Scene.

Then comes the scene of the Drawing-room in which, contrary to expectation, no sort of parody is attempted. The Royal household, and the various Court officials, correct to a button, occupy their proper places, and, amid the strains of a stately gavotte, a procession of ladies in such wondrous Court costumes that no mere male would be bold enough to describe them, pass along the stage, every detail of the presentation being carried out practically as it is at Buckingham Palace.
Daily News

As a spectacle alone, *Utopia* would be well worth witnessing.
The Globe

The scene would later raise some questions as to its exact purpose in a comic opera (*Daily News*). At the opening, however, the majority of the audience did not question it and Gilbert's extraordinary visual presentation had a stunning effect.

At the end of the performance the house, which had so warmly welcomed the composer at the beginning of the evening, became even more excited. Both Gilbert and Sullivan had a double call. Even D'Oyly Carte was cheered by the audience. At the very end both Gilbert and Sullivan took a call together. As they were being applauded, they turned to each other and shook hands. The audience went wild. It was one of those rare human moments which occur only a few times in a lifetime of theatre-going. An era was summed up in that curtain call. An era which may well have come to its end.

Even if *Utopia, Limited* was not ultimately as successful as the earlier Savoy operas, the opening night itself was far from a failure.

This was the first Gilbert and Sullivan première that Mr D'Oyly Carte's 'exceptional audience' had been able to witness for four years, and they were determined to see that the 'event' was a successful one.

Everybody was glad to see Mr Gilbert, Sir Arthur Sullivan and Mr Carte working together again; everybody was prejudiced in favour of the production; and everybody joined in making it a success.
The Globe

. . . a more complete success has never been achieved in comic opera at the Savoy.
Standard

Both composer and librettist came in for their share of raves.

In none of his previous works has the composer shown the resources of the orchestra more fully.
News of the World

The book has Mr Gilbert's lighter qualities without his faults.
GEORGE BERNARD SHAW *The Saturday Review*

The critic for *The Globe* summed it up.

The world already knows that the new Gilbert and Sullivan opera is a triumph for all concerned.

The dissents from this opinion, however, were formidable, the leading dissenter being F. C. Burnand, editor of *Punch*, and Sullivan's ex-librettist. He had written the lyrics for *Cox and Box* twenty-seven years earlier and was still jealous that Sullivan had subsequently adopted Gilbert for his partner.

Mr D'Oyly Carte is to be heartily congratulated on his brilliant mounting of Messrs Gillivan and Sulbert's most recent production entitled *Utopia, Limited* . . . Sir Arthur Sullivan's muse, in which if there be nothing particularly new . . . there is at all events nothing dull, even though it may 'hardly ever' rise above mere commonplace.

Burnand went on to complain that Gilbert had stolen the idea for the Christy Ministrel scene from a twenty-five-year-old Burnand play called *Black-Eye'd Susan*:

Imitation being the sincerest flattery, the author of *Black-Eye'd Susan* must be indeed gratified by this tribute to his original success paid by the librettist and the composer of *Utopia*, and having no further use for this particular bit of humour, he will, no doubt, be willing to make a present of it, free of charge, for nightly use, to the distinguished Savoyards as a practical congratulation to the pair of them on their return to the scene of some of their former triumphs.

Burnand's anger may have been justifiable. *Black-Eye'd Susan* was an early 'nautical' ballad opera. In 1878 many thought *HMS Pinafore* had been derived from it. Now Gilbert had adopted another idea from it. A 'court martial' scene opening the last Act of *Black-Eye'd Susan* had been played by a group of Admirals seated in a semi-circle and speaking as minstrels. Gilbert's minstrel scene in its *final* form contained no dialogue (p. 162), only a song, the chorus of which was based more than loosely on one of Burnand's lyrics from the same work.

Gilbert's chorus:

> It really is surprising
> What a thorough Anglicizing
> We have brought about – Utopia's quite another land,
> In her enterprising movements
> She is England – with improvements,
> Which we dutifully offer to our mother-land!

Burnand's chorus:

> When the Sailors are invited
> They're delighted but excited,
> Be they Dicky, Nicky, Harry, Tom or Bob!
> If they dare to try to kiss me,
> I will give 'em – if they miss me –
> Such a wunner and a stunner on the nob.

But aside from the predictable hostility of Burnand's review the balance of the production came in for some pretty heavy attack.

One newcomer, soon to be one of the most important Savoyards of the 90s received a very cool welcome.

Mr Walter Passmore lent perhaps undue fussiness to the role of Tarara, the Public Exploder . . .
Daily Graphic

Gilbert must have seethed with anger at the following (not atypical) reception accorded his protégée.

Curiosity was of course centred on Nancy McIntosh who played the leading part . . . Of Miss McIntosh's singing, others shall decide . . . But she has a great deal to learn before she can be taken seriously as an actress. Even when the nervousness of a first night and the inadequacies of the part are allowed for liberally, it is impossible as yet to guess whether she has any gift for acting.

Gazette

Sullivan too must have been angry when he read his notices. Not since the decimating reception of *Kenilworth* at the Birmingham Festival *thirty years earlier* had a Sullivan score been vivisected so meticulously by the press:

It would be altogether unreasonable to expect the musician of more than a dozen comic operas to go on producing strains new in character and expression.

Daily Telegraph

The brief prelude which ushers in the piece calls for no notice.

Daily Graphic

. . . one early song for the King 'A King of Autocratic Power We' is almost a failure . . . .

Pall Mall Gazette

. . . nor does the setting of Lady Sophy's song, illustrating the course of courtship rise above the level of appropriateness.

Daily Graphic

The King's second song – on the text that life is a farce – is one of the weakest numbers in the score and made little impression.

Daily Graphic

Sir Arthur Sullivan's score . . . suffers from a dearth of fetching tunes which one looks for in a work of this kind while the instrumentation is of the sketchiest and most perfunctory description.

Daily Graphic

It was true, however, that *Utopia, Limited* was the least romantic libretto that Gilbert ever wrote. The South Sea Island setting was difficult to evoke musically, and Sullivan failed to characterize the exotic milieu as evocatively as he had in *Princess Ida* or *The Gondoliers*. Occasionally a dramatic moment would thunder out of the orchestra, but on the whole, the score was disappointing. Sullivan was no longer looking forward to writing greater music as he had been when he composed *The Yeomen of the Guard* and *The Gondoliers*. *Ivanhoe* was now behind him, and with the score to *Utopia, Limited* Sullivan had begun looking backward in his music.

But Gilbert's libretto had failed to inspire Sullivan, and it also failed to inspire much of the audience.

As to dramatic plot – well, strictly speaking, there is none; and it would be difficult to name a single telling 'situation' in *Utopia*.

Punch

The most penetrating analysis of the libretto, however, appeared in *The Gazette*.

Mr Gilbert . . . has, it may be said, drawn the outline of a comic opera, but he has left it to the beholders to fill in all that he meant to put in, that he might have put in. Even the most extravagant fantasy is bound to have a certain order, a certain sequence, a certain adherence of purpose if it is to be regarded as a work of art. And *Utopia, Ltd.* has no coherence, no ordered sequence. Nothing comes of anything. Characters appear that promise to amuse or amaze, and then trail feebly off like an unsuccessful firework.

The reviewer was absolutely correct. *Utopia, Limited*, which had promised at the outset to be a satire on monarchy and corruption in government, fulfilled very little. The plottings of the two old ministers for the love of Princess Zara, the *process* by which the English gentlemen anglicize the mores of Utopia, the evil machinations by which Scaphio, Phantis and Tarara *bring about* the final chaos of the social order – none of these lines of action was developed by Mr Gilbert onstage. The opera had absolutely no continuity of action in its final version and it could not fail to disappoint.

Rutland Barrington said the Second Act 'was not as full of fun as usual.' The *Daily Graphic* called the dénouement 'about the bitterest thing Mr Gilbert has ever penned.' There was little question that a new 'dark side' of Gilbert's humour was now coming to the fore – no doubt as a result of the strain of his recent relations with his partners. The public, however, was in no mood for 'dark humour' at the Savoy, and *Utopia, Limited* had elements in it that were frankly distasteful to them.

King Paramount, the central character in *Utopia, Limited*, is unique in the Savoy roster. He is a victim, he is unhappy, but his unhappiness is not, like that of Katisha or Lady Jane, the result of his own self-indulgence, and we may not laugh at it. King Paramount is publicly humiliated by Scaphio and Phantis, and the cruelty which they exhibit towards him can not be regarded as *fun* by anybody's standards. King Paramount is helpless in a way that Ko-Ko and Robin Oakapple had not been helpless in the earlier operas. Scaphio and Phantis are evil in a way that the Mikado had not been evil, even in his most Gothic pronouncements. One is never quite certain as to how one should react to certain of the events in *Utopia, Limited*, for one has never seen totally dislikeable characters in a Gilbert libretto before. But Gilbert had never before collaborated with partners against whom he was still quietly embittered.

Of all the critics who wrote of *Utopia, Limited*, at its opening night, only the reviewer for *The Theatre* recognized the fact that Gilbert and Sullivan's satire had changed as a result of their estrangement.

The famous collaborators are no longer the same men. They have grown sager, soberer; their art has gained in avoirdupois . . . Mr Gilbert has gone too far afield for his whimsicality and Sir Arthur has suffered from his journey in pursuit.

In 1893 few critics understood exactly what had happened.

Immediately after the opening of the opera, a number of changes were made, largely at Gilbert's insistence.

The most important change was the elimination of Princess Zara's song 'Youth is a Boon Avowed' (p. 144). It had been tentatively cut before the opening, and omitted from both the public dress rehearsal of the opera, and the first edition of the libretto. It was reinstated for the opening performance only. After the mediocre impression made by Nancy McIntosh, the song was permanently deleted.

The only other important alterations that were made affected the very end of the opera. Gilbert disliked the Finale;* Sullivan thought there was too much closing dialogue; and the press objected to many of Gilbert's bitter lines.

'We *must* finish the piece coherently,' Gilbert wrote to Sullivan. He was keenly aware of the press criticism. 'I notice, by the way, that nearly all the papers quote Scaphio and Phantis's speech – and also

---

* The Finale performed on the first night appears on pp. 205–206

Zara's last speech. God only knows how I am to finish the piece if these are to be cut out.'*

Gilbert did, however, make the following concessions to the press. In Zara's speech about 'Government by Party' he deleted the lines:

. . . inexperienced civilians will govern your Army and your Navy; no social reforms will be attempted, because out of vice, squalor, and drunkenness no political capital is to be made . . .

And in Scaphio's speech about the 'boons' conferred by the Flowers of Progress, Gilbert deleted the line in italics:

> Utopia, swamped by dull Prosperity
> *Stifled with benefits, all English born,*
> Demands that these detested Flowers of Progress
> Be sent about their business . . .

Sullivan had wanted the chorus, 'Down With the Flowers of Progress' to follow *directly* after the Tarantella, eliminating a few lines of intervening dialogue (see p. 180). Gilbert disagreed, but was so displeased with the Finale, that he offered Sullivan the following proposition two days after the opera opened:

I do most certainly hope that you will see your way to setting the words I originally wrote. – 'there's a (something) little isle beyond the wave.' . . . If you will do this, I will endeavour to carry out your suggestions as to dialogue even if I don't agree with them.

Sullivan accepted Gilbert's offer and composed the new Finale the same day. It was rehearsed and put into the opera on Friday, the thirteenth.† Six days after *Utopia, Limited* had opened, it achieved its final shape.

---

* These quotations and the one following are from letters from Gilbert to Sullivan written shortly after the opera's opening, and are now at the Pierpont Morgan Library.

† Sullivan and Flower, p. 227.

5

Separate Ways Again

AFTER the opening of *Utopia, Limited* it was not immediately apparent that the opera would be less successful than its predecessors, for Richard D'Oyly Carte was doing all in his power to arouse and maintain the public's interest in the new opera. The Duke of Edinburgh saw *Utopia, Limited* during its first week and the public was promptly informed of the fact. Articles appeared frequently telling the public how quickly tickets were selling. And on 24 October the following curious piece of information found its way into the *St James Gazette:*

Probably very few of the audience who witness the nightly interviews between Mr Gilbert's 'King of Utopia, Ltd.' and her Majesty's Life Guards are aware that the latest hero of the Labour party, King Lobengula of Matabeleland* actually received a real deputation of Life Guards at Bulawayo a few years ago. The Colonial Office authorities of the period thought that the sight of some officers of the Guards might conciliate Lobengula and establish a Union of Hearts.

Three British officers in *full uniform* visited the King who was said to have been a good deal impressed at the time!

The fact that the operas (especially in the 80s) were able to create this kind of awareness in the public was responsible for their authors' becoming, as Gilbert once remarked, 'as much an institution as Westminster Abbey'.

Somewhere along the line word got out that the Queen had commanded a performance of *Utopia, Limited* at Windsor Castle. Practically every newspaper in the country carried the same report:

The Queen might perhaps be amused by seeing the most stately of court ceremonials good-naturedly burlesqued, and she would also be greatly shocked at

---

* The phonetic structure of these African names suggests that Gilbert's design of the Utopian language, spoken briefly in the First Act of his opera, was not altogether spurious!

seeing individuals in the uniforms of the highest State Functionaries indulging in the most fantastic antics.

The book as it exists contains some rather 'strong meat' for Royalty.

The lines singled out as 'strong meat' for the Queen were:

> No peeress at our drawing room before the presence passes
> Who wouldn't be accepted by the lower middle classes.

This kind of anxiety in the press was always good for business.

By the middle of November the first production of *Utopia, Limited* opened in Australia. Three weeks later the touring company reached New Zealand. *The Brisbane Courier*, an Australian financial journal thought that the economic humour of Gilbert's opera was tame!!

Richard D'Oyly Carte opened the first provincial production of *Utopia, Limited* in Cambridge on 1 December; a month later it was in the repertory of *five* provincial companies. The November issue of *Housekeeper* declared:

The dramatic event of the year has been the production of the comic opera at the Savoy Theatre.

an opinion which the public did not share.

At the beginning of December Sullivan was in Berlin. He had hoped to make arrangements for the 'European première of *Ivanhoe* for February. He didn't. The opera was not performed abroad until 1895.

While in Germany, however, Sullivan heard that a well-known Hungarian soprano, Mme Ilka von Palmay, was appearing at the Theatre Unter den Linden as Nanki-Poo in *The Mikado*! Sullivan communicated this information to Carte, and an injunction was obtained to prevent her from appearing in a man's role in a Gilbert and Sullivan opera.

But Mme Palmay's Gilbert and Sullivan début, bizarre as it may have been, was *nothing* compared to the confusion she was to cause in her next Gilbert and Sullivan appearance, in London two years later.

By the time Sullivan returned from Germany it was obvious that *Utopia, Limited* would *not* have a run equal to that of *The Yeomen of the Guard* or *The Gondoliers*, and so Gilbert arranged to meet Sullivan to discuss the future. Gilbert was anxious to begin work on a new opera. (Gilbert had *always* been eager to begin work on a new opera as soon as his last one opened.)

Sullivan was not indifferent, but two problems had to be dealt with. First, Sullivan wanted it understood that if they were to work together again, no matter *what* disagreements might arise between them, Gilbert would *not* resort to the courts of law to settle them.

And second, Gilbert wanted the understanding that no matter what opera they eventually decided to collaborate on, there would be a role in it for Nancy McIntosh.

Sullivan did not jump at the idea. The next Gilbert and Sullivan opera was left in abeyance, and a few weeks later Gilbert visited Sullivan at Queen's Mansions and said:

We have worked for seventeen years together; we have put many thousands into each others' pockets. Now I appeal to you by our old friendship, by our long and honourable collaboration, by the regard and respect that I have for you and you, I hope, for me, as a *favour*, to write a female part in the next piece for Miss McIntosh and save her from starvation. *

Sullivan did not say yes or no. The fate of the 'next piece' was far from settled, and Sullivan was not going to bind himself to any conditions in advance.

By February, however, it became obvious that *Utopia, Limited's* days were numbered, and even if Sullivan was not making plans for his next opera, Gilbert was, and one by one reports of it began to creep into the press.

Gilbert wanted to follow the closing of *Utopia, Limited* with a revival and so did Carte. Such in fact was the plan although Gilbert had not as yet signed back to Carte the London rights to his operas. Nevertheless on 17 February a report appeared in *Figaro* that either *The Yeomen of the Guard* or *The Mikado* would be revived after *Utopia, Limited* closed.

Three days later the following bizarre report appeared in *Echo*:

The famous Gilbert and Sullivan combination will not end with the run of *Utopia, Limited*, for already another opera by the same writers is in contemplation; and though nothing has as yet been written, Sir Arthur has taken the *scenario* with him to the South of France. The scenes of this opera will be laid in Egypt, a country to which Mr Gilbert has made more than one pleasure trip and playgoers will be pleased to learn that Mr George Grossmith will probably return

* Sullivan's diary, 5 January 1894.

to the Savoy in a prominent part when this is produced. Meanwhile, upon the withdrawal of *Utopia* the interval will be filled by a revival of some of the older works of the same author and composer. In all probability *Iolanthe* or *Princess Ida* will be selected.

Ten days later this story was corrected in *Truth:*

According to the original report . . . Mr Gilbert proposed to reanimate a British Museum mummy thus bringing a daughter of the Pharoahs to life in the midst of British 19th Century civilization. It may nevertheless interest the public to know that the whole announcement is an extraordinary confusion of fact and error.

The origin of this curious report is still a mystery. Gilbert of course eventually wrote an opera about 'revival from the dead' (*The Grand Duke*) but in April of 1893 the idea had not even occurred to him.

The only fact which the press had thus far reported correctly was that George Grossmith had been contacted, and had expressed a willingness to go on the boards again.

On 21 March Gilbert gave an interview which was printed in *Cassell's Saturday Journal* under the title *Collaborating With Sir Arthur Sullivan* in which he stated that he and Sullivan were working on a new opera for the autumn. When asked what the subject was to be, Gilbert replied,

That is, I needn't say, a secret. If the subject were to leak out, it would very likely be anticipated, and we should then lay ourselves open to the charge of having copied our copiers.

Gilbert would have made this reply whether he had a new opera planned with Sullivan or not. As it happened, he had not. Everything was breaking down again.

As *Utopia, Limited* was about to close, the three partners were trying to arrange to follow it with a revival of *The Mikado*. Had it been satisfactorily settled, Sullivan would have agreed to set Gilbert's next opera, *His Excellency*. But the revival of *The Mikado* was not settled at all.

Gilbert refused to allow *The Mikado* to be played unless Nancy McIntosh appeared as Yum-Yum.

Sullivan wasn't having any of that. He refused to allow *The Mikado* to be performed if Miss McIntosh had to appear in the role.

That being the case, Gilbert refused to allow *The Mikado* (or any other opera by him and Sullivan) to be revived at the Savoy.

THE SAVOY.

MR. GEORGE GROSSMITH, TO MR. D'OYLY CARTE:—"WHAT DO YOU SAY, D'OYLY? SHALL I COME AND GIVE YOU A LEG-UP AGAIN?"

George Grossmith and Richard D'Oyly Carte. Cartoon in The Entr'acte, *31 March 1894.* (*Newspaper Library, Colindale.*)

That being the case, Sullivan refused to collaborate on Gilbert's next opera and that was the end of that round of negotiations.

Needless to say there was no shortage of press coverage when *this* little story got out.

That spring the two collaborators went their separate ways and Carte had no opera by either Gilbert or Sullivan to present at the Savoy. Carte had lost a fortune by producing Sullivan's grand opera *Ivanhoe* in 1891. Thereafter Sullivan came under constant pressure from the Cartes to come up with something, *anything*, that they could produce at the Savoy with his name on it. Something was required for the autumn. Sullivan had nothing in mind.

And then one evening Sullivan got together with F. C. Burnand whose self-righteous review of *Utopia, Limited* had recently done little to help the opera. Burnand had always been jealous of Gilbert for 'stealing' Sullivan away from him as a collaborator. Burnand may also have had reason to be angry with Gilbert for developing many ideas originally appearing in Burnand plays (and, one might add, improving them). Down through the years the reviews in *Punch*, which F. C. Burnand edited, traditionally criticized the Savoy operas more severely than any other magazine in London. Burnand would apparently have given anything to have had an opera of *his* playing at the Savoy during the last ten years. Finally fate was giving him his chance.

He and Sullivan had dinner at the Garrick Club and during the meal Sullivan must have explained his predicament, for by the time dinner was over, Burnand had proposed that they revise their 1868 production of *The Contrabandista* for the Savoy and Sullivan agreed. *
It is unbelievable that Mr Burnand, who had criticized Gilbert so harshly for his lack of originality in *Utopia, Limited*, could not come up with an *original* idea himself when presented with the opportunity to supply a libretto for the same theatre!
What Sullivan could have been thinking of that evening, nobody can tell. His old opera with Burnand had not been particularly successful in 1868. And in the years that followed, the public taste in light opera had become a bit more sophisticated – largely as a result of

---

* Herbert Sullivan's biography of Arthur Sullivan is the source of this account of the origin of *The Chieftain*.

Arthur Sullivan's contribution to the field. In any case the Sullivan–
Burnand work was produced with the new title *The Chieftain*. It was
the worst libretto that Sullivan ever set. It ran thirteen weeks.

But the most unfortunate aspect of Sullivan's part in *The Chieftain*
was the fact that it made him unavailable to set the opera that
Gilbert was writing that year, *His Excellency*. Unlike *The Mountebanks* two years earlier, *His Excellency* was 100 per cent in the
Savoy tradition. George Grossmith and Jessie Bond came back to the
boards to appear in it; Rutland Barrington took a leave of absence
from the Savoy to do so. Rosina Brandram was unwilling to leave the
Savoy, however, and so, in her place Gilbert engaged Alice Barnett
who had opened at the Savoy twelve years earlier as the Queen of the
Fairies in *Iolanthe*.

The inevitable Nancy McIntosh was also in the cast of *His Excellency*. She did not weaken the libretto this time for Gilbert had
designed it from the beginning with her in mind, but she did compromise the *score* to *His Excellency* inasmuch as her presence in the
cast had prevented Sullivan from composing it.

The story was Gilbert at his best. It concerned the adventures of a
practical-joking governor (George Grossmith) of a small town in
Denmark – a man whose practical jokes have lately begun to be just
a bit unpleasant. He is ultimately brought to terms by the Regent
(Rutland Barrington) who appears in the town in the unsuspected
guise of a strolling player.

The libretto is generally free from politics although it is thought
that the Regent may have been intended as a gentle caricature of
the Prince of Wales who was genuinely popular with the people and
had often visited parts of London incognito!

His Excellency was filled with patter songs, sentimental songs, and
ensembles in the best Savoy tradition. The problem with the production was the score. Had Sullivan written it, he would have found some
way of musically characterizing the milieu of Gilbert's Danish village,
as he had so successfully for Gilbert's Japan and Venice. Gilbert had
engaged Dr Osmond Carr to score the piece. Carr was twenty-two
years younger than Gilbert. He was in his early thirties, and had had
a few musical successes in the 90s including *Joan of Arc* and *Morocco
Bound*. In 1894 he looked like *the* up-and-coming *younger* composer –
something which may very well have appealed to Gilbert inasmuch
as his previous composer Alfred Cellier, had died while he was scoring

The Mountebanks.

But Frank Osmond Carr's strength had been in setting individual numbers. He had never had to meet the challenge of creating an entire milieu musically to the extent that a Gilbert libretto required. The score to *His Excellency* fell flat, and Osmond Carr did very little of importance thereafter.

His Excellency did not have a long run by Savoy standards, and the reason was generally conceded to have been the music. Even Gilbert knew it. '*His Excellency* started out well,' he wrote to Mrs Carte years later, 'and if it had had the benefit of your expensive friend Sullivan's music, it would have been a second *Mikado.*'

The end of 1894 was probably the most frustrating period in the entire Gilbert and Sullivan collaboration. *The Chieftain* opened on 12 December at the Savoy Theatre and on 27 December, a few streets away at the Lyric, *His Excellency* began its run. The two productions divided up England's favourite composer and librettist, as well as the leading singers who had been so much a part of their joint success the decade before. Neither opera ran through the spring.

Sullivan spent the rest of the winter (1894–1895) in his usual round of socializing, gambling and idleness. Gilbert spent his time developing his next libretto in the hope that it would be quickly produced and profitably so.

It was inevitable then, as the summer of 1895 rolled around, that the three partners should find themselves talking to each other again, resolving their new old differences, and agreeing to have one last shot at it.

Poster by Dudley Hardy.

6

The Writing of
The Grand Duke

ON Thursday 8 August 1895, Gilbert read Sullivan the first sketch of his latest opera, and left the copy with him to read over at his leisure. On Sunday, Sullivan read the outline again, and wrote to Gilbert and Carte to say that he would set it. Four days later, on Friday, 16 August 1895, the three of them met at Carte's home and agreed to produce *The Grand Duke* at the Savoy the following year. 'Went to Adelphi Terrace,' Sullivan wrote in his diary. 'All settled satisfactorily.'

All had indeed been settled satisfactorily. Gilbert, who had been withholding the London rights to his operas since 1891, signed an agreement which allowed D'Oyly Carte to present them once again at the Savoy. At the same time the delicate (or indelicate) question of Miss McIntosh was settled as well. It was tacitly understood that she would *not* appear in the new piece. (Gilbert however was not precluded from finding another ingénue to star in the opera if he chose to do so.)

For the moment at least things looked promising. Gilbert went to work and Sullivan went to Europe. From Luzon he cabled Mrs Carte that he could *not* have the new opera ready by November. Things were promising, but they were not as promising as all that. Sullivan went on to the Spas in Switzerland. His health was *very* bad.

While abroad, Sullivan travelled to Berlin where he supervised the long-delayed European première of *Ivanhoe*. It was not a great success, but it was not a failure. Gone were the days when every Sullivan performance caused a sensation.

Appropriately enough Sullivan began the score to *The Grand Duke* in Germany. While he was in Berlin he found time to compose the first two numbers. When he returned to London he was anxious to begin working on the opera full time. The outline had pleased him.

'I have studied the sketch plot very carefully,' Sullivan had written to Gilbert during the summer, 'it comes out as clear and bright as possible.'

'Clear and bright' indeed!

In February of 1893 Sullivan had declared Gilbert's sketch plot to *Utopia, Limited* to be the *best* he'd ever done.

Now the summer before the opening of *The Grand Duke* Sullivan pronounced the outline to this opera to be 'clear and bright'. The libretto to *The Grand Duke* was certainly *not* 'clear and bright' by the time it opened. One longs to ask the question, *What went wrong this time?*

The answer is not simple.

First, however, it is necessary to establish precisely what the sketch plot that Sullivan declared to be 'clear and bright' was like before it is possible to relate the unhappy course through which its brightness and clarity were compromised.

The evolution of Gilbert's libretto to *The Grand Duke* is quite different from the development of *Utopia, Limited*. In *Utopia, Limited* Gilbert started with a brilliant and original premise which he never succeeded in realizing. In *The Grand Duke* he began with a fully realized plot which he proceeded to weaken, confuse and embitter.

GILBERT'S SOURCES

Any popular writer, once he has become established, is bound to receive a considerable number of letters from his public, often from very far afield. Requests for collaboration, ideas for new operas, and manuscripts submitted for criticism all came to Gilbert with varying frequency and were generally not taken seriously.

But late in 1894 one letter to Gilbert from America received far more consideration than was generally accorded to fan mail. Mr Bertram Ellis, editor of a small newspaper in Keene, New Hampshire, wrote to Gilbert as follows:

Dear Sir,
    Enclosed you will find an editorial on Electrical execution written by myself for the *Keene Evening Sentinel*. I think you more capable of writing a comic opera that I could possibly be and should be very much pleased if you would take up my suggestion which is entirely original.

The electric chair had recently been invented and Mr Ellis's editorial reads as follows:

Dead, Yet Alive.

The resuscitation of an executed criminal furnishes a theme for the plot of a comic opera worthy the pen of the wittiest, most talented librettist. The legal, financial and social situations and predicaments are complex enough to tax the ingenuity of the most cunning. Suppose the governor of New York should grant the request for permission to experiment upon the next victim of the electrical chair and suppose the victim should be brought back to life after he had been declared dead by the proper authorities, then what would result?

The executed man would be dead. His wife if he had one, would logically be a widow. Could she marry another man without committing bigamy? Would she be obliged to marry him again in order to be his wife? The man's position would be equally puzzling. His children would be orphans and his wife would be a widow but he would not be a widower. For his wife would not be dead. He therefore could not marry again.

His property, if he had any: where would the title to that be? His death could be proved by the record of the execution. His heirs and next of kin would take the property, perhaps, and the poor resuscitated man would be penniless. An administrator or executor would be appointed and his estate would be settled. But suppose the man were insolvent. Could the creditors collect anything from the man? If he should accumulate property after his revival and should be sued for a former debt, could he prove his own death as a defense?

The poor unfortunate, more dead than alive, would be sorry that he had been brought back to life. Without family or fortune he would be tempted to commit suicide were it not for the fact that, being dead, it would be impossible. The only way left for him would be to begin life anew, to be christened again, to take a new name and seek new fortunes, to be in fact another man, who it is to be hoped would learn a lesson from his first existence and not place himself in a similar predicament a second time by committing another murder and being executed over again.

Gilbert appreciated Mr Ellis's reasoning for he pasted Mr Ellis's editorial on the first page of the plot-book for *The Grand Duke*. It is not known whether Mr Ellis of New Hampshire ever learned that his idea inspired the last Gilbert and Sullivan opera!

Gilbert decided to employ some of the Ellis logic in *The Grand Duke*, but he needed a story which took place in an exotic locale – one that would lend itself to the topsy-turvydom of the legal resuscitation of a 'dead' man. Gilbert's search for a suitable plot took him very far afield.

In contriving the plot for *The Grand Duke*, Gilbert drew upon two works by other authors. The first was a short story called *The Duke's Dilemma* which had appeared in *Blackwood's Magazine* in September 1853. The second was a musical (based on the *Blackwood's* story) which had played at the Avenue Theatre as recently as 1889, billed as follows:

The Prima Donna, Opera Comique in three acts adopted from a well known story by H. B. Farnie and Alfred Murray, music composed by Tito Mattei.

The Prima Donna, which did not have a long run, had been originally titled *The Grand Duke*. The first page of the Lord Chamberlain's copy bears the title *The Grand Duke*. It was changed to *The Prima Donna* because another play had been produced in Dundee in 1886 called *The Grand Duke* and the title was still controlled.

Blackwood's short story *The Duke's Dilemma* is an amusing tale of about twenty-five pages relating the problems of Grand Duke Leopold of Niesenstein whose treasury has become depleted and who faces financial ruin if he is unable to effect a marriage with Princess Wilhelmina, sister to the wealthy and influential Prince of Hanau. The Prince and Princess are soon to pay a visit to the Grand Duke's court and are sure to cancel the marriage when they learn of the Grand Duke's finances. His court is empty. His courtiers and guard have left the palace for non-payment of wages.

But the Grand Duke's problems are solved when Balthasar, the leader of a French theatrical company, offers the services of his actors as substitute courtiers. The plan is implemented and, after a bit of typical court intrigue, the marriage between Grand Duke Leopold and Princess Wilhelmina is arranged and all ends happily.

Besides several plot elements, there were other ideas in the *Blackwood's* story which Gilbert used. The satire on the royalty of Germany's countless duchies, electorates and principalities was suggested in one speech by Balthasar, the French actor:

'Last summer, having a little leisure, I made an excursion to Baden-Baden. As usual, it was crowded with fashionables. One rubbed shoulders with princes and trod upon highnesses' toes; one could not walk twenty yards without meeting a sovereign. All these crowned heads, kings, grand-dukes, electors, mingled easily and affably with the throng of visitors.'

Elsewhere in the story Gilbert found the seed for another theme which he was to develop:

The Grand Duke . . . began to suspect that the government of a grand duchy is a much easier matter than the management of a company of actors.

Gilbert found a few more useful ideas in Farnie's play *The Prima Donna* and apparently had no compunction about helping himself to them.

THE DUKE'S DILEMMA.

A CHRONICLE OF NIESENSTEIN.

THE close of the theatrical year, which in France occurs in early spring, annually brings to Paris a throng of actors and actresses, the disorganised elements of provincial companies, who repair to the capital to contract engagements for the new season. Paris is the grand centre to which all dramatic stars converge —the great bazaar where managers recruit their troops for the summer campaign. In bad weather the mart for this human merchandise is at an obscure coffeehouse near the Rue St Honoré; when the sun shines, the place of meeting is in the garden of the Palais Royal. There, pacing to and fro beneath the lime-trees, the high contracting parties pursue their negotiations and make their bargains. It is the theatrical Exchange, the histrionic *Bourse.* There the conversation and the company are alike curious. Many are the strange discussions and original anecdotes that there are heard; many the odd figures there paraded. Tragedians, comedians, singers, men and women, young and old, flock thither in quest of fortune and a good engagement. The threadbare coats of some say little in favour of recent success or present prosperity; but only hear them speak, and you are at once convinced that *they* have no need of broadcloth who are so amply covered with laurels. It is delightful to hear them talk of their triumphs, of the storms of applause, the rapturous bravos, the boundless enthusiasm, of the audiences they lately delighted. Their brows are oppressed with the weight of their bays. The south mourns their loss; if they go west, the north will be envious and inconsolable. As to themselves—north, south, east, or west— they care little to which point of the compass the breeze of their destiny may waft them. Thorough gypsies in their habits, accustomed to make the best of the passing hour, and to take small care for the future so long as the present is provided for, like soldiers they heed not the name of the town so long as the quarters be good.

It was a fine morning in April. The sun shone brightly, and, amongst the numerous loungers in the garden of the Palais Royal were several groups of actors. The season was already far advanced; all the companies were formed, and those players who had not secured an engagement had but a poor chance of finding one. Their anxiety was legible upon their countenances. A man of about fifty years of age walked to and fro, a newspaper in his hand, and to him, when he passed near them, the actors bowed—respectfully and hopefully. A quick glance was his acknowledgment of their salutation, and then his eyes reverted to his paper, as if it deeply interested him. When he was out of hearing, the actors, who had assumed their most picturesque attitudes to attract his attention, and who beheld their labour lost, vented their ill-humour.

"Balthasar is mighty proud," said one; "he has not a word to say to us."

"Perhaps he does not want anybody," remarked another; "I think he has no theatre this year."

"That would be odd. They say he is a clever manager."

"He may best prove his cleverness by keeping aloof. It is so difficult nowadays to do good in the provinces. The public is so fastidious! the authorities are so shabby, so unwilling to put their hands in their pockets. Ah, my dear fellow, our art is sadly fallen!"

Whilst the discontented actors bemoaned themselves, Balthasar eagerly accosted a young man who just then entered the garden by the passage of the Perron. The coffeehouse-keepers had already begun to put out tables under the tender foliage. The two men sat down at one of them.

"Well, Florival," said the manager, "does my offer suit you? Will you make one of us? I was glad to hear you had broken off with Ricardin.

The first page of The Duke's Dilemma, *as it appeared in* Blackwood's Edinburgh Magazine, *one of Gilbert's sources for* The Grand Duke. (*British Library.*)

Prima Donna

THE ~~GRAND DUKE.~~

Opera Comique in Three Acts.

BY

H. B. FARNIE AND ALFRED MURRAY.

MUSIC BY

TITO MATTEI.

Title page of The Prima Donna (*showing original title as* The
Grand Duke), *another of Gilbert's sources. (British Library.)*

In the libretto to *The Prima Donna*, the Grand Duke again receives the aid of the actors in staffing his palace. The wealthy Prince of Hanau makes a highly theatrical entrance in Act I. He is greeted by the Grand Duke and presented formally to ladies and gentlemen of 'the court' who are played by members of the acting company appearing in their own Shakespearian costumes.

In *The Prima Donna* the Grand Duke has a rival, the Elector of Hesse-Hausen who also desires the hand of the Princess of Hanau. But two young actors, Florival and Delia (who are engaged to each other) become involved in court intrigues which eventually bring about the failure of the Elector's suit and the successful union between the Grand Duke and the Princess of Hanau.

What Gilbert did was to transfer the Prince and Princess of Hanau to Monte Carlo and move their entrance to the last Act. The ritual with which they are greeted in Gilbert's version is not a formal presentation of the Court but a travesty on court formality. Gilbert's theatrical company does not appear in costumes from various Shakespearian plays to celebrate the Prince's arrival. They appear in *Troilus and Cressida* costumes to open the second Act. Florival and Delia, the young lovers in *The Prima Donna* become Ludwig and Lisa in *The Grand Duke* and they are implicated in a conspiracy to *overthrow* the Grand Duke and not to perpetuate his rule.

After Gilbert had completed his study of the *Blackwood's*–Farnie plot, he added a few ideas of his own, and sketched out his first outline as follows:

The Grand Duchy of Hesse Halbpfennig is governed by the Grand Duke Wilhelm. This Grand Duchy is only 10 acres in extent, and it has one small town – Spiesesaal. The Grand Duke is not at all popular – he is practically penniless and imposes dreadful taxes which cripple his fifty subjects.

In babyhood he was betrothed to Casilda, daughter of the Prince and Princess of Monaco. He and she have never met for he has never been able to afford to travel to Monaco and the Prince of Monaco has never been able to afford to travel to Hesse Halbpfennig. But Casilda is now of age and as the Prince has just won a large sum of money at a game called Roulette which he has just invented, he makes up his mind to pay his future son-in-law a visit, accompanied by his wife and daughter.*

---

* This and subsequent excerpts from Gilbert's plot-book of *The Grand Duke* are from the Gilbert papers, British Library, MS 49290.

The table below shows the evolution of the names of the characters and places as they appear first in the short story, then in the musical, next in Gilbert's earliest surviving libretto, and finally in the version that opened at the Savoy Theatre on 7 March 1896.

It is interesting to note that one German name which appeared in the 1853 story, Saxe-Topelhausen, was *not* adopted either in *The Prima Donna* or *The Grand Duke*, as apparently it was too close to Saxe-Coburg, the family of Prince Albert.

Characters in *The Duke's Dilemma* Blackwood's *Magazine*, September 1853	Characters in *The Prima Donna* Avenue Theatre, London, 1889

Leopold
    Grand Duke of Niesenstein
	Leopold
	    Grand Duke of Nierstein

Maximilian
    Prince of Hanau
	Maximilian
	    Prince of Hanau

The Princess Wilhelmina
    Sister to Maximilian
	The Princess Mina
	    Sister to Maximilian

Balthasar, manager of a troupe
    of French players
	Ballard, manager of a troupe
	    of French players

Florival, the lover	Florival, Jeune-Premier
Delia, the prima donna	Delia, Prima Donna

This outline makes mention of a conspiracy to overthrow the Grand Duke, however the reasons for it are vague. But Gilbert was working with broad strokes at the beginning, and with other men's ideas.

In the outlines that follow, Gilbert's own ideas make their appearance one after the other until, at last, the story takes recognizable shape.

The sausage roll appears next in Gilbert's notes, and with it, the accidental disclosure of the conspiracy.

Now by a rule of the Society, before one member addresses another, he has to take out a sausage roll and eat it. The other member does likewise and they converse . . . to Ernest and Notary, enters Ludwig (another conspirator) in great agitation. An awful thing has happened. Seeing a stranger and feeling doubtful whether he was a member, he challenged him by taking out a sausage roll and eating it. The stranger took out another sausage roll and ate that and Ludwig immediately entered into conversation with him, discussing freely the affairs of the conspiracy. He then discovered that the stranger was merely lunching and that his selecting a sausage roll for that purpose was a mere coincidence.

In the same draft, the Statutory Duel is introduced together with the legal consequences of 'reviving' a dead man.

Gilbert's original 'Grand Duke Wilhelm of Hesse Halbpfennig' was based on an eighteenth-century member of the royal family: a grandson of George III, the Landgrave Wilhelm of Hesse Cassel. It is recorded that, as ruler of his Duchy, he was able to increase his revenues 120 thalars by forbidding the practice of omitting fractions of $\frac{1}{2}$ of a penny in the accounting procedures of one of his dairies. This and other economic practices earned him the unflattering nickname of 'Halbpfennig'.

Characters in an early draft of Gilbert's libretto	*The Grand Duke* by W. S. Gilbert Savoy Theatre, final version
Wilhelm, Grand Duke of Hesse Halbpfennig	Rudolph, Grand Duke of Pfennig Halbpfennig
The Prince of Monte Carlo	The Prince of Monte Carlo
The Princess of Monte Carlo	The Princess of Monte Carlo
Daughter of the Prince	Daughter of the Prince
Ernest Dummkopf	Ernest Dummkopf,
A theatrical manager	A theatrical manager
Ludwig, his leading comedian	Ludwig, his leading comedian
Elsa, a soubrette	Lisa, a soubrette

The Notary advises them to avail themselves at once of the law passed 100 years ago to abolish duelling . . . when two men quarrelled to the duelling point, instead of fighting they were to draw two cards in the presence of a notary and the one who drew the best card was to be henceforth civilly and socially dead, the survivor taking upon himself all the debts and other responsibilities incurred by the civilly defunct. By this means one of them will escape the penalty, and as the law has only a fortnight to run – when it will expire as a matter of course (unless revived which is unlikely) the defunct will then come to life again and (having once died) cannot be proceeded against.

This logic was a skilful blend of Mr Ellis's and Mr Gilbert's.

In the next draft the character of the Grand Duke is developed.

Wilhelm a mean (rich) shabby fellow – quite a miser.
Was betrothed in infancy to daughter of Prince of Monaco.
Prince very poor, very proud.
Princess very pretty.
Wilhelm resents having to marry her.
When he marries he means to marry money and Princess is poor – penniless.

A few pages later Gilbert begins to develop the idea of the theatrical company. All the elements of Gilbert's First Act are now present and

[The Grand Duke]

14

The Grand Duchy of Hesse Halbpfennig is governed by the Grand Duke Wilhelm. This Grand Duchy is only 10 acres in extent, & it has one small town – Spiessesaal. The Grand Duke is not at all popular – he is practically penniless & imposes dreadful taxes which cripple his fifty subjects.

In babyhood he was betrothed to the ~~Princess~~ Casilda, daughter of the Prince & Princess of Monaco ~~King & Queen of Castile~~. He & she have never met for he has never been able to afford to travel to ~~Castile~~ Monaco; & the ~~King~~ Prince of ~~Castile~~ Monaco; Casilda has never been able to afford to travel to Hesse ~~Halbpfennig~~. But the ~~Princess~~ Casilda is now of age & as the Prince has just won a large sum of money at a game called Roulette which he has just invented, he makes up his mind to pay his future son in law a visit, accompanied by his wife & daughter. This visit is a source of dreadful inconvenience to Wilhelm – who is ashamed to let the Prince & Princess know how poor & insignificant he is, & who, moreover, having fallen in love with one Bertha – a beautiful villager, is altogether anxious to escape from his troth to Casilda.

His Court consists of a Chamberlain, a Chaplain, a Treasurer, a Lady Housekeeper, a Minister of Police & a Commander in Chief. There are, besides some domestic servants – including 3 housemaids – & there is a garrison of 6 soldiers. There is great discontent among these people for none of them have received any pay for several months. The piece may open with a meeting of these people – called by the Commander in chief – who suggests to them that the approaching visit of the ~~Grand~~ Prince & Princess of Monaco & their daughter will afford an excellent opportunity for them to

A page from Gilbert's plot-book of The Grand Duke. (*British Library.*)

this draft of the sketch plot ends at Ludwig's unexpected revival of the law.

At this point Gilbert makes his own outline of the legal rights of the 'revived' dead man. Gilbert followed Mr Ellis's article very closely with the intention of using it as the basis of the Second Act.

Position of a man resuscitated after Civil Death:

He would be obliged to marry his wife again – or allow her to remain as widow – or let her marry another man.

His heirs and next of kin would take his property and he would be penniless.

If sued on any contract he could plead his own death as a defence.

He might be tempted under these distressing circumstances to commit suicide, but he couldn't, having already died.

The course is to begin life anew, be christened again, take new name, and seek new fortunes – to be another man who would learn a lesson from his past experience.

If this idea is to be exploited, the dead man must be resuscitated much earlier in the piece – and his resuscitation must be through the agency of the Alteration of the Calendar. Therefore the Calendar incident must be introduced much earlier into the piece to give time for development of complicated and various consequences.

The 'calendar incident' was a plot device whereby the effects of the Statutory Duel would be annulled owing to the arrival of a dispatch from the Pope obliterating fourteen days from the calendar.

But this line of development was hastily abandoned as being too complicated for even a Gilbert plot!

Most of the latter half of the plot-book is spent developing other themes for Act II. In one outline Gilbert considered centring the Act about the adventures of the newly installed Grand Duke Ludwig and the four 'Grand Duchesses', Lisa, Julia, the Baroness von Krackenfeld and the Princess of Monte Carlo who, in that order, try to claim his hand. This plot line is clear, bright, witty, full of delightful surprises and worthy of the librettist at his best. To the extent that Gilbert used it he was completely successful.

The plot-book suggests quite clearly that Gilbert intended to give far more prominence to the Prince and Princess of Monte Carlo than he ultimately did. It is intended that their impending visit be announced to the Grand Duke in the First Act. In the last Act a scene is plotted in which the 'deceased' Grand Duke and Ernest have a meeting and resolve to return to life and reclaim their rights. Had Gilbert implemented *these* ideas he would have wound up with a much more coherent and solidly structured story.

One of the final sketches in the plot-book begins as follows:

Ernest has just been married to Lisa. They enter accompanied by congratulatory chorus. Ludwig has also been married to Elsa, but Elsa had to go home to change her dress and this had delayed them. However they will be here presently and and the Notary (who is also solicitor to the Conspirators) is present and takes part in the ensuing Dialogue from which it appears that Ernest is proprietor of theatrical troupe. That he has married his leading lady . . . He is uneasy for other reasons. Hesse Halbpfennig is ruled by a highly unpopular Grand Duke – a shabby miserly cowardly creature who, among other enormities has abolished the State Theatre. This has induced Ludwig to form a conspiracy for his deposition.

There is no mention at all in this final plot-book sketch of the murky German milieu that came to dominate Gilbert's opera. There is no suggestion of the backstage politics of Ernest's troupe that divert so much of Gilbert's First Act. And there is not a trace of an ingénue named Julia Jellicoe who eventually takes over the opera.

In the sketch plot that Gilbert left with Sullivan in the summer of 1895, he had brought together all of the elements for a delightful satire on gambling, capital punishment, and the royalty of the *smaller* courts of Europe. An outline based on these ideas easily strikes one, as it did Arthur Sullivan, as 'clear and bright'.

The degeneration of Gilbert's plot from the one which he showed to Sullivan in 1895 to the one which he produced at the Savoy in 1896 resulted from the introduction of three elements not contemplated by the original sketch plot:

1 satire on backstage politics *
2 the character of Julia Jellicoe *
3 the Gilbertian Germany

As Gilbert developed his libretto from August to December one by one these elements began to take control.

GILBERT'S GERMANY

When Bismarck brought about the unification of Germany in the 1860s, a major identity crisis was created for many of the smaller German duchies, protectorates, electorates, houses and royal families. The tiny German courts, in a desperate effort to retain autonomous

* These themes are discussed in the next chapter.

identity, became well-known for their rigid insistence on etiquette and ceremony and eventually, as need would have it, economy.

In *The Gondoliers* the Duke of Plaza Toro represented a Spanish grandee whose fortunes had fallen, but who was still able to support his family by hiring out the use of his name. England too had her 'descending' aristocrats, forced year after year to sell more and more of their land in order to support themselves.

The choice of the aristocratically poor Duchy of Pfennig Halbpfennig, and the use of the Roulette wheel as the agency whereby the Prince of Monte Carlo regains his family's fortune, are two variations on an old Gilbertian theme.

The choice of *Germany*, however, as the locale of the last Gilbert and Sullivan opera, was made to facilitate a particularly bitter bit of satire, and one which was to a large extent emasculated before the opera opened.

In the earliest extant version of the libretto,* for example, Grand Duke Rudolph is originally designated as Grand Duke Wilhelm, no doubt a dig at Kaiser Wilhelm II who, like Gilbert's Grand Duke, was fond of composing his own musical pieces (i.e. 'The Wedding Anthem') and promoting their sales.

In Gilbert's first printed version the Duchy of Pfennig Halbpfennig was originally the Duchy of Hesse Halbpfennig.

The Grand Duke's entrance was originally heralded by seven chamberlains singing the following verse:

> The good Grand Duke of Hesse Halbpfennig,
> Though he may be of German Royalty a sprig,
> In point of fact he's nothing but a miserable pig
> Is the good Grand Duke of Hesse Halbpfennig.

The word pig was changed to prig and the line 'though he may be of German Royalty a sprig' was rewritten completely. Hesse Halbpfennig was changed to Pfennig Halbpfennig, and Wilhelm was changed to Rudolph in order to avoid all reference to *another* Wilhelm, Landgrave of Hesse Cassel, an obscure German relative of Queen Victoria's, who was known for his miserly ways. Gilbert's satire was often open to more than one interpretation.

---

* The American Copyright Deposit copy at the Library of Congress, Washington, D.C. See p. 211.

But one of Gilbert's major devices of Anglo-German satire, which was not cut, was Julia Jellicoe, the one 'English' character in the opera, who was made to speak with a German accent! All of the ostensibly German characters spoke with English accents. Much was made of this in the dialogue. Julia says:

Ach, what a crackjaw language this German is.

O, I should like to talk to you in my own language for five minutes – only five minutes. I know some good, strong, energetic English remarks that would shrivel your trusting nature into raisins.

Later in the opera, Ernest Dummkopf says to her in desperation:

We will fly to your native country and I'll play broken-English in London as you play broken-German here!

Mme Palmay who played the 'German' Englishwoman had a European accent. The reviewers praised her performance and were amused by the fact that she used typically English gestures – Gilbert's direction.

Victoria. A German Queen on the English Throne.　　*Victoria. An English Queen on the German Throne.*

But by the time *The Grand Duke* opened, the opera had been bowdlerized of its more specific German references and it never occurred to anyone that Gilbert had somebody specific in mind when he made his references to 'sprigs of German Royalty' or 'playing broken-English in London'.

One wants to proceed very cautiously after this point, but the fact remains that Gilbert did delete his questionable German topicalities during rehearsals, so there must have been someone whom Gilbert was trying *not* to offend.

It is known that Queen Victoria once made a phonograph recording of her voice giving Christmas greetings to a European relative. She ordered that the cylinder be destroyed after it was played – her reason being that she did not want the voice of the Queen to be available to the common people. She may also have chosen not to preserve the cylinder in order to prevent future generations from being able to hear the former Queen of England speaking fluent German or heavily accented English.

But Queen Victoria would not have been the only royal personage who could have inspired Julia Jellicoe's Anglo-Germanic dyslexia. Queen Victoria's eldest daughter, the Princess Royal, whose name was also Victoria, had married Emperor Frederick III (the son of Kaiser Wilhelm I). Princess Victoria was the mother of Kaiser Wilhelm II and was living in Germany. There was thus a German-speaking Queen in England and an English-speaking Queen in Germany when Gilbert was writing *The Grand Duke*.

But there is a further parallel between the careers of the Princess Royal and Julia Jellicoe. The Princess Royal of England had been Crown Princess of Germany for well over twenty years before Kaiser Wilhelm, her husband's father, died and she became Empress. Her husband, however, died after a reign of only three months, whereupon her son was proclaimed Kaiser Wilhelm II. The Princess Royal thus went from Crown Princess to Dowager Empress in less than half a year – a career not unlike that of Julia Jellicoe, whose reign of Grand Duchess lasts half a day. Julia sings the following verse after losing her place as Grand Duchess:

> So ends my dream – so fades my vision fair!
> Of hope no gleam – distraction and despair!
> My cherished dream, the Ducal throne to share,
> That aim supreme has vanished into air!

81

Gilbert may well have had the Princess Victoria in mind.

Another member of Queen Victoria's family whose career may also be satirically represented in *The Grand Duke* is the Duke of Kent, the fourth son of George III, and Queen Victoria's father.

The Duke of Kent had a moderate income from the British government and had married late in life at a time when there was no direct heir to the British throne. He had hoped to increase his income by marrying for the express purpose of providing the Crown with an heir. He married the Princess of Leiningen who was sister to the Duke of Saxe-Coburg. Saxe-Coburg was a small duchy which had been impoverished by the Napoleonic wars. The Duke himself, like the Prince of Monte Carlo, was heavily in debt. In fact, after his marriage, the Duke of Kent declared himself too poor to live in England and remained instead on the Continent.

But when his wife became pregnant (with a child who would one day ascend the British throne) the Duke determined that the child should be born in England and, organizing his family somewhat shabbily, proceeded to London. Lytton Strachey describes the Duke's trip to England:

Funds were lacking for the journey, but his determination was not to be set aside. Come what may, he declared his child must be English born. A carriage was hired, and the Duke himself mounted the box. Inside were the Duchess, her daughter, Feodora, a girl of fourteen, with maids, nurses, lap-dogs, and canaries. Off they drove – through Germany, through France: bad roads, cheap inns were nothing to the rigorous Duke and the equable abundant Duchess.

It would be very difficult to find a model more suggestive of the arrival of Gilbert's Prince and Princess of Monte Carlo (suddenly freed from debt) attended by a miserly assortment of servants hired from a local theatre at eighteenpence a day to claim the throne of Pfennig Halbpfennig.

This is bitter satire indeed. Gilbert was not fond of Queen Victoria. But he had never expressed his feelings angrily before. The man who had written 'He Is An Englishman' could hardly have been proud of the German heritage of his monarch. And so when Gilbert decided to write an opera that took place in a mythical country which typified the things that Germany represented to him, it is little wonder that the milieu of Pfennig Halbpfennig became a murky one.

7

The Production Period

BUT it was not only the German satire which changed Gilbert's libretto from what Sullivan had once regarded as 'clear and bright'. The introduction of the character of Julia Jellicoe did just as much damage to the original outline. Sullivan's letter to Gilbert of 11 August 1895 makes it clear from his discussion of the plot that this character had not been included in the outline which Gilbert first read to Sullivan.

. . . There is one very important suggestion I should like to make . . . Of course I speak from the musical point of view. How would it do to make Lisa the principal soprano part and Elsa the contralto. She might be the leading tragedy lady of Ludwig's troupe, and contralto of the Operatic company – not necessarily old, but (if played by Brandram) staid and earnest, a suitable wife for the manager . . . Perry would make an admirable young shrewish, no-nonsense-about-her Countess Krackenfeld.*

Without the character of Julia Jellicoe, Gilbert had created an amusing satire on petty royalty, gambling and duelling. With the introduction of Julia Jellicoe Gilbert added nothing to his plot. He merely interrupted it with one aria, one recitation and three duets – a great deal of irrelevant singing for a character who was not even contemplated when Sullivan agreed to score the opera.

Immediately prior to the opening of *The Grand Duke*, Gilbert and Sullivan and Carte had agreed to present a revival of *The Mikado* at the Savoy. *The Mikado* would play at night while the new opera was rehearsed in the morning as in the old days.

The new production of *The Mikado* was in every way as brilliant as the original. Gilbert directed; Rutland Barrington and Rosina Brandram, who were still contract players at the Savoy, appeared in

* Pearson, p. 185.

the production, and Richard Temple and Jessie Bond, who had been absent for several seasons, returned to recreate their original roles.

As Gilbert put the finishing touches on his new libretto he tailored the leading roles to the talents of these four actors whose performances had been responsible for so much of his success in the past. Not having had a success for seven years, Gilbert was determined, in his production of *The Grand Duke*, to have as much going for him as possible. Unfortunately, at the final moment, Mr Temple and Miss Bond broke the news to Gilbert that they would not be appearing in the new opera. Why Richard Temple declined to appear in *The Grand Duke* is not clear, but Jessie Bond explains her absence from the cast in her memoirs:

> When 'Mikado' was revived, none of us knew that when its run was over, Jessie Bond would leave the stage forever. I kept the bitter fact secret as far as possible, for it *was* bitter, though I was going to make a happy marriage. When I told Gilbert he was so angry that I don't think he ever quite forgave me; he would not accept my health as an excuse, he was unreasonable as, alas, he often was!
>
> 'You are a little fool!' he said.
>
> . . . Neither he nor Arthur Sullivan sent me a wedding present.

Jessie Bond *did* keep her plans to retire a secret for too long. Her announcement caught Gilbert unawares. He had counted on her very much. The entrance of her and Richard Temple, two old Savoyards, *together* in the *last* Act of the opera would have had an electric effect on the audience.

Gilbert's anger was so great that it crept into his libretto! In the First Act Finale Julia Jellicoe, in horror, gives up her engagement to Ernest, and agrees, out of professional obligation, to play the Grand Duchess of Pfennig Halbpfennig (to Ludwig's Grand Duke). The Notary explains that theatrical engagements are more binding than marital ones:

> Though marriage contracts – or whate'er you call 'em – are very solemn,
> Dramatic contracts (which you all adore so) are even more so.

Jessie Bond was one of the few performers who had always been able to have her way with Gilbert. She was able to get rises, extra songs and solo entrances pretty much as she pleased. It would appear that when she abandoned Gilbert as the rehearsals for *The Grand Duke* approached, Gilbert, who never was one to keep his displeasure to himself, put his anger into his libretto. There is much humour at the expense of leading ladies. This point of view is not developed in the plot-book and probably did not occur to Gilbert until Jessie Bond made her untimely departure.

It may also have been at that time that Gilbert cancelled one of his better lyrics in favour of an inferior one. Among Gilbert's papers there survives a 'lost' lyric from *The Grand Duke*, prepared presumably for Ernest to sing in the First Act when he bases his qualifications to run a Grand Duchy on his experience in the theatre.

'THE STROLLER'S SONG'

The Stroller's life is freedom true – a fact
   I'm now attesting.
The King, well he's an actor too – hard worked
   and never resting.
From eight to ten your strollers play – say twelve
   to be within time.
The King plays fifty parts a day, from dawn to
   turning in time.
The King dies once and dies outright, then
   flies to regions upper.
The Stroller, he dies every night, and toddles
   home to supper.
With dangers dark and dangers drear your modern
   monarch grapples.
The deadliest missiles strollers fear are
   oranges and apples.
      On Kingly crimes falls vengeance dread;
      A king may sometimes lose his head.
      If fairly clever in the biz,
      An actor never loses his.

The monarch who resentment shows – his country
   always blames him.
The actor stabs a dozen foes and no policeman
   claims him.
When kings disburse their subjects' gold, they
   rouse the papers weekly;
When actor gives 'a sum twice told' the
   country hears it meekly.
A King from Royalty deposed finds life a
   dull chimera.
The Actor, when his theatre's closed turns
   lightly to the 'Era.'

In short to sum in brief degree my
   argument preceedent,
A King must always Kingly be – a light
   Comedian needn't.
      Oh don't suppose a Monarch's crown
      Is bed of rose or bed of down.
      Condemned to State as Monarchs are,
      A stroller's fate is fairer far!

This lyric was replaced by another one in which Mr Gilbert took out some of his hostilities against actors and actresses. The new lyric is much less amusing than 'The Stroller's Song'.

'ERNEST'S SONG'

Were I a king in very truth,
And had a son – a guileless youth –
   In probable succession;
To teach him patience, teach him tact,
How promptly in a fix to act,
He should adopt, in point of fact,
   A manager's profession.
To that condition he should stoop
   (Despite a too fond mother),
With eight or ten 'stars' in his troupe,
   All jealous of each other!
Oh, the man who can rule a theatrical crew,
Each member a genius (and some of them two),
And manage to humour them, little and great,
   Can govern this tuppenny State!

Both A and B rehearsal slight –
They say they'll be 'all right at night'
   (They've both to go to school yet);
C in each act must change her dress,
D will attempt to 'square the press';
E won't play Romeo unless
   His grandmother plays Juliet;
F claims all hoydens as her rights
   (She's played them thirty seasons);
And G must show herself in tights
   For two convincing reasons –
   Two very well-shaped reasons!
Oh, the man who can drive a theatrical team,
With wheelers and leaders in order supreme,

A lyric from The Grand Duke *with corrections in Gilbert's hand.*
(*British Library.*)

> Can govern and rule, with a wave of his fin,
> All Europe – with Ireland thrown in!

Already the brightness of Gilbert's original libretto was beginning to tarnish.

But introducing a certain amount of bitter satire upon theatrical life was not the only thing which Gilbert did as a result of the unexpected loss of Richard Temple and Jessie Bond. He shortened their parts. Two songs, which had originally been written with them in mind, 'He was my Maiden Heart's First Prince' and 'You Forward Minx' were cut at an early stage of rehearsals. *

The part of Grand Duke Rudolph appears to have been written with George Grossmith in mind. Grossmith had appeared in *His Excellency* in 1894, and was to return to the Savoy (albeit briefly) in *His Majesty* in 1897. Why he did not appear in *The Grand Duke* is unclear. But the title role appears to have been cut down considerably. Rudolph has practically nothing to do in the last Act, although he figures prominently in Gilbert's plot-book outlines.

It would be fair to assume that when George Grossmith, Richard Temple and Jessie Bond proved unavailable for *The Grand Duke*, Gilbert decided to edit their parts rather than entrust the roles *in toto* to their understudies. Gilbert then decided that he needed a 'guest star' to carry the show. The 'guest star' in Gilbert's last two operas had been Nancy McIntosh. Nan was out of the question for the Savoy, of course, but if Gilbert wanted to hire *another* ingénue, and build her up as a star, he knew that he would have the Cartes' support, for they were always of the opinion that the *right* ingénue could generally be counted on to sell a great number of tickets.

Gilbert's talent hunt ended with the discovery of the Hungarian soprano whom Sullivan had had enjoined from appearing as Nanki-Poo in Berlin a few years before. Mme Ilka von Palmay had appeared in *Der Vogelhändler* at the Drury Lane Theatre that summer and Gilbert engaged her for his new opera.

Countess Palmay was an unquestionably fine performer. She has left behind several very fine gramophone records and photographs which prove it. Mme Palmay had a strong European accent which Gilbert had to 'accommodate' if he was going to use her in a Savoy production. As all of the other members of the Savoy troupe were

---

* These songs appear on pp. 274 and 276.

BEHIND THE SCENES AT THE SAVOY.

MR. **RUTLAND BARRINGTON**, TO MR. GEORGE GROSSMITH:—"SORRY YOU'RE NOT WITH US, GEORGE."

Rutland Barrington and George Grossmith. Cartoon in The Entr'acte, *4 April 1896.* (*Newspaper Library, Colindale.*)

Madame Palmay, offstage, St Paul's *27 March 1896. (News-paper library, Colindale.)*

English, and as the opera was set in Germany, it appealed to Gilbert's sense of the ridiculous to have the one Savoyard with an accent portraying the one 'English' character in the opera.

Thus Gilbert created the role of Julia Jellicoe the 'English' com-medienne with the German accent, and her role grew and grew and grew. When it finished growing, the libretto which Sullivan had initially thought to be 'clear and bright' was utterly unrecognizable.

Gilbert always developed his ideas from one opera to another. In the 80s the Dragoons Chorus in *Patience* became the Peers Chorus in *Iolanthe*; the Mikado's Second Act entrance became Sir Roderic's Second Act entrance an opera later. In the 90s it was Nancy McIntosh, the ingénue for whom Gilbert weakened the plot of *Utopia, Limited* who, two and a half years later became Ilka von Palmay, the soprano for whom he destroyed the libretto of *The Grand Duke*.

The revival of *The Mikado* opened on 6 November 1895, and was a tremendous success.

The rehearsals for *The Grand Duke* began in January 1896, and could not possibly have gone smoothly. Gilbert was again suffering from gout, and had to be carried to and from the stage. It must have been a great source of irritation to him to know that Jessie Bond and Richard Temple were appearing in his old opera in his theatre every night, and yet they were not available to him to rehearse his new opera by day.

Sullivan had gone to the Continent the previous summer for his health, and prior to his return to London he had been afflicted by a further series of kidney attacks. He was in a greatly weakened state and forced to resort to morphine fairly regularly.

Richard D'Oyly Carte too had been recently incapacitated by illness.

Sullivan's diary for the rehearsal period is empty. This is a bad sign. The only other times when Sullivan had failed to make diary entries were during periods of illness, depression, or the rehearsals of *The Chieftain*. Sullivan could tell in advance when something wasn't working.

As the rehearsals progressed, Gilbert seemed to rely less and less upon the chorus and soloists of the Savoy Company and more and more upon lavishness, spectacle and visual effects, things which he had exploited heavily, and with little success, in *Utopia, Limited*. Gilbert was relying on his technique as a stage director, and not as a satirist, in the production of his last two Savoy operas, and his audiences did not go to the Savoy solely for visual effects.

In *The Grand Duke* the visual splendour of the Greek Wedding Procession approached the impact of the Drawing Room Scene in *Utopia, Limited*. In both operas Gilbert achieved a dramatic visual effect by a costume change between Acts I and II. In *Utopia, Limited* the wild native garb changed to well-tailored English uniforms and

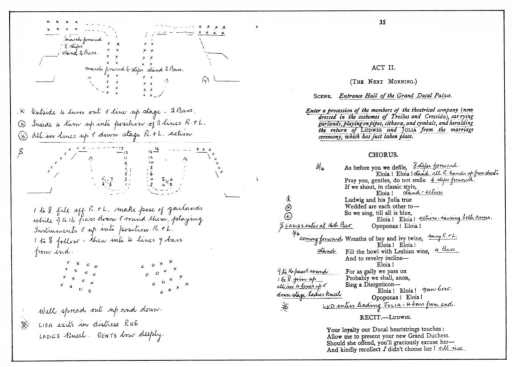

Pages from the prompt copy of The Grand Duke *showing Gilbert's stage directions for the Greek Wedding Chorus at the opening of Act II. (Bridget D'Oyly Carte.)*

dresses. In *The Grand Duke* the close-fitting European costumes gave way to loose gowns and Greek robes.

Gilbert made much of the entrance of Princess Zara and the Life Guards in *Utopia, Limited*, and much more of the entrances of Rudolph and his Chamberlains and the Monte Carlos and their attendants in *The Grand Duke*.

A tarantella in the last Act of *Utopia, Limited*, became a wild dance in the last Act of *The Grand Duke*.

Gilbert had very little faith in himself when he produced his last two operas with Sullivan. After one lawsuit with his partners, five years of painful illness, and three less than successful productions, he no longer trusted his life-long ability to amuse. If only he had retained enough confidence in 1893 or 1896 to believe that his innate wit as a writer was sufficient (as it had been for twenty years) to hold the interest of his audience, his final operas with Sullivan would have been successful. But there was a curse on Gilbert and Sullivan in the 90s, and nothing they did worked out properly.

8

The Opening of
The Grand Duke

THERE had been eight Gilbert and Sullivan premières in London in the 80s; so far in the 90s there had only been one. The opening of *The Grand Duke* would be a social event whether the opera succeeded or not.

Prior to the opening there was much rejoicing that Gilbert and Sullivan were again working together on a new piece. The successful revival of *The Mikado* had whetted everyone's appetite.

Mme Palmay made excellent copy, and articles and interviews with her appeared in numerous newspapers and periodicals, as articles about Miss McIntosh had appeared three years before.

The afternoon before the opening Gilbert held another public dress rehearsal for the benefit of the press. This time, unlike the public rehearsal of *Utopia, Limited*, the opera was performed straight through without interruptions, and with no clowning by Sullivan or Gilbert for the benefit of the audience.

The opening itself was characterized by all the excitement and glamour typical of Victorian England.

It was as difficult to get a stall for the Savoy first night as for the scriptural camel to thread the needle.

Man of the World

The guests at the première included the Lord Chamberlain and Lady Latham, Lord and Lady Londesborough, Lord and Lady Donoughmore, Sir Francis and Lady Lockwood, George Edwardes and Julia Gwynne, Jessie Bond, Mr and Mrs Pinero, Signor Tosti, Kate Rorke, Ernest Ford and many more notables.

Sullivan entered the pit at 8.15. He was unusually nervous (as usual), he was well received by the faithful audience (as usual) and

93

THIS EVENING, SATURDAY, MARCH 7th, at 8.15, will be produced a NEW AND ORIGINAL COMIC OPERA, entitled—

THE GRAND DUKE,

Or, The Statutory Duel.

Written by W. S. GILBERT.   Composed by ARTHUR SULLIVAN.

RUDOLPH (Grand Duke of Pfennig-Halbpfennig)	MR. WALTER PASSMORE
ERNEST DUMMKOPF (a Theatrical Manager)	MR. CHARLES KENNINGHAM
LUDWIG (his Leading Comedian)	MR. RUTLAND BARRINGTON
DR. TANNHÄUSER (a Notary)	MR. SCOTT RUSSELL
THE PRINCE OF MONTE CARLO	MR. R. SCOTT FISHE
VISCOUNT MENTONE	MR. E. CARLETON
BEN HASHBAZ (a Costumier)	MR. C. HERBERT WORKMAN
HERALD	MR. JONES HEWSON
THE PRINCESS OF MONTE CARLO (Betrothed to Rudolph) ..	MISS EMMIE OWEN
THE BARONESS VON KRAKENFELDT (Betrothed to Rudolph) ..	MISS ROSINA BRANDRAM
JULIA JELLICOE (an English Comedian)	MDME. ILKA VON PALMAY
LISA (a Soubrette)	MISS FLORENCE PERRY
OLGA	MISS MILDRED BAKER
GRETCHEN	MISS RUTH VINCENT
BERTHA (Members of Ernest Dummkopf's Theatrical Company) ..	MISS JESSIE ROSE
ELSA	MISS ETHEL WILSON
MARTHA	MISS BEATRICE PERRY

Chamberlains, Nobles, Actors, Actresses, etc.

PRODUCED UNDER THE PERSONAL DIRECTION OF THE AUTHOR AND THE COMPOSER.

STAGE DIRECTOR   ..   ..   MR. CHARLES HARRIS.

The last Gilbert and Sullivan First Night Programme, 7 March 1896.

the performance ran smoothly (as usual). Sullivan was tremendously relieved when the performance was over. The production had not been easy and everyone's nerves were frayed. Sullivan remarked in his diary that the piece had dragged a little, but that its success had been genuine.

The opera's reception on the first night had been great. (After that it was quite a different story.) The first nighters had a great stake in making the evening a success, and most of the people present were determined to do so.

Mr W. S. Gilbert and Sir Arthur Sullivan's new opera was bought out at the Savoy last night and received with the utmost enthusiasm by a crowded house.
Sunday Times

Many of the reviewers were determined to see only the good things in the opera.

1896 31 Days   **7 SATURDAY** [67–299]   [7] **March**

Earliest Day for commencement of
Spring Quarter Sessions

Busy all day - shopping &c. auntie called for Bertie time at ¼ to 8. to go to theatre - Began new opera "Grand Duke" at ¼ past 8 - usual reception - Opera went well - over at 11.15. Parts of it dragged a little - dialogue too rehearsed but success great and genuine I think. Supped at Savoy with Oppenheim &c - then home. Thank God Opera is finished + out.

Sullivan's diary entry for 7 March 1896, the opening of The Grand Duke. (*Beinecke Rare Book and Manuscript Library.*)

. . . The fact remains that *The Grand Duke* is from first to last a delightful entertainment.
The Theatre

Mr Gilbert's libretto is, if possible, more brilliant than it has ever been before.
Cork Daily Herald

Sir Arthur Sullivan's music is tuneful and excellent, far above all other living composers . . .
Modern Society

There seems to have been a great deal to praise, in the performance at least. Favourites such as Rutland Barrington and Rosina Brandram, as well as such relative newcomers as Emmie Owen and Walter Passmore, were singled out for special mention.

First page of the Overture to The Grand Duke *in Sullivan's hand,
establishing the fact that he composed it himself.*

The low comedy part of *The Grand Duke* is played by Walter Passmore who has
the reversion of Grossmith's place in the company and always brings an accurate
sense of character into his parts.

Man of the World

Miss Rosina Brandram is as artistic as ever in the part of the Baroness, adding yet
another to her series of careful portraits of elderly and amorous ladies.

The Times

All eyes of course were on the début of the evening, which belonged
to Mme Palmay. Unlike Nancy McIntosh, Mme Palmay was a sea-
soned artist. The talent which Gilbert had recognized in her was

indeed present in abundance. She had stolen the libretto in rehearsals; she stole the show in performance.

The histrionic success of the piece is the English actress *Julia Jellicoe* of Mme Ilka von Palmay . . . Mme von Palmay has a pleasing voice of rare freshness and her acting quite lifted the piece when she was on the stage.
Musical Standard

Even Gilbert's effects proved impressive enough on one viewing:

. . . the droll entrance of Rudolph's chamberlains took the house by storm in the first act.
Cork Daily Herald

. . . the 'job lot' of noblemen hired from a Jew costumier by the Prince of Monte Carlo [is] among the best things in the piece.
Man of the World

The scenery, dresses and mounting are as usual irreproachable, and the street perspective in the first scene is one of the most successful things of its kind ever to be seen on the stage.
The Times

There were six encores taken on the first night:

> 'By the Mystic Regulation' (Barrington)
> 'Strange the Views Some People Hold' (Quintet)
> 'At the Outset I may Mention' (Barrington)
> 'Take Good Care of Him' (Perry)
> 'So Ends My Dream' (Palmay)
> 'The Prince of Monte Carlo' (Jones Hewson)

One reviewer felt too many encores were given; another noted that Sullivan had difficulty restraining the audience from demanding more of them.

The Greek Chorus was conceded to be the musical highlight of the evening. The *Era* liked the 'Wagnerian procession' preceding Rudolph's entrance. The Herald's song in Act II was likened to the Herald's song in *Lohengrin*. The orchestral effects in 'When You Find You're a Broken Down Critter' amused many critics.

Opinion was divided on the 'Drinking Song'. Opinion was divided on the 'Roulette Song'. And a few critics agreed that the opera could have done with less of Mme Palmay and more of Walter Passmore.

Sullivan noted in his diary the first night that Gilbert's dialogue seemed redundant. One critic remarked that the First Act ran one and one half hours, and the reviewer from *Punch* observed that a third of the First Act could be omitted with advantage. Most agreed that the second half played better.

The costumes were so impressive that they became the subject of an entire article in *Sketch*. We are told that the girls in the bridal quartet were dressed in pale green gowns gently contrasting with darker green velvet bodices trimmed with old silver buttons.

Lisa, the bride, wore a white satin dress with a square-cut bodice draped with chiffon and lace, trimmed with orange blossoms.

Miss Brandram wore a richly stiff costume consisting of a black watered moiré skirt with an over-dress of pompadour brocade and pink flowers on a fawn-coloured ground.

The most impressive dress in the First Act however was worn by Mme von Palmay – a full skirt of white satin bedecked with many rows of turquoise-blue satin ribbon set off by a shimmering white cape decorated with an appliqué of blue satin and silver embroidery.

The critic is careful to point out that the colouring of the scenery provided a delightful background for the exquisite groupings of colour chosen by the costume designer.

In the Second Act the chic smartness of tightly laced corselets and high-heeled shoes was displaced by the corsetless grace of Greek draperies and sandals.

The most striking costume, however, seems to have been worn by the Herald: one red and one black stocking with odd sleeves to match, adorning his brilliant red satin suit with overhanging herald's cape which was decorated with roulette-balls, hearts and diamonds, crowns and dice in black or red. He wore a white satin neck-ruffle, edged in gold and a three-cornered black hat with white plumes.

But when all was said and done, there was a great deal of critical opinion that did not reflect the opening night magic.

The librettist becomes tiresome in his dialogue.
Musical Standard

Mr Gilbert has lost all his gaiety and nearly all his old brilliance.
The City

A rare full stage photograph of the Second Act set of The Grand Duke. (*Bridget D'Oyly Carte.*)

Arthur Sullivan too has coarsened in his methods.

One thinks of *The Grand Duke* and one is only dimly conscious of melodious music.
Musical Standard

Like so many much anticipated functions *The Grand Duke* fell somewhat flat.
Modern Society

Tickets did not sell well at all.

A pathetic attempt was made to exploit the good reviews and the tremendous reception which Mme Palmay was getting. The woman *was* effective on stage.

The Grand Duke has 'caught on' tremendously at the Savoy Theatre, where the demand for seats to witness Gilbert and Sullivan and Carte's production outbids all previous records. It must in all fairness be said that the enormous success achieved in the principal soprano role by the gifted Hungarian artiste Madame von

Palmay, has almost as much to do with the rush for the new opera as the merits of the work itself.

People

But the Savoy audiences did not want a *tour de force*. For twenty years Gilbert had been teaching them the unimportance of the star system, and they were not about to allow him to reverse himself at this late date.

During the first week after the opening, Gilbert cut three numbers from the Second Act.

'The Drinking Song' for the Baroness
'The Roulette Song' for the Prince
The patter song for Rudolph

Each of these songs had been particularly enjoyed by at least one critic. 'The Roulette Song', the staging of which included an exciting Can-Can, had been especially successful. Each of these numbers had a certain relevance to the plot. The opera could have been far better served if *other* numbers had been cut.

But Gilbert realized the piece was too long and decided to eliminate these songs which occurred near the end of the opera where apparently the audience's attention level was at its lowest point. As with the majority of his decisions regarding *The Grand Duke*, Gilbert made the *safe* choice, instead of the effective one.

9

The Very End

A FEW days after the opening of *The Grand Duke*, Sullivan went to the Riviera to recover from the ordeal of rehearsing a new opera with Gilbert in his now weakened condition. Shortly after his arrival he received a stinging letter from his still jealous former collaborator F. C. Burnand on the subject of Gilbert's libretto. 'Why reproach me? *I* didn't write the book!!' Sullivan replied to him. 'Another week's rehearsal with W. S. G. and I should have gone raving mad.'*

The production period had been dangerously difficult for Sullivan, and he didn't recover from it in Monte Carlo. He succumbed to it.

When he returned to London in early May, a new series of kidney attacks kept him in bed for many weeks. It was a reaction to the strain of overwork and the disappointment of creating another unsuccessful opera. When he left England in June for St Moritz, he knew that he could never work with Gilbert again.

The Grand Duke closed after a breathtakingly short run of 123 performances.

It was followed by the revival of *The Mikado*, and a renewal of public interest in the earlier operas of Gilbert and Sullivan. D'Oyly Carte had the rights to present them in London now, and one by one he began to re-mount them at the Savoy.

At the same time Sullivan began to fall under increasing pressure from Mr and Mrs D'Oyly Carte to turn out additional operas for the Savoy, albeit not by Gilbert. The Cartes would continue to pressure Sullivan into writing operas for them as long as there was a breath of life left in his body.

By the end of 1896, however, there was considerably more life left in Gilbert's body, and he managed to preserve it by beating a hasty

* Letter dated 12 and 13 March 1896, in Pierpont Morgan Library.

retreat from London.

He had one more libretto in his plot-books in 1897, an adaptation of a comedy which he had written in 1872 (*The Wicked World*) now transformed into an opera called *Selene*, another vehicle for Nancy McIntosh. Fortunately for Gilbert, he could not find a composer to set it in 1897. 'A Gilbert is no good without a Sullivan,' he conceded many years later 'and I can't find one.' And in this spirit he abandoned further plans to produce his final opera at the Savoy in the 90s. He put his plot-books and early drafts aside for twelve years. He designed no further comic operas at all. His life work virtually complete, he abandoned himself at long last to a well deserved retirement at his elaborate country home, Grim's Dyke.

Sullivan completed two more operas, both of which were produced at the Savoy in the late 90s. *The Beauty Stone* was not a success at all; *The Rose of Persia*, compared with other Savoy productions of the 90s was relatively popular. But as the century ended, the golden age at the Savoy came to an end.

Sullivan died in November of 1900.
D'Oyly Carte died five months later.
A year later Gilbert's gout left him for good, and he lived out the rest of his life in the best of health.

After her husband died, Mrs D'Oyly Carte produced five more operas at the Savoy, and finally, in May of 1903, leased the theatre and sent the opera company off on tour. For three and a half years London was without Gilbert and Sullivan and without a D'Oyly Carte Opera Company.

In 1906 Mrs D'Oyly Carte planned to bring the Company back to the Savoy, and Gilbert, then aged seventy, agreed to come out of retirement to stage the new London productions. The return of the Gilbert and Sullivan operas to the Savoy Theatre was a triumphant success, and the D'Oyly Carte Opera Company made further appearances there in 1907 and 1908.

Gilbert's return to the theatre late in his life fired up all of his old enthusiasm. He took his final opera off of the shelf, finished it after ten years, re-titled it *Fallen Fairies*, and once again cast about for a composer. This time he found Edward German.

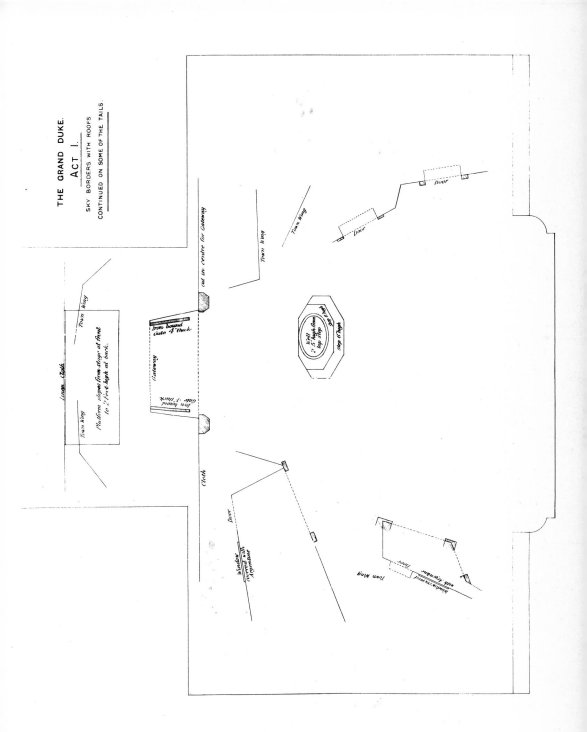

The Grand Duke, *Act I.* (*Mander & Mitchenson.*)

The original stage settings for Utopia, Limited. *Hawes Craven, one of Henry Irving's designers at the Lyceum, did all of the Savoy premières from* The Mikado *to* Utopia, Limited. *These are the earliest known photographs of an original Gilbert and Sullivan set. They were taken by Martin & Sallnow, Strand, and coloured by hand. It is unlikely that the sets of the earlier operas were ever photographed, for it was not customary to take a camera inside a theatre before the 1890s.*

Hawes Craven's original stage design for Utopia, Limited, *Act I.*

Utopia, Limited, *Act II*.

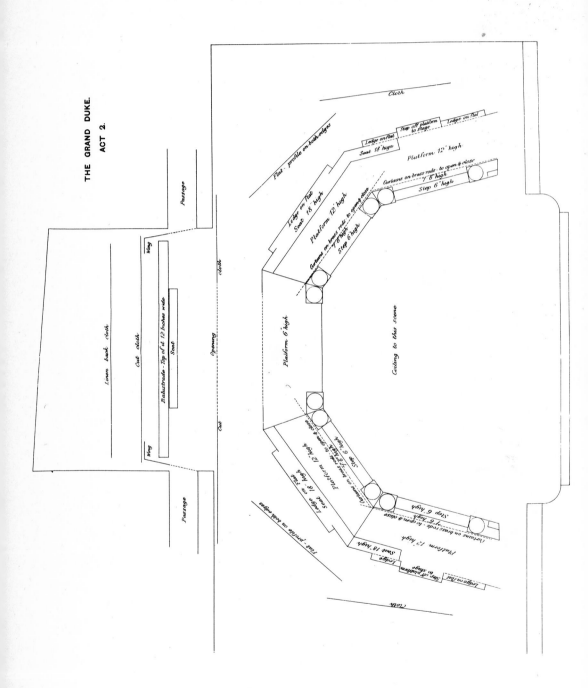

The Grand Duke, *Act II. (Mander & Mitchenson.)*

Charles Workman, who had played the principal comedian's parts for Gilbert with great success during the Savoy seasons of 1906–07 and 1908–09, had secured the backing that he needed to form an opera company of his own. He leased the Savoy Theatre for the 1909–10 season with the intention of producing a series of light operas there including *Fallen Fairies*, to be followed by productions of *Ruddigore*, *Utopia, Limited* and *The Grand Duke*. Gilbert had agreed to revise his librettos for the last three operas, a most exciting prospect.

But a decade and half later Gilbert was still very much the same Gilbert, and had not profited from the lessons of the past one whit.

Fifteen years later Gilbert was still writing leading roles for Nancy McIntosh, and still forcing her upon his producers. Charles Workman, who was the effective producer of *Fallen Fairies*, agreed to engage Miss McIntosh, probably because at the time he saw no way of getting round Gilbert. But Workman was not happy with her performance, and neither were his backers. The opera opened, and at the end of the first week of its run the ill-starred Miss McIntosh was fired.

Gilbert was furious. He felt used, cheated and betrayed. He threatened to sue and in fact initiated proceedings. But the opera was not successful and it closed in six weeks. Gilbert dropped his lawsuit. But the *affaire* McIntosh effectively terminated Gilbert's working relationship with Mr Workman. There would be no further season of Gilbert and Sullivan operas at the Savoy. There would be no future productions of Gilbert and Sullivan operas managed by Mr Workman. And there would be no productions in 1909 of *Utopia, Limited* and *The Grand Duke*, with librettos newly rewritten by their author.

What Gilbert's plans were for the revisions of *Utopia, Limited* and *The Grand Duke* in 1909 has not been recorded, but it is worth noting that Gilbert, to the end of his life, considered these librettos worthy of further consideration.

They are *still* worthy of further consideration, and it may be that now, with additional information available, the public is finally in a position to appreciate these two works which have, for so long, been practically unknown.

Gilbert's audience of the 1890s was unused to allegory at the Savoy, and not one person who saw his later operas there understood what they were really about.

No critic recognized Queen Victoria's foreign accent in the character of Julia Jellicoe. No journalist drew any parallel between Pfennig Halbpfennig and the heritage of Saxe-Coburg. And no contemporary writer realized that the Limited Company that Mr Goldbury sang about was really the Palace Theatre of Varieties. The two final operas which Gilbert wrote with Sullivan were understood by none but their author – and the two operas which Gilbert had *intended* to write were understood by no one at all.

The laws of Pfennig Halbpfennig run for a hundred years. Almost that much time has elapsed since these operas were first produced – and if it has taken nearly a century before they could be properly understood, it is probably just as well. Had their real meaning been clear when they opened, it would have taken almost a hundred years for the storm to clear.

PART TWO

The Rehearsal Texts
of
Utopia, Limited
and
The Grand Duke

including all subsequently

cancelled passages

Introduction

IN the late nineteenth century it was a relatively simple matter for a writer to have his works set in type, and it was W. S. Gilbert's invariable procedure to do so.

From the earliest days of his career, whenever he finished a play or a libretto, Gilbert immediately had a small number of copies printed – an investment which he felt inevitably repaid itself many-fold. It was one thing which he claimed to have learned from his father.

Gilbert frequently cited the example of his production of *An Old Score* at the Gaiety Theatre in 1868. It was produced because it had been printed! John Holingshead, the manager of the Gaiety, had a pile of unproduced scripts on his desk and needed a one-act play in a hurry. Gilbert's script caught his eye because it was *printed* and there-fore easier to read than the others, which were all hand-written. Holingshead later admitted that he only produced Gilbert's play because he had read it – and the only reason that he read it was because it had been in *print*! As it turned out the production was *not* successful and both author and producer learned something from the experience. Gilbert learned the value of having his scripts printed.

As the years went by, however, Gilbert's procedure became more sophisticated. By the 80s Gilbert and Sullivan had become so impor-tant to Chappell & Company, their publisher, that whenever a new opera went into rehearsal, an entire printing press and operator were put at Mr Gilbert's disposal. Before rehearsals for a new opera began, a small edition of the libretto would be printed so that the principals would all have copies at the first rehearsal. The entire libretto was then kept *in type* at Chappell's, and as changes were made in rehearsals, the rewrites would be rushed down to Gilbert's press, the corrections made in the plates, and the new sheets run off as needed. Librettos thus issued before the opera opened were bound in grey wrappers carrying no advertising, and stamped 'Advance Proof' in large red letters across the title page.

It was customary to sell librettos in the theatre on the first night of each opera, and the version of the libretto in the press at the time of the first performance became the 'First Edition' of the libretto. Frequently further changes were made during the first week of an opera's run. Those too were hurried into print, and the earlier copies of the libretto were withdrawn. First editions of Gilbert's librettos are rare, and 'Advance Proof' editions, which were probably collected at the end of rehearsals and destroyed, are practically unknown outside libraries.

Before a play could be licensed to open in London in Gilbert's day, a copy had to be deposited with the Lord Chamberlain – for the purposes of determining whether the play contained any 'offensive' passages. The licensing procedure was not complicated, and usually the librettos were sent over during the last week of rehearsals. The Lord Chamberlain's copies are now at the British Library and many of Gilbert's librettos there contain lyrics subsequently deleted, and known in no other copies.

In many cases, however, *earlier* and more unusual issues of Gilbert's text can be found at the Library of Congress in America.

Before 1900 a copyright could only be secured in America on a work which had been printed from plates which had been set in the United States. It was also necessary to secure the American copyright *before* the first English performance.

This meant that the libretto sent to America for registration had to leave England many weeks before the opera opened there, in order to cross the ocean by ship, be set in type, proof-read, printed and finally delivered to the Library of Congress in Washington *before* the London première.

The librettos which were copyrighted in America, therefore, were generally versions which had *not* benefited from changes made during the last three weeks of rehearsals. In some cases the changes were considerable. For this reason many of the earliest extant texts of

Gilbert's librettos are preserved at the Library of Congress in America. It is these librettos which have been reprinted here. They represent, as well as can be established, the version of the operas which Gilbert and Sullivan themselves used when they began their rehearsals at the Savoy.

The rehearsal text of *Utopia, Limited* is reasonably close to the version performed on opening night. Few changes were made during the rehearsal period of this opera. Gilbert and Sullivan were working well together in 1893, and they were both pretty much satisfied with the text before the rehearsals began. Most of the cancelled lyrics which survive from *Utopia, Limited* were cancelled *before* the opera went into production, and therefore do not appear in the rehearsal text itself. These lyrics have been printed in the Appendix.

The rehearsal text of *The Grand Duke*, on the other hand, differs greatly from that performed at the Savoy on opening night. Gilbert and Sullivan were *not* working well together in 1896. Most of the rewrites for *The Grand Duke* were made *after* rehearsals had begun. Therefore, most of the subsequently cancelled lyrics from this opera which still survive, appear *in the rehearsal text itself*.

The original cast photographs were taken by Alfred
Ellis, a leading Victorian Theatrical photographer.
It was customary for the Savoy Company to go down
to his studio to pose in costume in front of a painted
backdrop which resembled part of the actual set.

UTOPIA, LIMITED

GILBERT began writing the libretto to *Utopia, Limited* in the beginning of February 1893. By 4 March he informed Sullivan that he had seven or eight lyrics completed. These he sent over to Sullivan a few at a time, to be set to music. Sullivan saved the lyrics to this opera as he received them from Gilbert. They are preserved today at the Pierpont Morgan Library in New York. They include the words to many songs that were never published.

By late July, Gilbert was preparing a clean manuscript copy of *Utopia, Limited* to be sent to Chappell & Company his printer. A fair copy of *Utopia, Limited*, in Gilbert's hand, survives among the Gilbert Papers at the British Library (MS 49300); it can be dated late July 1893. In all probability it was the copy that he sent over to be typeset before he left England for medical treatment in Germany.

While he was abroad, he and Sullivan discussed, in correspondence, several changes to be made in the text as Gilbert had left it (MS 49300). These changes included basically the addition of the chorale, 'Eagle High', p. 164, the elimination of the quartet, p. 196, the elimination of the 'Fire-flies' lyric, *et seq.*, p. 192, and the transplanting of Zara's solo to Act I, p. 144.

These changes (plus a few smaller ones) were made in the type being set at Chappell's, and the first printed text was run off for use at rehearsals on 4 September. The same text was sent to Washington for copyright purposes. It is this 'advance proof' or rehearsal text that is printed here.

Whenever this text differs significantly from the manuscript version that Gilbert prepared for the printer, or from the lyric sheets that he prepared for Sullivan, the variant, or cancelled passages have been printed in the Appendix. Minor variations in dialogue and versification have not been collated. Passages in the printed text which Gilbert eliminated after the first performance have been footnoted.

𝔄n 𝔒riginal 𝔆omic 𝔒pera

IN TWO ACTS,

ENTITLED

UTOPIA, (LIMITED);

OR,

THE FLOWERS OF PROGRESS.

WRITTEN BY	COMPOSED BY
W. S. GILBERT.	**ARTHUR SULLIVAN.**

PRICE TWENTY-FIVE CENTS.

London :

CHAPPELL & CO., 50, NEW BOND STREET, W.

31198

AGENTS :

New York: **NOVELLO, EWER & CO.**

UTOPIA, (LIMITED);

OR,

THE FLOWERS OF PROGRESS.

ACT I.

SCENE.—*Gardens of* KING PARAMOUNT'S *Palace, showing a picturesque and luxuriant Tropical landscape, with the sea in the distance.* SALATA, MELENE, PHYLLA, *and other Maidens discovered, thoroughly enjoying themselves in lotos-eating fashion.* 1

OPENING CHORUS.

In lazy languor—motionless,
We lie and dream of nothingness;
  For visions come
  From Poppydom
    Direct at our command:
Or, delicate alternative,
In open idleness we live,
  With lyre and lute
  And silver flute,
    The life of Lazyland!

SOLO.—PHYLLA.

The song of birds
  In ivied towers;
    The rippling play
    Of waterway;
The lowing herds;
  The breath of flowers;
    The languid loves
    Of turtle doves—
These simple joys are all at hand
Upon thy shores, O Lazyland!

CHORUS.

In lazy languor, &c.

Enter CALYNX.

CALYNX. Good news! Great news! His Majesty's eldest daughter, Princess Zara, who left our shores five years since to go to England —the greatest, the most powerful, the wisest country in the world

---

1. For Gilbert's original stage direction see Appendix, no. 1.

4

(*he uncovers at the name of England*)—has taken a high degree at Girton, and is on her way home again, having achieved a complete mastery over all the elements that have tended to raise that glorious country to her present pre-eminent position among civilized nations!

SALATA. Then in a few months Utopia may hope to be completely Anglicized?

CAL. Absolutely and without a doubt.

MELENE (*lazily.*) We are very well as we are. Life without a care —every want supplied by a kind and fatherly monarch, who, despot though he be, has no other thought than to make his people happy— what have we to gain by the great change that is in store for us?

SAL. What have we to gain? English institutions, English tastes, and oh, English fashions!

CAL. England has made herself what she is because, in that favoured land, every one has to think for himself. Here we have no need to think, because our monarch anticipates all our wants, and our political opinions are formed for us by the journals to which we subscribe. Oh, think how much more brilliant this dialogue would have been, if we had been accustomed to exercise our reflective powers! They say that in England the conversation of the very meanest is a coruscation of impromptu epigram!

Enter TARARA *in a great rage.*

TARARA. Lalabalele talala! Callabale lalabalica falahle!

CAL. (*horrified.*) Stop—stop, I beg! (*All the ladies close their ears.*)

TARARA. Callamalala galalate! Caritalla lalabalee kallalale poo!

LADIES. Oh, stop him! stop him!

CAL. My Lord, I'm surprised at you. Are you not aware that His Majesty, in his despotic acquiescence with the emphatic wish of his people, has ordered that the Utopian language shall be banished from his court, and that all communications shall henceforward be made in the English tongue?

TARARA. Yes, I'm perfectly aware of it, although—(*suddenly presenting an explosive "cracker"*). Stop—allow me.

CAL. (*pulls it*). Now, what's that for?

TARARA. Why, I've recently been appointed Public Exploder, and as I'm constitutionally nervous, I must accustom myself by degrees to the startling nature of my duties. Thank you. I was about to say that although, as Public Exploder, I am next in succession to the throne, I nevertheless do my best to fall in with the royal decree. But when I am over-mastered by an indignant sense of overwhelming wrong, as I am now, I slip into my native tongue without knowing it. I am told that in the language of that great and pure nation,

5

strong expressions do not exist, consequently when I want to let off steam I have no alternative but to say, "Lalabalele molola lililah kallalale poo!"

CAL.   But what is your grievance?

TARARA.   This—by our Constitution we are governed by a Despot who, although in theory, absolute—is, in practice, nothing of the kind—being watched day and night by two Wise Men whose duty it is, on his very first lapse from political or social propriety, to denounce him to me, the Public Exploder—allow me (*presenting a cracker which* CALYNX *pulls*) thank you—and it then becomes my duty to blow up His Majesty with dynamite, and, as some compensation to my wounded feelings, I reign in his stead.

CAL.   Yes.   After many unhappy experiments in the direction of an ideal Republic, it was found that what may be described as a Despotism tempered by Dynamite provides, on the whole, the most satisfactory description of ruler—an autocrat who dares not abuse his autocratic power.

TARARA.   That's the theory—but in practice, how does it act? Now, do you ever happen to see the Palace Peeper? (*producing a newspaper*).

CAL.   Never even heard of the journal.

TARARA.   I'm not surprised, because His Majesty's agents always buy up the whole edition; but I have an aunt in the publishing department, and she has supplied me with a copy.   Well, it actually teems with circumstantially convincing details of the King's abominable immoralities!   If this high-class journal may be believed, His Majesty is one of the most Heliogabalian profligates that ever disgraced an autocratic throne!   And *do* these Wise Men denounce him to me?   Not a bit of it!   They wink at his immoralities!   Under the circumstances I really think I am justified in exclaming "Lalabalele molola lililah kalabalele poo!" (*all horrified.*)   I don't care—the occasion demands it.   [*Exit* TARARA.]

March.   Enter Guard, escorting SCAPHIO *and* PHANTIS.

CHORUS.

O make way for the Wise Men!
They are prizemen—
Double-first in the world's university!
For though lovely this island,
(which is *my* land,)
She has no one to match them in *her* city.
They're the pride of Utopia—
Cornucopia
Is each in his mental fertility.
O they never make blunder,
And no wonder,
For they're triumphs of infallibility!

W. H. Denny as Scaphio and John le Hay as Phantis, Act I.
(British Library.)

6

DUET.—Scaphio *and* Phantis.

Sca.	In every mental lore,
Phan.	(The statement smacks of vanity),
Sca.	We claim to rank before
Phan.	The wisest of humanity.
Sca.	As gifts of head and heart
Phan.	We're wasted on "utility,"
Sca.	We're "cast" to play a part
Phan.	Of great responsibility.
Sca.	Our duty is to spy
Phan.	Upon our King's illicities,
Sca.	And keep a watchful eye
Phan.	On all his eccentricities.
Sca.	If ever a trick he tries
Phan.	That savours of rascality,
Sca.	At our decree he dies
Phan.	Without the least formality.
Phan.	We fear no rude rebuff,
Sca.	Or newspaper publicity,
Phan.	Our word is quite enough,
Sca.	The rest is electricity.
Phan.	A pound of dynamite
Sca.	Explodes in his auriculars;
Phan.	It's not a pleasant sight—
Sca.	We'll spare you the particulars.
Sca.	It's force all men confess,
Phan.	The King needs no admonishing—
Sca.	We may say its success
Phan.	Is something quite astonishing.
Sca.	Our despot it imbues
Phan.	With virtues quite delectable:
Sca.	He minds his P's and Q's,—
Phan.	And keeps himself respectable.

Both.
> Of a tyrant polite
> He's a paragon quite.
> He's as modest and mild
> In his ways as a child;
> And no one ever met
> With an autocrat, yet,
> So delightfully bland
> To the least in the land!

Chorus.   It's force all men confess, &c.

Exeunt all but Scaphio *and* Phantis.   Phantis *is pensive.*

Sca.   Phantis, you are not in your customary exuberant spirits.
What is wrong?

7

[PHAN. Nothing—nothing—a little passing anxiety, that's all. *

SCA. Why, what have we to be anxious about? Are not all our little secret commercial ventures doing tremendously? Our time bargains, our betting-office, our cheap wine business, our Army clothing concern, our Matrimonial agency, our Advertising office, our Roulette tables, our Exchange and Mart?

PHAN. Hush—pray be careful! If it should ever be known that these are our speculations, and that we have compelled the King to place his Royal authority and influence ot our disposal for their advancement, we should be ruined!

SCA. As to our Society paper—why its circulation has increased ten-fold since we compelled His Majesty to contribute every week a couple of pages of disreputable attacks on his own moral character! As to our theatre, why since we insisted on his writing a grossly personal Comic Opera, in which he is held up, nightly, to the scorn and contempt of overwhelming thousands, we have played to double prices!

PHAN. Your keen commercial instincts have been invaluable to us; but my anxiety has nothing to do with our unacknowledged business ventures.] Scaphio, I think you once told me that you have never loved?

SCA. Never! I have often marvelled at the fairy influence which weaves its rosy web about the faculties of the greatest and wisest of our race; but I thank Heaven I have never been subjected to its singular fascination. For, O Phantis! there is that within me that tells me that when my time *does* come, the convulsion will be tremendous! When *I* love, it will be with the accumulated fervour of sixty-six years! But I have an ideal—a semi-transparent Being, filled with an inorganic pink jelly—and I have never yet seen the woman who approaches within measurable distance of it. All are opaque—opaque—opaque!

PHAN. Keep that ideal firmly before you, and love not until you find her. Though but fifty-five, I am an old campaigner in the battle-fields of Love; and, believe me, it is better to be as you are, heart-free and happy, than as I am—eternally racked with doubting agonies! Scaphio, the Princess Zara returns from England to-day!

SCA. My poor boy, I see it all.

PHAN. Oh! Scaphio, she is so beautiful. Ah! you smile, for you have never seen her. She sailed for England three months before you took office.

SCA. Now tell me, is your affection requited?

PHAN. I do not know—I am not sure. Sometimes I think it is, and then come these torturing doubts! I feel sure that she does not regard me with absolute indifference, for she could never.look at me without having to go to bed with a sick headache.

*The next five lines were deleted after the opening.

8

Sca. That is surely something. Come, take heart, boy! you are young and beautiful. What more could maiden want?

Phan. Ah! Scaphio, remember she returns from a land where every youth is as a young Greek god, and where such poor beauty as I can boast is seen at every turn.

Sca. Be of good cheer! Marry her, boy, if so your fancy wills, and be sure that love will come.

Phan. (*overjoyed*). Then you will assist me in this?

Sca. Why, surely! Silly one, what have you to fear? We have but to say the word, and her father must consent. Is he not our very slave? Come, take heart. I cannot bear to see you sad.

Phan. Now I may hope, indeed! Scaphio, you have placed me on the very pinnacle of human joy!

DUET.—Scaphio *and* Phantis.

Sca.
> Let all your doubts take wing—
> Our influence is great.
> If Paramount our King
> Presumes to hesitate,
> Put on the screw,
> And caution him
> That he will rue
> Disaster grim
> That must ensue
> To life and limb,
> Should he pooh-pooh
> This harmless whim.

Both.
> This harmless whim—this harmless whim,
> It is, as $\begin{Bmatrix} I \\ you \end{Bmatrix}$ say, a harmless whim.

Phan. (*dancing*).
> Observe this dance
> Which I employ,
> When I, by chance,
> Go mad with joy.
> What sentiment
> Does this express?

(Phantis *continues his dance while* Scaphio *vainly endeavours to discover its meaning.*)
> Supreme content
> And happiness!

Both.
> And happiness—and happiness—
> Of course it does—and happiness!

9

PHAN.   Your friendly aid conferred,
       I need no longer pine.
     I've but to speak the word,
       And lo! the maid is mine!
     I do not choose
       To be denied.
     Or wish to lose
       A lovely bride—
     If to refuse
       The King decide,
     The Royal shoes
       Then woe betide!

BOTH.   Then woe betide—then woe betide
     The Royal shoes then woe betide!

SCA. *(dancing.)*   This step to use
       I condescend
     Whene'er I choose
       To serve a friend.
     What it implies
       Now try to guess;

[SCA. *continues his dance while* PHANTIS *is vainly endeavouring to discover its meaning.*]
     It typifies
       Unselfishness!

BOTH *(dancing.)* Unselfishness!   Unselfishness!
     Of course it does—unselfishness!
     This step to use
     We condescend! etc.
       [*Exeunt* SCAPHIO *and* PHANTIS.

March. Enter KING PARAMOUNT, *attended by guards and nobles, and preceded by girls dancing before him.*

CHORUS.

Quaff the nectar—cull the roses—
     Gather fruit and flowers in plenty!
For our King no longer poses—
     Sing the songs of *far niente!*
Wake the lute that sets us lilting,
     Dance a welcome to each comer;
Day by day our year is wilting—
     Sing the sunny songs of summer!
       La, la, la, la!

SONG.—KING.   2

A King of autocratic power we—
     A despot whose tyrannic will is law,

2. For Paramount's original entrance verse see Appendix, no. 2.

Whose rule is paramount o'er land and sea,
　　A Presence of unutterable awe!
But though the awe that I inspire
Must shrivel with imperial fire
　　All foes whom it may chance to touch,
To judge by what I see and hear,
It does not seem to interfere
　　With popular enjoyment, much.

Chorus. 　　　No, no—it does not interfere
　　　　　With our enjoyment much.

Stupendous when we rouse ourselves to strike—
　　Resistless when our tyrant thunder peals—
We often wonder what obstruction's like,
　　And how a contradicted monarch feels!
But as it is our Royal whim
Our Royal sails to set and trim
　　To suit whatever winds may blow,
What buffets contradiction deals,
And how a thwarted monarch feels,
　　We probably shall never know.

Chorus. 　　　No, no—what thwarted monarch feels
　　　　You'll never, never know.

RECIT.—KING.

My subjects all, it is your wish emphatic
That all Utopia shall henceforth be modelled
Upon that glorious country called Great Britain—
To which some add—but others do not—Ireland.

ALL. 　It is!

KING. 　That being so, as you insist upon it,
　　We have arranged that our two younger daughters
　　Who have been "finished" by an English Lady—
(tenderly) A grave, and good, and gracious English Lady—
　　Shall daily be exhibited in public,
　　That all may learn what, from the English stand-point,
　　Is looked upon as maidenly perfection!
　　Come hither, daughters!

Enter NEKAYA *and* KALYBA. *They are twins, about fifteen years old; they are very modest and demure in their appearance, dress, and manner. They stand with their hands folded and their eyes cast down.*

CHORUS.

How fair! how modest! how discreet!
　　How bashfully demure!
　　　　See how they blush, as they've been taught,
　　　　At this publicity unsought!
　　How English and how pure!

Rutland Barrington as King Paramount, in native Utopian dress,
Act I. (British Library.)

11

DUET.—Nekaya *and* Kalyba.

Both.	Although of native maids the cream,
	We're brought up on the English scheme—
	The best of all
	For great and small
	Who modesty adore.

Nek.	For English girls are good as gold,
	Extremely modest (so we're told),
	Demurely coy—divinely cold—

Kal.	And we are that—and more.
	To please papa, who argues thus—
	All girls should mould themselves on us
	Because we are,
	By furlongs far
	The best of all the bunch,
	We show ourselves to loud applause
	From ten to four without a pause—

Nek.	Which is an awkward time because
	It cuts into our lunch.
Both.	Oh, maids of high and low degree,
	Whose social code is rather free,
	Please look at us and you will see
	What good young ladies ought to be!

Nek.	And as we stand, like clockwork toys,
	A lecturer whom papa employs
	Proceeds to praise
	Our modest ways
	And guileless character—

Kal.	Our well-known blush—our downcast eyes—
	Our famous look of mild surprise

Nek.	(Which competition still defies)—

Kal.	Our celebrated "Sir!!!"
	Then all the crowd take down our looks
	In pocket memorandum books.
	To diagnose
	Our modest pose
	The Kodaks do their best:

Nek.	If evidence you would possess
	Of what is maiden bashfulness,
	You only need a button press—

Kal.	And *we* do all the rest!

12

Enter LADY SOPHY—*an English lady of mature years and extreme gravity of demeanour and dress. She carries a lecturer's wand in her hand. She is led on by the* KING, *who expresses great regard and admiration for her.*

RECIT.—LADY SOPHY.

This morning we propose to illustrate
A course of maiden courtship, from the start
To the triumphant matrimonial finish.

(*Through the following song the two princesses illustrate in gesture the description given by* LADY SOPHY.)

SONG.—LADY SOPHY.

Bold-faced ranger.
(Perfect stranger)
Meets two well-behaved young ladies.
He's attractive,
Young and active—
Each a little bit afraid is.
Youth advances,
At his glances
To their danger they awaken;
They repel him
As they tell him
He is very much mistaken.
Though they speak to him politely,
Please observe they're sneering slightly,
Just to show he's acting vainly.
This is Virtue saying plainly,
"Go away, young bachelor,
We are not what you take us for!"
When addressed impertinently,
English ladies answer gently,
"Go away, young bachelor,
We are not what you take us for!"

As he gazes,
Hat he raises,
Enters into conversation.
Makes excuses—
This produces
Interesting agitation.
He, with daring,
Undespairing,
Gives his card—his rank discloses—
Little heeding
This proceeding,

*Emmie Owen (left) and Florence Perry (right) as Princess Nekaya
and Princess Kalyba, Act II. (British Library.)*

13

They turn up their little noses.
Pray observe this lesson vital—
When a man of rank and title
His position first discloses,
Always cock your little noses.
   When at home, let all the class
   Try this in the looking-glass.
English girls of well-bred notions,
Shun all unrehearsed emotions,
   English girls of highest class
   Practise them before the glass.

  His intentions
  Then he mentions.
Something definite to go on—
  Makes recitals
  Of his titles,
Hints at settlements, and so on.
  Smiling sweetly,
  They, discreetly,
Ask for further evidences.
  Thus invited,
  He, delighted,
Gives the usual references.
This is business.   Each is fluttered
When the offer's fairly uttered.
"Which of them has his affection?"
He declines to make selection.
  Do they quarrel for his dross?
  Not a bit of it—they toss.
Please observe this cogent moral—
English ladies never quarrel.
  When a doubt they come across,
  English ladies always toss.

CHORUS.

Quaff the nectar—cull the roses—
 Bashful girls will soon be plenty!
Maid who thus at fifteen poses
 Ought to be divine at twenty!

(*Exeunt* LADY SOPHY *and the two Princesses, followed by
Chorus. Manent* KING, SCAPHIO, *and* PHANTIS, *who
re-enter as the previous scene finishes.*)

SCA. Your Majesty wished to speak with us, I believe. You—
you needn't keep your crown on, on our account, you know.

KING. I beg your pardon (*removes it*). I always forget that!
Odd, the notion of a King not being allowed to wear one of his own
crowns in the presence of two of his own subjects.

PHAN. Yes—bizarre, is it not?

KING. Most quaint. But then it's a quaint world.

PHAN. Teems with quiet fun. I often think what a lucky thing it is that you are blessed with such a keen sense of humour!

KING. Do you know, I find it invaluable. Do what I will, I *cannot* help looking at the humorous side of things—for, properly considered, everything has its humorous side—even the Palace Peeper (*producing it*). See here—"Another Royal Scandal," by Junius Junior. "How long is this to last?" by Senex Senior. "Ribald Royalty," by Mercury Major. "Where is the Public Exploder?" by Mephistopheles Minor. When I reflect that all these outrageous attacks on my morality are written by me, at your command—well, it's one of the funniest things that have come within the scope of my experience.

SCA. Besides, apart from that, they have a quiet humour of their own which is simply irresistible.

KING (*gratified*). Not bad, I think. Biting, trenchant sarcasm— the rapier, not the bludgeon—that's my line. But then it's so easy —I'm such a good subject—a bad King but a good Subject—ha! ha! —a capital heading for next week's leading article! (*makes a note*). And then the stinging little paragraphs about our Royal goings-on with our Royal Second Housemaid—delicately sub-acid, are they not?

SCA. My dear King, in that kind of thing no one can hold a candle to you.

[KING (*doubtfully*). Ye—yes. You refer, of course, to the literary * quality of the paragraphs?

SCA. Oh, of course—

KING. Because the essence of the joke lies in the fact that instead of being the abominable profligate they suggest, I'm one of the most fastidiously respectable persons in my whole dominions!]

PHAN. But the crowning joke is the Comic Opera you've written for us—"King Tuppence, or A Good deal Less than Half a Sovereign"—in which the celebrated English tenor, Mr. Wilkinson, burlesques your personal appearance and gives grotesque imitations of your Royal peculiarities. It's immense!

KING. Ye—es—That's what I wanted to speak to you about. Now I've not the least doubt but that even *that* has its humorous side, too—if one could only see it. As a rule, I'm pretty quick at detecting latent humour—but I confess I do *not* quite see where it comes in, in this particular instance. It's so horribly personal!

SCA. Personal? Yes, of course it's personal—but consider the antithetical humour of the situation.

KING. Yes. I—I don't think I've quite grasped that.

*The next three lines were deleted after the opening.

Sca. No? you surprise me. Why consider. During the day thousands tremble at your frown, during the night (from 8 to 11) thousands roar at it. During the day your most arbitrary pronouncements are received by your subjects with abject submission—during the night, they shout with joy at your most terrible decrees. It's not every monarch who enjoys the privilege of undoing by night all the despotic absurdities he's committed during the day.

King. Of course! now I see it! Thank you very much. I was sure it had its humorous side, and it was very dull of me not to have seen it before. But, as I said just now, it's a quaint world!

Phan. Teems with quiet fun.

King. Yes. Properly considered, what a farce life is, to be sure!

SONG.—King.

First you're born—and I'll be bound you
Find a dozen strangers round you.
"Hallo," cries the new-born baby,
"Where's my parents? which may they be?"
    Awkward silence—no reply—
    Puzzled baby wonders why!
Father rises, bows politely—
Mother smiles, (but not too brightly)—
Doctor mumbles like a dumb thing—
Nurse is busy mixing something.—
    Every symptom tends to show
    Your decidedly *de trop*—

All. Ho! ho! ho! ho! ho! ho! ho! ho!
        Time's teetotum,
            If you spin it
        Gives its quotum
            Once a minute.
            I'll go bail
            You hit the nail,
        And if you fail
            The deuce is in it!

You grow up, and you discover
What it is to be a lover.
Some young lady is selected—
Poor, perhaps, but well-connected,
    Whom you hail (for Love is blind)
    As the Queen of fairy kind.
Though she's plain—perhaps unsightly,
Makes her face up—laces tightly,
In her form your fancy traces
All the gifts of all the graces.
    Rivals none the maiden woo,
    So you take her and she takes you!

16

ALL.
>Ho! ho! ho! ho! ho! ho! ho! ho!
>Joke beginning,
>>Never ceases,
>Till your inning
>>Time releases,
>On your way
>You blindly stray,
>And day by day
>>The joke increases!

>Ten years later—Time progresses—
>Sours your temper—thins your tresses;
>Fancy, then, her chain relaxes;
>Rates are facts and so are taxes.
>>Fairy Queen's no longer young—
>>Fairy Queen has got a tongue.
>Twins have probably intruded—
>Quite unbidden—just as you did—
>They're a source of care and trouble—
>Just as you were—only double.
>>Comes at last the final stroke—
>>Time has had his little joke!

ALL.
>Ho! ho! ho! ho! ho! ho! ho! ho!
>Daily driven
>>(Wife as drover)
>Ill you've thriven—
>>Ne'er in clover:
>Lastly, when
>Three-score and ten
>(And not till then,)
>>The joke is over!
>Ho! ho! ho! ho! ho! ho! ho! ho!
>Then—and then
>>The joke is over!

[Exeunt SCAPHIO *and* PHANTIS. *Manet* KING.

KING *(putting on his crown again.)* It's all very well. I always like to look on the humorous side of things; but I do *not* think I ought to be required to write libels on my own moral character. Naturally, I see the joke of it—anybody would—but Zara's coming home to-day; she's no longer a child, and I confess I should *not* like her to see my Opera—though it's uncommonly well written; and I should be sorry if the Palace Peeper got into her hands—though it's certainly smart—very smart indeed. It is almost a pity that I have to buy up the whole edition, because it's really too good to be lost. Besides, one never knows; a copy might leak out, and that would be very confusing, although, of course, great fun. And Lady Sophy —that blameless type of perfect womanhood! Great Heavens, what would *she* say if the Second Housemaid business happened to meet *her* pure blue eye!

17

Enter LADY SOPHY.

LADY S.   My monarch is soliloquizing.   I will withdraw *(going.)*

KING.   No—pray don't go.   Now I'll give you fifty chances, and you won't guess whom I was thinking of.

LADY S.   Alas, sir, I know too well.   Ah! King, it's an old, old story, and I'm well nigh weary of it!   Be warned in time—from my heart I pity you, but I am not for you! *(going.)*

KING.   But hear what I have to say.

LADY S.   It is useless.   Listen.   In the course of a long and adventurous career in the principal European Courts, it has been revealed to me that I unconsciously exercise a weird and super-natural fascination over all Crowned Heads.   So irresistible is this singular property, that·there is not a European Monarch who has not implored me, with tears in his eyes, to quit his kingdom, and take my fatal charms elsewhere. [As there is not a civilized king who is *
sufficiently single to realize my ideal of Abstract Respectability, I extended my sphere of action to the Islands of the South Pacific—only to discover that the monarchs of those favoured climes are at least as lax in their domestic arrangements as the worst of their European brethren.] As time was getting on it occured to me that by descending several pegs in the scale of Respectability I might qualify your Majesty for my hand.   Actuated by this humane motive and happening to possess Respectability enough for Six, I consented to confer Respectability enough for Four upon your two younger daughters—but although I have, alas, only Respectability enough for Two left, there is still, as I gather from the public press of this country *(producing the·Palace Peeper)*, a considerable balance in my favour.

KING *(aside.)* Da—! *(Aloud.)* May I ask how you came by this?

LADY S.   It was handed to me by the officer who holds the position of Public Exploder to your Imperial Majesty.

KING.   And surely, Lady Sophy, surely you are not so unjust as to place any faith in the irresponsible gabble of the Society press!

LADY S. *(referring to paper.)*   I read on the authority of Senex Senior that your Majesty was seen dancing with your Second House-maid on the Oriental Platform of the Tivoli Gardens.   That is untrue?

KING.   Absolutely.   Our Second Housemaid has only one leg.

LADY S. *(suspiciously.)*   How do you know that?

KING.   Common report, I give you my honour.

LADY S.   It may be so.   I further read—and the statement is vouched for. by no less an authority than Mephistopheles Minor—that your Majesty indulges in a bath of hot rum-punch every morning.   I trust I do not lay myself open to the charge of displaying an indelicate curiosity as to the mysteries of the royal dressing-room when I ask if there is any foundation for this statement?

*This sentence about the 'civilized king' was deleted after the opening.

Rosina Brandram as Lady Sophy, Act I. (British Library.)

18

KING. None whatever. When our medical adviser exhibits rum-punch it is as a draught, not as a fomentation. As to our bath, our valet plays the garden hose upon us every morning.

LADY S. (*shocked.*) Oh, pray—pray spare me these unseemly details. Well, you are a Despot—have you taken steps to slay this scribbler?

KING. Well, no—I have *not* gone so far as that. After all, it's the poor devil's living, you know.

LADY S. It is the poor devil's living that surprises me. If this man lies, there is no recognized punishment that is sufficiently terrible for him.

KING. That's precisely it. I—I am waiting until a punishment is discovered that will exactly meet the enormity of the case. I am in constant communication with the Mikado of Japan, who is a leading authority on such points; and, moreover, I have the ground plans and sectional elevations of several capital punishments in my desk at this moment. Oh, Lady Sophy, as you are powerful, be merciful!

DUET.—KING *and* LADY SOPHY.

KING.
Subjected to your heavenly gaze
    (Poetical phrase),
My brain is turned completely.
    Observe me now,
    No Monarch, I vow,
      Was ever so far afflicted!

LADY S.
I'm pleased with that poetical phrase,
    "A heavenly gaze,"
But though you put it neatly,
    Say what you will,
    These paragraphs still
      Remain uncontradicted.

Come, crush me this contemptible worm
    (A forcible term),
If he's assailed you wrongly.
    The rage display,
    Which, as you say,
      Has moved your Majesty lately.

KING.
Though I admit that forcible term,
    "Contemptible worm,"
Appeals to me most strongly,
    To treat this pest
    As you suggest
      Would pain my Majesty greatly!

LADY S.   This writer lies!

KING.   Yes, bother his eyes!

19

LADY S.	He lives, you say?
KING.	In a sort of a way.
LADY S.	Then have him shot.
KING.	Decidedly not.
LADY S.	Or crush him flat.
KING.	I cannot do that.
BOTH.	O royal Rex,

$\begin{Bmatrix} \text{My} \\ \text{Her} \end{Bmatrix}$ blameless sex

    Abhors such conduct shady.

$\begin{Bmatrix} \text{You} \\ \text{I} \end{Bmatrix}$ plead in vain,

$\begin{Bmatrix} \text{You} \\ \text{I} \end{Bmatrix}$ never will gain

    Respectable English lady!

[Dance of repudiation by LADY SOPHY. *Exit, followed by* KING.]

March. Enter all the Court, heralding the arrival of the PRINCESS ZARA, *who enters, escorted by* CAPTAIN FITZBATTLEAXE *and four troopers, all in the full uniform of the First Life Guards.*

CHORUS.   3

Oh, maiden, rich
   In Girton lore,
That wisdom which
   We prized before,
We do confess
Is nothingness,
And rather less,
   Perhaps, than more.
On each of us
   Thy learning shed.
On calculus
   May we be fed.
And teach us, please,
To speak with ease
All languages,
   Alive and dead!

SOLO—PRINCESS *and* CHORUS.

| ZARA. | Five years have flown since I took wing— |

    Time flies, and his footstep ne'er retards—
I'm the eldest daughter of your king.

| TROOPERS. | And we are her escort—First Life Guards! |

    On the royal yacht,
      When the waves were white,

3. Gilbert wrote an additional chorus to be sung before Princess Zara's entrance. See Appendix, no. 3.

20

In a helmet hot
And a tunic tight,
And our great big boots,
We defied the storm:
For we're not recruits,
And his uniform
A well-drilled trooper ne'er discards—
And we are her escort—First Life Guards!

ZARA.　These gentlemen I present to you,
The pride and boast of their barrack-yards;
They've taken O such care of me!

TROOPERS.　For we are her escort—First Life Guards!
When the tempest rose,
And the ship went *so*—
Do you suppose
We were ill? No, no!
Though a qualmish lot
In a tunic tight,
And a helmet hot,
And a breastplate bright
(Which a well-drilled trooper ne'er discards),
We stood as her escort—First Life Guards!

FULL CHORUS.

Knightsbridge nursemaids—serving fairies—
Stars of proud Belgravian airies;
At stern duty's call you leave them,
Though you know how that must grieve them!

ZARA.　Tantantarara-rara-rara!
CAPT. FITZ.　Trumpet-call of Princess Zara!
CHORUS.　That's trump-call, and they're all trump cards—
They are her escort—First Life Guards!

ENSEMBLE.

CHORUS.	PRINCESS ZARA *and* FITZBATTLE-
LADIES.　Knightsbridge nurse-maids, &c. MEN.　When soldier seeks, &c.	AXE (*aside*). Oh! the hours are gold, And the joys untold, When my eyes behold 　My beloved Princess; And the years will seem But a brief day dream, In the joy extreme 　Of our happiness!

FULL CHORUS.　Knightsbridge nursemaids, serving fairies, &c.

Enter KING, PRINCESSES NEKAYA *and* KALYBA, *and* LADY SOPHY.

KING.　Zara! my beloved daughter! Why, how well you look, and how lovely you have grown! (*embraces her*).

Nancy McIntosh, the cause of a great deal of trouble, as Princess
Zara. (British Library.)

ZARA. My dear father! (*embracing him*). And my two beautiful little sisters! (*embracing them*).

NEK. Not beautiful.

KAL. Nice looking.

ZARA. But first let me present to you the English warrior who commands my escort, and who has taken such care of me during the voyage—Captain Fitzbattleaxe!

TROOPERS. The First Life Guards.
When the tempest rose,
And the ship went *so*—

(CAPT. FITZBATTLEAXE *motions them to be silent. The Troopers are now standing in the four corners of the stage, immovably as if on sentry. Each is surrounded by an admiring group of young ladies, of whom they take no notice.*)

KING (*to* CAPT. FITZ.). Sir, you come from a country where every virtue flourishes. We trust that you will not criticise too severely such shortcomings as you may detect in our semi barbarous society.

FITZ. (*looking at* ZARA). Sir, I have eyes for nothing but the blameless and the beautiful.

KING. We thank you—he is really very polite! (LADY SOPHY, *who has been greatly scandalized by the attentions paid to the Lifeguardsmen by the young ladies, marches the* PRINCESSES NEKAYA *and* KALYBA *towards an exit.*) Lady Sophy, do not leave us.

LADY S. Sir, your children are young, and, so far, innocent. If they are to remain so, it is necessary that they be at once removed from the contamination of their present disgraceful surroundings. (*She marches them off.*)

KING (*whose attention has thus been called to the proceedings of the young ladies—aside*). Dear, dear! They really shouldn't. (*Aloud.*) Captain Fitzbattleaxe—

FITZ. Sir.

KING. Your Troopers appear to be receiving a troublesome amount of attention from those young ladies. I know how strict you English soldiers are, and I should be extremely distressed if anything occurred to shock their puritanical British sensitiveness.

FITZ. Oh, I don't think there's any chance of that.

KING. You think not? They won't be offended?

FITZ. Oh no! They are quite hardened to it. They get a good deal of that sort of thing, standing sentry at the Horse Guards.

KING. It's English, is it?

FITZ. It's particularly English.

KING. Then, of course, it's all right. Pray proceed, ladies, it's particularly English. Come, my daughter, for we have much to say to each other.

ZARA. Farewell, Captain Fitzbattleaxe! I cannot thank you too emphatically for the devoted care with which you have watched over me during our long and eventful voyage.

DUET.—ZARA *and* CAPTAIN FITZBATTLEAXE.

ZARA.
> Ah! gallant soldier, brave and true
> > In tented field and tourney,
> I grieve to have occasioned you
> > So very long a journey.
> A British soldier gives up all—
> > His home and island beauty—
> When summoned by the trumpet-call
> > Of Regimental Duty!

ALL.
> Tantantarara-rara-rara!
> Trumpet-call of Princess Zara!

ENSEMBLE.

MEN.	FITZBATTLEAXE *and* ZARA (*aside*).
A British warrior gives up all, &c.	Oh my joy, my pride,
	My delight to hide,
LADIES.	Let us sing, aside,
Knightsbridge nursemaids, &c.	What in truth we feel.
	Let us whisper low
	Of our love's glad glow,
	Lest the truth we show
	We would fain conceal.

FITZ.
> Such escort duty, as his due,
> > To young Lifeguardsman falling
> Completely reconciles him to
> > His uneventful calling.
> When soldier seeks Utopian glades
> > In charge of Youth and Beauty,
> Then pleasure merely masquerades
> > As Regimental Duty!

ALL.
> Tantantarara-rara-rara!
> Trumpet-call of Princess Zara!

ENSEMBLE.

CHORUS.	FITZBATTLEAXE *and* ZARA (*aside*).
MEN.	Oh the hours are gold
A British Warrior, &c.	And the joys untold
	When my eyes behold
WOMEN.	My beloved Princess;
Knightsbridge nursemaids, &c.	And the year will seem
	But a brief day-dream
	In the joy extreme
	Of our happiness!

[*Exeunt* KING *and* PRINCESS *in one direction, Lifeguards-*   4
men and crowd in opposite direction. Enter
SCAPHIO *and* PHANTIS. SCAPHIO *is seated, shaking*
violently, and obviously under the influence of some
strong emotion.]

PHAN.   There—tell me Scaphio, is she not beautiful?   Can you
wonder that I love her so passionately?

SCA.   No.   She is extraordinarily—miraculously lovely!   Good
heavens! what a singularly beautiful girl!

PHAN.   I knew you would say so!

SCA.   What exquisite charm of manner!   What surprising delicacy
of gesture!   Why she's a goddess! a very goddess!

PHAN. (*rather taken back*).   Yes—she's—she's an attractive
girl.

SCA.   Attractive?   Why you must be blind!—She's entrancing—
enthralling!   Her walk—her smile—her play of feature!   What
eyes—what lips!   Why it's bewildering—dazzling—intoxicating!
(*aside*).   God bless my heart, what's the matter with me?

PHAN. (*alarmed*).   Yes.   You—you promised to help me to get
her father's consent, you know.

SCA.   Promised!   Yes, but the convulsion has come, my good
boy!   It is she—my ideal!   My ideal, did I say?

PHAN. (*much disconcerted*).   Yes, you said so.

SCA.   Then I lied, for by all that's dazzling I had no conception
that the world contained such transcendent loveliness!   Why, what's
this? (*staggering.*)   Phantis!   Stop me—I'm going mad—mad with
the love of her!   What an eye! what an ear! what shoulders!

PHAN.   Scaphio, compose yourself, I beg.   The girl is perfectly
opaque!   Besides, remember—each of us is helpless without the
other.   You can't succeed without my consent, you know.

SCA.   And you dare to threaten?   Oh ungrateful!   When you
came to me, palsied with love for this girl, and implored my assistance, did I not unhesitatingly promise it?   And this is the return
you make?   Out of my sight, ingrate! (*Aside*) Dear! dear! what
is the matter with me?

Enter CAPTAIN FITZBATTLEAXE *and* ZARA.

ZARA.   Dear me.   I'm afraid we are interrupting a *tête-à-tête.*

SCA. (*breathlessly*).   No, no.   You come very appropriately.   To
be brief, we—we love you—this man and I—madly—passionately!

ZARA.   Sir!

SCA.   And we don't know how we are to settle which of us is to
marry you.

4. Gilbert wrote a song for King Paramount about the origin of his interest in English
culture. It was meant to follow here. See Appendix No. 4.

Fitz. Zara, this is very awkward.

Sca. (*very much overcome*). I—I am paralyzed by the singular radiance of your extraordinary loveliness. I know I am incoherent. I never was like this before—it shall not occur again. I—shall be fluent, presently.

Zara. (*aside*). Oh, dear Captain Fitzbattleaxe, what *is* to be done?

Fitz. (*aside*). Leave it to me—I'll manage it. (*aloud*) It's a common situation. Why not settle it in the English fashion?

Both. The English fashion? What is that?

Fitz. It's very simple In England, when two gentlemen are in love with the same lady, and until it is settled which gentleman is to blow out the brains of the other, it is provided, by the Rival Admirers' Clauses Consolidation Act, that the lady shall be entrusted to an officer of Household Cavalry as stakeholder, who is bound to hand her over to the survivor (on the Tontine principle) in a good condition of substantial and decorative repair.

Sca. Reasonable wear and tear and damages by fire excepted?

Fitz. Exactly.

Phan. Well, that seems very reasonable. [But why is an officer   *
of Household Cavalry selected for this delicate duty?

Fitz. Why the officers of Household Cavalry are a very exclusive body, and do not consider any lady worthy of matrimonial consideration until she has acquired at least sixty-two years of unblemished experience in the very highest ranks of English society. If she comes out of this ordeal unscathed she is—well, she is eligible, but even then the officers of Household Cavalry are not very keen about it.

Phan. Why, bless my heart, in Utopia we scarcely look at a girl over eighteen.

Fitz. Ah, it's a tropical country, you see. We cold Northerners —you know——]

Phan. Ah, true. (*To* Scaphio.) Well, what do you say— Shall we entrust her to this cold Northerner? It will give us time.

Sca. (*trembling violently*). I—I am not at present in a condition to think it out coolly—but if he is a *very* cold Northerner, and if the Princess consents——

Zara. Alas, dear sirs, I have no alternative—under the Rival Admirers' Clauses Consolidation Act!

Fitz. Good—then that's settled.

*These four lines were deleted before the opening.

QUARTETTE.

FITZBATTLEAXE, ZARA, SCAPHIO, *and* PHANTIS.

FITZ.
It's understood, I think, all round
That, by the English custom bound,
I hold the lady safe and sound
    In trust for either rival,
Until you clearly testify
By sword or pistol, by and bye,
Which gentleman prefers to die,
    And which prefers survival.

ENSEMBLE.

SCA. *and* PHAN.	ZARA *and* FITZ. (*aside*).
It's clearly understood, all round,	We stand, I think, on safish ground ;
That, by your English custom bound,	Our senses weak it will astound
He holds the lady safe and sound	If either gentleman is found
In trust for either rival,	Prepared to meet his rival.
Until we clearly testify	Their machinations we defy ;
By sword and pistol, by and bye,	We won't be parted, you and I—
Which gentleman prefers to die,	Of bloodshed each is rather shy—
And which prefers survival.	They both prefer survival !

PHAN.
(*aside to* FITZ.).
If I should die and he should live,
To you, without reserve, I give
Her heart so young and sensitive,
    And all her predilections.

SCA.
(*aside to* FITZ.).
If he should live and I should die,
I see no kind of reason why
You should not, if you wish it, try
To gain her young affections.

ENSEMBLE.

SCA. *and* PHAN. (*angrily to each other*).	FITZ. *and* ZARA (*aside*).
If I should die and you should live,	As both of us are positive
To this young officer I give	That both of them intend to live,
Her heart so soft and sensitive,	There's nothing in the case to give
And all her predilections.	Us cause for grave reflections.
If you should live and I should die,	As both will live and neither die
I see no kind of reason why	I see no kind of reason why
He should not, if he chooses, try	I should not, if I wish it, try
To win her young affections.	To gain your young affections !

[*Exeunt* SCAPHIO *and* PHANTIS *together.*

DUET.—ZARA *and* FITZBATTLEAXE.   5

ENSEMBLE.

Oh admirable art !
    Oh neatly-planned intention !
    Oh happy intervention—
        Oh well-constructed plot !
When sages try to part
    Two loving hearts in fusion,
    Their wisdom's a delusion,
        And learning serves them not !

*N.B. Pages 25–28, containing the omitted song 'Youth is a boon avowed', etc. were ripped out of the Library of Congress copy several years ago by a pathetic Savoyard who was apparently incapable of copying out the lyric by hand. The missing pages were supplied from an English pre-production libretto in the Pierpont Morgan Library. Fortunately the pages, although typographically slightly different, are textually identical.

5. Gilbert's original version of this duet was very short. See Appendix, no. 5.

26

FITZ.   Until quite plain
     Is their intent,
    These sages twain
     I represent.
    Now please infer
     That, nothing loth,
    You're henceforth, as it were,
     Engaged to marry both—
   Then take it that I represent the two—
   On that hypothesis, what would you do?

ZARA (*aside*). What would I do? what would I do?

ZARA.   In such a case,
     Upon your breast,
    My blushing face
     I think I'd rest— (*doing so*).
    Then perhaps I might
     Demurely say—
    " I find this breastplate bright
     Is sorely in the way!"
   That is, supposing it were true
   That I'm engaged to both—and both were you!

ENSEMBLE.

Our mortal race
 Is never blest—
There's no such case
 As perfect rest ;
Some petty blight
 Asserts its sway—
Some crumpled roseleaf light
 Is always in the way!

    (*Exit* FITZBATTLEAXE. *Manet* ZARA.)

ZARA. Poor, trusting, simple-minded, and affectionate old gentlemen! I'm really sorry for them! How strange it is that when the
flower of a man's youth has faded, he seems to lose all charm in a
woman's eyes; and how true are the words of my expurgated
Juvenal
    " — *Festinat decurrere velox*
 Flosculus, angusta, miseræque brevissima vitæ
  Portio!"
Ah, if we could only make up our minds to invest our stock of youth
on commercial principles instead of squandering it at the outset, old
age would be as extinct as the Dodo!

27

SONG.—ZARA.*

Youth is a boon avowed—
      A gift of priceless worth
To rich and poor allowed—
      With which all men at birth—
            The lowly and the proud—
            Are equally endowed.
But sorrow comes anon,
      For Man's a prodigal
Who madly lives upon
      His little capital.
            As this, alas, goes on
            Till every penny's gone:
He finds himself, at Life's concluding stage,
With no Youth left to comfort his old age!

      Ah, dame improvident,
            If you, in very sooth
      In infancy had lent
            Your Capital of Youth
                  At four or five per cent.—
                  (As Nature doubtless meant),
      Resolved, within your breast,
            To do as others do
      Who Capital invest,
            And live a lifetime through,
                  With modest comfort blest,
                  Upon the interest—
You might be still in girlhood's mid-career
A merry madcap maid of fourscore year!

Enter KING.

KING. My daughter! At last we are alone together.

ZARA. Yes, and I'm glad we are, for I want to speak to you very seriously. Do you know this paper?

KING (*aside*). Da——! (*Aloud.*) Oh, yes—I've—I've seen it. Where in the world did you get this from?

ZARA. It was given to me by Lady Sophy—my sister's governess.

KING (*aside*). Lady Sophy's an angel, but I do sometimes wish she'd mind her own business! (*Aloud*) It's—ha! ha!—it's rather humorous.

ZARA. I see nothing humorous in it. I only see that you, the despotic King of this country, are made the subject of the most scandalous insinuations. Why do you permit these things?

KING. Well, they appeal to my sense of humour. It's the only really comic paper in Utopia, and I wouldn't be without it for the world.

*This lyric was slightly re-written by Gilbert at Sullivan's request. The original version appeared in Act II. See Appendix, no. 14.

28

ZARA. If it had any literary merit I could understand it.

KING. Oh, it *has* literary merit. Oh, distinctly, it has literary merit.

ZARA. My dear father, it's mere ungrammatical twaddle.

KING. Oh, it's not ungrammatical. I can't allow that. Unpleasantly personal, perhaps, but written with an epigrammatical point that is very rare now-a-days—very rare indeed.

ZARA (*looking at cartoon*). Why do they represent you with such a big nose?

KING. Why, the fact is that, in the cartoons of a comic paper, the size of your nose always varies inversely as the square of your popularity. It's the rule.

ZARA. Then you must be at a tremendous discount, just now! I see a notice of a new piece called " King Tuppence," in which an English tenor has the audacity to personate you on a public stage. I can only say that I am surprised that any English tenor should lend himself to such degrading personalities.

KING. Oh, he's not really English. As it happens he's a Utopian, but he calls himself English.

ZARA. Calls himself English?

KING. Yes. Bless you, they wouldn't listen to any tenor who didn't call himself English.

ZARA. And you permit this insolent buffoon to caricature you in a pointless burlesque!

KING. Oh, it's not pointless—it's very smartly written. If it were pointless. I wouldn't allow it, but the piece really has very remarkable literary merit. Now listen—this gets a double encore. (*Sings.*)   *

> Oh, I'm a kind of a King—
>   A sort of a Despot bold—
> An utterly unsignificant thing
>   Who does whatever he's told—
> Oh, cruel is my lot,
>   My fate unkind I call—
> For I'm a Kingly Never Mind What
> A Royal Nothing at All!

(*Breaks down, and sinks sobbing into a chair.*)

ZARA. My dear father—there's something wrong here. If you were a free agent, you would never permit these outrages.

KING (*almost in tears*). Zara—I—I admit I am not altogether a free agent. I—I am controlled. I try to make the best of it, but sometimes I find it very difficult—very difficult indeed. Nominally a Despot, I am, between ourselves, the helpless tool of two unscrupulous Wise Men, who insist on my falling in with all their wishes and threaten to denounce me for immediate explosion if I remonstrate! (*Breaks down completely.*)

---

*This line, including the verse, was deleted prior to the opening.

145

Enes Blackmore, as Sir Baily Barre. (British Library.)

ZARA. My poor father! Now listen to me. With a view to remodelling the political and social institutions of Utopia, I have brought with me six Representatives of the principal causes that have tended to make England the powerful, happy and blameless country which the consensus of European civilization has declared it to be. Place yourself unreservedly in the hands of these gentlemen, and they will reorganize your country on a footing that will enable you to defy your persecutors. They are all now washing their hands after their journey. Shall I introduce them?

KING. My dear Zara, how can I thank you? I will consent to anything that will release me from the abominable tyranny of these two men. (*Calling.*) What ho! Without there! (*Enter* CALYNX.) Summon my court without an instant's delay! (*Exit* CALYNX.)

FINALE.   6 7

Enter Everyone, except the Flowers of Progress.

CHORUS.

Although your Royal summons to appear
From courtesy was singularly free,
Obedient to that summons we are here—
What would your Majesty?

RECIT.—KING.

My worthy people, my beloved daughter
Most thoughtfully has brought with her from England
The types of all the causes that have made
That great and glorious country what it is.

CHORUS.   Oh joy unbounded!

SCA., TAR., *and* PHAN. (*aside.*) Why, what *does* this mean?

RECIT.—ZARA.

Attend to me, Utopian populace,
Ye South Pacific Island viviparians;
All, in the abstract, types of courtly grace,
Yet, when compared with Britain's glorious race,
But little better than half-clothed barbarians!

CHORUS.

That's true—we South Pacific viviparians,
Contrasted when
With Englishmen,
Are little better than half-clothed barbarians!

Enter all the Flowers of Progress, led by FITZBATTLEAXE.

---

6. The Finale was originally preceded by two lines which were cut for obvious reasons. See Appendix, no. 6.

7. An earlier draft of the First Act Finale (up to 'Some Seven Men') appears in Appendix, no. 7.

30

SOLO.—ZARA. (*Presenting* CAPT. FITZBATTLEAXE.)

When Britain sounds the mighty trump of war
(And Europe trembles,)
The army of that doughty conqueror
In serried ranks assembles;
'Tis then this warrior's eyes and sabre gleam
For our protection—
He represents a military scheme
In all its proud perfection!

FITZ.   Yes—yes—
I represent a military scheme
In all its proud perfection!

CHORUS.   Ulahlica!   Ulahlica!   Ulahlica!

SOLO.—ZARA. (*Presenting* SIR BAILEY BARRE, Q.C.

A complicated gentleman allow me to present,
Of all the arts and faculties the terse embodiment,
He's a great arithmetician who can demonstrate with ease
That two and two are three, or five, or anything you please;
An eminent logician who can make it clear to you
That black is white—when looked at from the proper point of view;
A marvellous philologist who'll undertake to show
That "yes" is but another and a neater form of "no."

SIR BAILEY.   Yes—yes—yes—
Oh "yes" is but another and a neater form of "no."
All preconceived ideas on any subject I can scout,
And demonstrate beyond all possibility of doubt,
That whether you're an honest man or whether you're a thief
Depends on whose solicitor has given me my brief.

CHORUS.   Yes—yes—yes—
That whether you're an honest man, &c.
Ulahlica! Ulahlica! Ulahlica!

SOLO.—ZARA. (*Presenting Lord Chamberlain and County
Councillor.*)

What these may be, Utopians all
Perhaps you'll hardly guess—
They're types of England's physical
And moral cleanliness.
This is a Lord High Chamberlain
Of purity the gauge—
He'll cleanse our Court from moral stain,
And purify our Stage.

LORD C.   Yes—yes—yes—
Court reputations I revise,

Scott Russell as Lord Dramaleigh, a British Lord Chamberlain.
(British Library.)

Herbert Ralland as Mr Blushington. (*British Library.*)

31

And presentations scrutinize,
New plays I read with jealous eyes,
And purify the Stage.

CHORUS.   Yes—yes—yes—
New plays, &c.

ZARA.   This County Councillor acclaim,
Great Britain's latest toy—
On anything you like to name
His talents he'll employ—
All streets and squares he'll purify
Within your city walls,
And keep meanwhile a modest eye
On wicked music halls.

C. C.   Yes—yes—yes—
In towns I make improvements great,
Which go to swell the County Rate—
I dwelling-houses sanitate
And purify the Halls!

CHORUS.   Yes—yes—yes—
He'll dwelling-houses, &c.
Ulahlica! Ulahlica! Ulahlica!

SOLO.—ZARA. (*Presenting* MR. GOLDBURY.)

A Company Promoter this, with special education
Which teaches what Contango means and also
Backwardation—
To speculators he supplies a grand financial leaven,
Time was when *two* were company—but now it must
be seven.

MR. GOLD.   Yes—yes—yes—
Stupendous loans to foreign thrones
I've largely advocated;
In ginger-pops and peppermint-drops
I've freely speculated;
Then mines of gold, of wealth untold,
Successfully I've floated,
And sudden falls in apple-stalls
Occasionally quoted:
And soon or late I always call
For Stock Exchange quotation—
No schemes too great and none to small
For Companification!

Then soon or late, &c.
Ulahlica! Ulahlica! Ulahlica!

3²

ZARA. (*Presenting* CAPT. SIR EDWARD CORCORAN, R.N.)
> And lastly I present
> > Great Britain's proudest boast,
> Who from the blows
> Of foreign foes
> > Protects her sea-girt coast—
> And if you ask him in respectful tone,
> He'll show you how you may protect your own!

SOLO.—CAPTAIN CORCORAN.

> I'm Captain Corcoran, K.C.B.,
> I'll teach you how we rule the sea,
> > And terrify the simple Gaul.
> And how the Saxon and the Celt
> Their Europe-shaking blows have dealt
> With Maxim gun and Nordenfelt
> > (Or will, when the occasion calls)
> If sailor-like you'd play your cards
> Unbend your sails, and lower your yards,
> > Unstep your masts—you'll never want 'em more.
> Though we're no longer hearts of oak,
> Yet we can steer and we can stoke,
> And, thanks to coal, and thanks to coke,
> > We never run a ship ashore!

ALL.   What never?

CAPT.   No, never!

ALL.   What, *never?*

CAPT.   Hardly ever!

ALL.   Hardly ever run a ship ashore!
> > Then give three cheers, and three cheers more,
> > For the tar who never runs his ship ashore;
> > Then give three cheers, and three cheers more,
> > For he never runs his ship ashore!

CHORUS.

> All hail, ye types of England's power—
> > Ye heaven-enlightened band!
> We bless the day, and bless the hour
> > That brought you to our land.

QUARTETTE.

> Ye wanderers from a mighty State
> Oh teach us how to legislate—
> Your lightest word will carry weight
> > In our attentive ears.

Laurence Gridley as Captain Corcoran, K.C.B. He stopped the show on opening night with an excerpt from HMS Pinafore. *(British Library.)*

33

Oh teach the natives of this land
(Who are not quick to understand)
How to work off their social and
      Political arrears!

CAPT. FITZ.   Increase your army!

LD. DRAMALEIGH.   Purify your Court!

CAPT. COR.   Get up your steam and cut your canvas short!

SIR B. BAR.   To speak on both sides teach your sluggish brains!

MR. B., C. C.   Widen your thoroughfares, and flush your drains!

MR. GOLD.   Utopia's much too big for one small head—
             I'll float it as a Company Limited!

KING.   A Company Limited? What may that be?
         The term, I rather think, is new to me.

CHORUS.   A Company Limited? &c.

SCA., PHAN., *and* TARARA (*aside*).
      What does he mean? What does he mean?
         Give us a kind of clue!
      What does he mean? What does he mean?
         What is he going to do?

SONG.—MR. GOLDBURY.

Some seven men form an Association,
    (If possible, all Peers and Baronets)
They start off with a public declaration
    To what extent they mean to pay their debts.
That's called their Capital: if they are wary
    They will not quote it at a sum immense.
The figure's immaterial—it may vary
    From eighteen million down to eighteenpence.
      I should put it rather low;
      The good sense of doing so
Will be evident at once to any debtor.
      When it's left to you to say
      What amount you mean to pay,
Why, the lower you can put it at, the better.

CHORUS.   When it's left to you to say, &c.

They then proceed to trade with all who'll trust 'em,
    Quite irrespective of their capital
(It's shady, but it's sanctified by custom);
    Bank, Railway, Loan, or Panama Canal.
You can't embark on trading too tremendous—
    It's strictly fair, and based on common sense—
If you succeed, your profits are stupendous—

34

And if you fail, pop goes your eighteenpence.
Make the money-spinner spin!
For you only stand to win,
And you'll never with dishonesty be twitted.
For nobody can know,
To a million or so,
To what extent your capital's committed!

CHORUS.   No, nobody can know, &c.

If you come to grief, and creditors are craving,
    (For nothing that is planned by mortal head
Is certain in this Vale of Sorrow—saving
    That one's Liability is Limited),—
Do you suppose that signifies perdition?
    If so you're but a monetary dunce—
You merely file a Winding-Up Petition,
    And start another Company at once!
        Though a Rothschild you may be
        In your own capacity,
As a Company you've come to utter sorrow—
        But the Liquidators say,
        "Never mind—you needn't pay,"
So you start another company to-morrow!

CHORUS.   But the Liquidators say, &c.

RECIT.

KING.   Well, at first sight it strikes us as dishonest,
                But if it's good enough for virtuous England—
                The first commercial country in the world—
                It's good enough for us.

SCA., PHAN., *and* TARARA.   You'd best take care—
(*aside to* KING.)   Please recollect *we* have not been consulted!

KING.   And do I understand you that Great Britain
(*not heeding them.*)   Upon this Joint Stock principle is governed?

MR. GOLD.   We haven't come to that, exactly—but
                We're tending rapidly in that direction.
                The date's not distant.

KING (*enthusiastically*).   We will be before you!
                We'll go down to Posterity renowned
                As the First Sovereign in Christendom
                Who registered his Crown and Country under
                The Joint Stock Company's Act of Sixty-Two!

ALL.   Ulahlica! Ulahlica! Ulahlica!

35

SOLO.—KING.

Henceforward, of a verity,
 With Fame ourselves we link—
We'll go down to Posterity
 Of sovereigns all the pink!

SCA., PHAN., *and* TAR. (*aside to* KING). If you've the
   mad temerity
 Our wishes thus to blink,
You'll go down to Posterity
 Much earlier than you think!

TARARA (*correcting them*). He'll go *up* to Posterity,
   If *I* inflict the blow!

SCA. *and* PHAN. (*angrily*). He'll go *down* to Posterity,
   We think we ought to know!

TARARA (*explaining*). He'll go *up* to Posterity,
   Blown up with dynamite!

SCA. *and* PHAN. (*apologetically*). He'll go *up* to Posterity,
   Of course he will, you're right!

CHORUS.

Let's seal this mercantile pact
 The step we ne'er shall rue—
It gives whatever we lacked—
 The statement's strictly true.
All hail, astonishing Fact!
 All hail, Invention new—
The Joint Stock Company's Act—
 The Act of Sixty-Two!

ENSEMBLE.

KING, LADY SOPHY, NEK., KAL., CALYX, *and* CHORUS.	SCA., PHAN., *and* TARARA (*aside*).	FITZBATTLEAXE *and* ZARA (*aside*).
Henceforward of a verity With fame ourselves we link, And go down to Posterity Of sovereigns all the pink!	If he has the temerity Our wishes thus to blink, He'll go up to Posterity Much earlier than they think!	Who love with all sincerity, Their lives may safely link; And as for our Posterity— We don't care what they think!

CHORUS. Let's seal this mercantile pact, &c.

CURTAIN.   8

END OF ACT I.

---

8. For Gilbert's original final stage direction, see Appendix, no. 8.

ACT II.

SCENE.—*Pavilion in the Palace, enclosed by curtains. Night.*
FITZBATTLEAXE *discovered, singing to* ZARA.

RECIT.—FITZ.

Oh Zara, my beloved one, bear with me!
Ah do not laugh at my attempted C!
Repent not, mocking maid, thy girlhood's choice—
The fervour of my love affects my voice!

SONG.—FITZ.

A tenor, all singers above,
    (This doesn't admit of a question),
       Should keep himself quiet,
       Attend to his diet
    And carefully nurse his digestion:
But when he is madly in love
    It's certain to tell on his singing—
       You can't do chromatics
       With proper emphatics
    When anguish your bosom is wringing!
When distracted with worries in plenty,
And his pulse is a hundred and twenty,
And his bosom the slave of mistrust is,
A tenor can't do himself justice.
    Now observe—(*sings a high note*),
You see, I can't do myself justice!

I could sing, if my fervour were mock,
    It's easy enough if you're acting—
       But when one's emotion
       Is born of devotion
    You mustn't be over-exacting.
One ought to be firm as a rock
    To venture a shake in *vibrato*,
       When fervour's expected
       Keep cool and collected
    Or never attempt *agitato*.
But, of course, when his tongue is of leather,
And his lips appear pasted together,
And his palate as dry as a crust is,
A tenor can't do himself justice.
    Now observe—(*sings a cadence*),
It's no use—I can't do myself justice!

37

ZARA. Why, Arthur, what *does* it matter? When the higher qualities of the heart are all that can be desired, the higher notes of the voice are matters of comparative insignificance. Who thinks slightingly of the cocoanut because it is husky? Besides (*demurely*) you are not singing for an engagement, (*putting her hand in his*) you have that already!

FITZ. How good and wise you are! How unerringly your practised brain winnows the wheat from the chaff—the material from the merely incidental!

ZARA. My Girton training, Arthur. At Girton all is wheat, and idle chaffs is never heard within its walls! But tell me, is not all working marvellously well? Have not our Flowers of Progress more than justified their name?

FITZ. We have indeed done our best. Captain Corcoran and I have, in concert, thoroughly remodelled the sister-services—and upon so sound a basis that the South Pacific trembles at the name of Utopia!

ZARA. How clever of you!

FITZ. Clever? not a bit. It's as easy as possible when the Admirality and Horse Guards are not there to interfere. And so with the others. Freed from the trammels imposed upon them by idle Acts of Parliament, all have given their natural talents full play and introduced reforms which, even in England, were never dreamt of!

ZARA. But perhaps the most beneficent change of all has been effected by Mr. Goldbury who, discarding the exploded theory that some strange magic lies hidden in the number Seven, has applied the Limited Liability principle to individuals, and every man, woman, and child is now a Company Limited with liability restricted to the amount of his declared Capital! There is not a christened baby in Utopia who has not already issued his little Prospectus!

FITZ. Marvellous is the power of a Civilization which can transmute, by a word, a Limited Income into an Income (*Limited*).

ZARA. Reform has not stopped here—it has been applied even to the costume of our people. Discarding their own barbaric dress, the natives of our land have unanimously adopted the tasteful fashions of England in all their rich entirety. Scaphio and Phantis have undertaken a contract to supply the whole of Utopia with clothing designed upon the most approved English models—and the first Drawing Room under the new state of things is to be held here this evening.

FITZ. But Drawing Rooms are always held in the afternoon.

ZARA. Ah, we've improved upon that. We all look so much better by candle-light! And when I tell you, dearest, that my court train has just arrived, you will understand that I am longing to go and try it on.

FITZ. Then we must part?

Charles Kenningham as Captain Fitzbattleaxe. (British Library.)

King Paramount dressed as a Field Marshal for the Drawing Room Scene, Act II. (British Library.)

38

ZARA. Necessarily, for a time.

FITZ. Just as I wanted to tell you, with all the passionate enthusiasm of my nature, how deeply, how devotedly I love you!

ZARA. Hush! Are these the accents of a heart that really feels? True love does not indulge in declamation, its voice is sweet, and soft, and low. The west wind whispers when he woos the poplars!

DUET.—ZARA *and* FITZBATTLEAXE.   9

ZARA.   Words of love too loudly spoken
        Ring their own untimely knell;
Noisy vows are rudely broken,
        Soft the song of Philomel.
Whisper sweetly, whisper slowly,
        Hour by hour and day by day;
Sweet and low as accents holy
        Are the notes of lover's lay!

BOTH.   Sweet and low, &c.

FITZ.   Let the conqueror, flushed with glory,
        Bid his noisy clarions bray;
Lovers tell their artless story
        In a whispered roundelay.
False is he whose vows alluring
        Make the listening echoes ring;
Sweet and low when all-enduring,
        Are the songs that lovers sing!

BOTH.   Sweet and low, &c.

[Exit ZARA.]

(*Enter* KING, *dressed as Field Marshal with his hair still in ringlets.*)

KING. To a Monarch who has been accustomed to the uncontrolled use of his limbs, the costume of a British Field Marshal is, perhaps, at first, a little cramping. Are you sure that this is all right? It's not a practical joke, is it? No one has a keener sense of humour than I have, but the First Statutory Cabinet Council of Utopia (*Limited*) must be conducted with dignity and impressiveness.

[FITZ. Your Majesty's hair is a little longer, perhaps, than according to strict regulation it should be. If you would permit me to send for the Court Barber—

KING. No, no! We draw the line at that. No liberties with a Monarch's toilette. We have placed our Royal body, arms, and legs at your entire disposal—and a pretty figure of fun you've made of us—but we still retain absolute control over our Royal *chevelure.*] Now, where are the other five who signed the Articles of Association?

FITZ. Sir, they are here.

9. For the original version of this song see Appendix, no. 9.
  *These two lines were deleted before the opening.

39

Enter LD. CHAMBERLAIN, CAPTAIN CORCORAN, SIR BAILEY BARRE, MR. BLUSHINGTON *and* MR. GOLDBURY *from different entrances.*

KING. Oh! (*addressing them.*) Gentlemen, our daughter holds her first Drawing Room in half an hour, and we shall have to make our half yearly report in the interval. I am necessarily unfamiliar with the forms of an English Cabinet Council—perhaps the Lord Chamberlain will kindly put us in the way of doing the thing properly, and with due regard to the solemnity of the occasion.

LD. C. Certainly—nothing simpler. Kindly bring your chairs forward—his Majesty will, of course, preside.

They range their chairs across stage like Christy Minstrels. KING *sits* C., LORD CHAMBERLAIN *on his* L., MR. GOLDBURY *on his* R., CAPT. CORCORAN L. *of* LORD CHAMBERLAIN, CAPT. FITZBATTLEAXE R. *of* SIR BAILEY BARRE, MR. BLUSHINGTON *extreme* R., SIR BAILEY BARRE *extreme* L.

KING. Like this?
LD. C. Like this.
KING. We take your word for it that this is all right. You are not making fun of us? This is in accordance with the practice at the Court of St. James's?
LD. C. It is in accordance with the practice at the Court of St. James's Hall.
KING. Oh! it seems odd, but never mind.

SONG.—KING.   10

Society has quite forsaken all her wicked courses,
Which empties our police courts and abolishes divorces.
CHORUS.   Divorce is nearly obsolete in England.

KING. No tolerance we show to undeserving rank and splendour;
For the higher his position is, the greater the offender.
CHORUS.   That's a maxim that is prevalent in England.

KING. No peeress at our Drawing Room before the Presence passes
Who wouldn't be accepted by the lower-middle classes.
Each shady dame, whatever be her rank, is bowed out neatly.

CHORUS. In short, this happy country has been Anglicized completely!
It really is surprising   11
What a thorough Anglicizing
We have brought about—Utopia's quite another land;
In her enterprising movements,
She is England—with improvements,
Which we dutifully offer to our mother-land!

10. A 'Minstrel scene' preceded the patter song. See Appendix, no. 10.
11. The original chorus to this song was slightly different. See Appendix, no. 11.

40

KING. Our city we have beautified—we've done it willy-nilly—
And all that isn't Belgrave Square is Strand and Picca-
dilly.

CHORUS. We haven't any slummeries in England!

KING. We have solved the labour question with discrimination
polished,
So poverty is obsolete and hunger is abolished—

CHORUS. We are going to abolish it in England!

KING. The Chamberlain our native stage has purged, beyond a
question,
Of "risky" situation and indelicate suggestion;
No piece is tolerated if it's costumed indiscreetly—

CHORUS. In short, this happy country has been Anglicized completely!
It really is surprising, &c.

KING. Our Peerage we've remodelled on an intellectual basis,
Which certainly is rough on our hereditary races—

CHORUS. We are going to remodel it in England.

KING. The Brewers and the Cotton Lords no longer seek admission,
And Literary Merit meets with proper recognition—

CHORUS. As Literary Merit does in England!

KING. Who knows but we may count among our intellectual
chickens
Like you, an Earl of Thackeray and p'r'aps a Duke of
Dickens—
Lord Fildes and Viscount Millais (when they come) we'll
welcome sweetly—

CHORUS. In short, this happy country has been Anglicized completely!
It really is surprising, &c.

(At the end all rise and replace their chairs.)   12

KING. Now then, for our First Drawing Room. Where are the
Princesses? What an extraordinary thing it is that since European
looking-glasses have been supplied to the Royal bed-rooms my
daughters are invariably late!

LD. DRAM. Sir, their Royal Highnesses await your pleasure in
the Ante-Room.

KING. Oh. Then request them to do us the favour to enter at
once.

MARCH.—*Enter all the Royal Household, including (besides the
Lord Chamberlain) the Vice-Chamberlain, the Master of the Horse,
the Lord High Treasurer, the Lord Steward, the Comptroller of the*

---

12. In Gilbert's manuscript, the 'Drawing Room' followed the patter song with no
spoken dialogue at all. The chorale ('Eagle High') was omitted. Gilbert's stage direction for
the Drawing Room Scene was slightly different. See Appendix, no. 12.

41

Household, the Lord-in-Waiting, the Groom-in-Waiting, the Field Officer in Brigade Waiting, the Gold and Silver Stick, and the Gentlemen Ushers. Then enter the three Princesses (their trains carried by Pages of Honour,) LADY SOPHY, and the Ladies-in-Waiting.

KING. My daughters, we are about to attempt a very solemn ceremonial, so no giggling, if you please. Now, my Lord Chamberlain, we are ready.

LD. DRAM. Then, ladies and gentlemen, places if you please. His Majesty will take his place in front of the throne, and will be so obliging as to kiss all the *débutantes*. (LADY SOPHY, *much shocked, again blindfolds the young Princesses*)

KING. What—must I really?

LD. DRAM. Absolutely indispensable.

KING (*aside.*) More jam for the Palace Peeper!

The KING takes his place in front of the throne, the PRINCESS ZARA on his left. The two younger Princesses on the left of ZARA.

KING. Now, is every one in his place?

LD. DRAM. Every one is in his place.

KING. Then let the revels commence.

> *The ladies to be presented then enter—give their cards to the Lord-in-Waiting, who passes them to the Vice-Chamberlain, who passes them to the Lord Chamberlain, who reads the names to the KING as each lady approaches. The ladies curtsey in succession to the KING and the three Princesses, and pass out, re-entering afterwards. When all the presentations have been accomplished the KING, Princesses, and LADY SOPHY come forward.*

RECIT.—KING.

This ceremonial our wish displays
To copy all Great Britain's courtly ways.
Though lofty aims catastrophe entail,
Will gloriously succeed or nobly fail!

SEXTETTE.

KING, PRINCESS ZARA, PRINCESSES NEKAYAH *and* KALYBA, LADY SOPHY, FITZBATTLEAXE, *and* CHORUS.

Eagle high in cloudland soaring—
    Sparrow twittering on a reed—
Tiger in the jungle roaring—
    Frightened fawn in grassy mead—
Let the eagle, not the sparrow,
Be the object of your arrow—

42

Fix the tiger with your eye—
Pass the fawn in pity by.
Glory then will crown the day—
Glory, glory, anyway!
If you hit it, song and story
Shrine you in a glow of glory:
If you miss it, why bewail?
For you gloriously fail!
Hit or miss it, as you may,
Glory still will crown the day!
Leave the sordid and the sorry—
Fiy your thoughts on nobler wings;
Keep your bolt for Royal quarry,
Fitted for the sport of Kings.
If you hit it, song and story
Shrine you in a glow of glory:
If you miss it, why bewail?
For you gloriously fail!
Hit or miss it, as you may,
Glory still will crown the day!

[*Then Exeunt all.*

Enter SCAPHIO *and* PHANTIS, *now dressed as judges in red and ermine robes and undress wigs. They come down stage melodramatically—working together.*

DUET.—SCAPHIO *and* PHANTIS.

SCA.   With fury deep we burn—
PHAN.   We do—
    We fume with smothered rage.
    These Englishmen who rule supreme
    Their undertaking they redeem
    By stifling every harmless scheme
        In which we both engage—
SCA.   They do—
    In which we both engage.

BOTH (*with great energy*). For this mustn't be, and this won't do,
If you'll back me, then I'll back you,
Let's both agree, and we'll pull things through,
For this mustn't be, and this won't do.
    No, this won't do,
    No, this won't do,
    No, this mustn't be,
    And this won't do.

Enter the KING.

KING. Gentlemen, gentlemen—really! This unseemly display of energy within the Royal Precincts is altogether unpardonable. Pray what do you complain of?

Scaphio and Phantis in judges' robes, Act II. (British Library.)

SCA. (*furiously*). What do we complain of? Why, through the innovations introduced by the Flowers of Progress all our harmless schemes for making a provision for our old age are ruined. Our Matrimonial Agency is at a standstill. Our Cheap Sherry business is in bankruptcy. Our Army Clothing contracts are paralyzed, and even our Society paper, the *Palace Peeper*, is practically defunct!

KING. Defunct? Is that so? Dear, dear, I am truly sorry.

SCA. Are you aware that Sir Bailey Barre has introduced a law of libel by which all editors of scurrilous newspapers are publicly flogged—as in England? And six of our editors have resigned in succession!

PHAN. Then our Burlesque Theatre is absolutely ruined!

KING. Dear me. Well, theatrical property is not what it was.

PHAN. Are you aware that the Lord Chamberlain, who has his own views as to the best means of elevating the national drama, has declined to license any play that is not in blank verse and three hundred years old—as in England?

SCA. And as if that wasn't enough, the County Councillor has ordered a four-foot wall to be built up right across the proscenium, in case of fire—as in England.

PHAN. It's so hard on the company—who are liable to be roasted alive—and this has to be met by enormously increased salaries—as in England.

KING. Really, gentlemen, this is very irregular. If you will be so good as to formulate a detailed list of your grievances in writing, addressed to the Secretary of Utopia (*Limited*), they will be laid before the Board, in due course, at their next monthly meeting.

SCA. Are we to understand that we are defied?

KING. That is the idea I intended to convey.

PHAN. Defied! We are defied!

SCA. (*furiously*). Take care—you know our powers. Trifle with us, and you die!

FURIOUS TRIO.—SCA., PHAN., *and* KING.   13

PHAN.   If you think that when banded in unity,
        We may both be defied with impunity,
                You are sadly misled of a verity!
        If you value repose and tranquility,
        You'll revert to a state of docility,
                Or prepare to regret your temerity!

SCA.   We'll apply, without quibble or quiddity,
        Such a powerful dose of acidity,
                It will act on your comfort corrosively—

13. The earlier design for this number was slightly different. See Appendix, no. 13.

44

We need only denounce your morality,
And then, in some public locality
    Your reign will be finished explosively!

KING.   If my speech is unduly refractory
You will find it a course satisfactory
    At an early Board meeting to show it up.
Though if proper excuse you can trump any,
You may *wind* up a Limited Company,
    You cannot conveniently *blow* it up!

(SCAPHIO *and* PHANTIS *thoroughly baffled.*)

KING. (*dancing quietly*).   Whene'er I chance to baffle you
    I, also, dance a step or two—
    Of this now guess the hidden sense:

(SCAPHIO *and* PHANTIS *consider the question as* KING *continues
dancing quietly—then give it up.*)

    It means—complete indifference!
ALL THREE. (*dancing quietly*.)   Indifference—indifference—
    Of course it does—indifference!
{ You }
{ We } might have guessed its hidden sense.
It means complete indifference!

KING. (*dancing quietly*).   SCA. *and* PHAN. *dancing furiously*).
    As we've a dance for every mood
    With *pas de trois* we will conclude.
    What this may mean you all may guess—

{ SCA. *and* PHAN. { It typifies remorselessness!
{   KING.   { It means unruffled cheerful-
                 ness!

KING *dances off placidly as* SCAPHIO *and* PHANTIS *dance furiously.*

PHAN. (*breathless*).   He's right—we are helpless! He's no longer a human being—he's a Corporation, and so long as he confines himself to his Articles of Association we can't touch him! What are we to do?

SCA.   Do? Raise a Revolution, repeal the Act of Sixty-Two, reconvert him into an individual, and insist on his immediate explosion! (TARARA *enters.*) Tarara, come here; you're the very man we want.

TAR.   Certainly, allow me. (*Offers a cracker to each, they snatch them away impatiently*). That's rude.

SCA.   We have no time for idle forms. You wish to succeed to the throne?

TAR.   Naturally.

SCA.   Then you won't unless you join us. The King has defied us, and, as matters stand, we are helpless. So are you. We must devise some plot at once to bring the people about his ears.

Walter Passmore in his Gilbert and Sullivan début as Tarara, the Public Exploder. (British Library.)

TAR. A plot?

PHAN. Yes, a plot of superhuman subtlety. Have you such a thing about you?

TAR. (*feeling*). No, I think not. There's one on my dressing-table.

SCA. We can't wait—we must concoct one at once, and put it into execution without delay. There is not a moment to spare.

TRIO.—SCAPHIO, PHANTIS, *and* TARARA.

ENSEMBLE.

With wily brain upon the spot
   A private plot we'll plan,
The most ingenious private plot
   Since private plots began.
That's understood. So far we've got
And, striking while the iron's hot,
We'll now determine like a shot
The details of this private plot.

SCA.   I think we ought—(*whispers*).

PHAN. *and* TAR. Such bosh I never heard.

PHAN.   Ah! happy thought!—(*whispers*).

SCA. *and* TAR. How utterly dashed absurd!

TAR.   *I'll* tell you how—(*whispers*).

SCA. *and* PHAN. Why, what put that in your head?

SCA.   I've got it now—(*whispers*).
       Oh, take him away to bed!

PHAN.   Oh, put him to bed!

TAR.   Oh, put him to bed!

SCA.   What! put *me* to bed?

PHAN. *and* TAR.   Yes, put him to bed!

SCA.   But, bless me, don't you see—

PHAN.   Do listen to me, I pray—

TAR.   It certainly seems to me—

SCA.   Bah—this is the only way!

PHAN.   It's rubbish absurd you growl—

TAR.   You talk ridiculous stuff!

SCA.   You're a drivelling barndoor owl—

PHAN.   You're a vapid and vain old muff!
      (*All coming down to audience.*)
So far we haven't quite solved the plot—
They're not a very ingenious lot—
   But don't be unhappy
   It' still on the *tapis*
We'll presently hit on a capital plot!

Scott Fishe as Mr Goldbury, Act I. (Bridget D'Oyly Carte.)

46

SCA.	Suppose we all—*(whispers).*
PHAN.	Now *there* I think you're right.
	Then we might all—*(whispers).*
TAR.	That's true—we certainly might.
	I'll tell you what—*(whispers).*
SCA.	We will if we possibly can.
	Then on the spot—*(whispers).*
PHAN. *and* TAR.	Bravo! a capital plan!
SCA.	That's exceedingly neat and new!
PHAN.	Exceedingly new and neat!
TAR.	I fancy that that will do.
SCA.	It's certainly very complete.
PHAN.	Well done, you sly old sap!
TAR.	Bravo, you cunning old mole!
SCA.	You very ingenious chap!
PHAN.	You intellectual soul! *(all shaking hands).*

(All, coming down, and addressing audience.)

At last a capital plan we've got;
Never mind why and never mind what:
    It's safe in my noddle—
    Now off we will toddle,
And slyly develop this capital plot!   14

                          [Business.   Exeunt all]

                                            15

       Enter LORD DRAMALEIGH *and* MR. GOLDBURY.

LORD D.   Well, what do you think of our first South Pacific Drawing Room? Allowing for a slight difficulty with the trains, and a little want of familiarity with the use of the rouge-pot, it was, on the whole, a meritorious affair?

GOLD.   My dear Dramaleigh, it redounds infinitely to your credit.

LORD D.   One or two judicious innovations, I think?

GOLD.   Admirable. The cup of tea and the plate of mixed biscuits were a cheap and effective inspiration.

LORD D.   Yes—my idea, entirely. Never been done before.

GOLD.   Pretty little maids, the King's youngest daughters, but shy.

LORD D.   That'll wear off. Young.

GOLD.   *That'll* wear off. Ha! here they come, by George! And without the Dragon! What can they have done with her?

       Enter NEKAYAH *and* KALYBA, *timidly.*

NEK.   Oh, if you please Lady Sophy has sent us in here, because Zara and Captain Fitzbattleaxe are going on, in the garden, in a manner which no well conducted young ladies ought to witness.

LORD D.   Indeed, we are very much obliged to her Ladyship.

---

14. Gilbert wrote a Quartet for Scaphio, Phantis, Zara and Fitzbattleaxe which originally followed here. See Appendix, no. 14.

15. Gilbert wrote another scene and song for Miss McIntosh which also came at this point. See Appendix, no. 15.

KAL. Are you? I wonder why.

NEK. Don't tell us if it's rude.

LORD D. Rude? Not at all. We are obliged to Lady Sophy because she has afforded us the pleasure of seeing you.

NEK. I don't think you ought to talk to us like that.

KAL. It's certain to turn our heads.

GOLD. Pray be reassured—you are in no danger whatever. But may I ask—is this extreme delicacy—this shrinking sensitiveness—a general characteristic of Utopian young ladies?

KAL. Oh no; we are crack specimens.

NEK. We are the pick of the basket.

KAL. *Would* you mind not coming quite so near? Thank you. Unfortunately, most young ladies are sadly lacking in that demure propriety which is so generally admired in us. *Would* you stand a little further off, please?

NEK. And please don't look at us like that; it unsettles us.

KAL. And we don't like it. At least, we *do* like it; but it's wrong.

NEK. *We* have enjoyed the inestimable privilege of being educated by a most refined and easily-shocked English lady, on the very strictest English principles.

GOLD. But my dear young ladies——

KAL. Oh don't! You mustn't. It's too affectionate.

NEK. It really does unsettle us.

GOLD. Are you really under the impression that English girls are so ridiculously demure? Why, an English girl of the highest type is the best, the most beautiful, the bravest, and the brightest creature that Heaven has conferred upon this world of ours. She is frank, open-hearted and fearless, and never shows in so favourable a light as when she gives her own blameless impulses full play!

NEK. *and* KAL. Oh, you shocking story!

GOLD. Not at all. I'm speaking the strict truth. I'll tell you all about her.

SONG.—MR. GOLDBURY.

A wonderful joy our eyes to bless,
In her magnificent comeliness,
Is an English girl of eleven stone two,
And five foot ten in her dancing shoe!
She follows the hounds, and on she pounds—
The "field" tails off and the muffs diminish—

48

Over the hedges and brooks she bounds
    Straight as a crow, from find to finish.
At cricket, her kin will lose or win—
    She and her maids, on grass and clover,
Eleven maids out—eleven maids in—
    And perhaps an occasional "maiden over"!
Go search the world and search the sea,
Then come you home and sing with me,
There's no such gold and no such pearl
As a bright and beautiful English girl!

With a ten mile spin she stretches her limbs,
She golfs, she punts, she rows, she swims—
She plays, she sings, she dances, too,
From ten or eleven till all is blue!
    At ball or drum, till small hours come,
        (Chaperon's fan conceals her yawning)
    She'll waltz away like a teetotum,
        And never go home till daylight's dawning.
    Lawn tennis may share her favours fair—
        Her eyes a-dance and her cheeks a-glowing— ·
    Down comes her hair, but what does she care?
        It's all her own and it's worth the showing!
        Go search the world, &c.

Her soul is sweet as the ocean air,
For prudery knows no haven there;
To find mock-modesty, please apply
To the conscious blush and the downcast eye.
    Rich in the things contentment brings,
        In every pure enjoyment wealthy;
    Blithe as a beautiful bird she sings,
        For body and mind are hale and healthy.
    Her eyes they thrill with right goodwill—
        Her heart is light as a floating feather—
    As pure and bright as the mountain rill
        That leaps and laughs in the Highland heather!
        Go search the world, &c.

NEK. Then I may sing and play?

LORD D.   You may!

KAL. And I may laugh and shout?

GOLD.   No doubt!

NEK. These maxims you endorse?

LORD D.   Of course!

KAL. You won't exclaim "Oh fie!"

GOLD.   Not I!

Emmie Owen. Act II. (British Library.)

Florence Perry, Act II. (*British Library.*)

GOLD. Whatever you are—be that:
  Whatever you say—be true:
   Straightforwardly act—
   Be honest—in fact
  Be nobody else but *you*.

LORD D. Give every answer pat—
  Your character true unfurl;
   And when it is ripe,
   You'll then be a type
  Of a capital English girl!

ALL. Oh sweet surprise—oh dear delight,
  To find it undisputed quite—
  All musty, fusty rules despite,
  That Art is wrong and Nature right!

NEK. When happy I,
  With laughter glad
   I'll wake the echoes fairly,
  And only sigh
   When I am sad—
   And that will be but rarely!

KAL. I'll row and fish,
  And gallop, soon—
   No longer be a prim one—
  And when I wish
   To hum a tune,
   It needn't be a hymn one?

GOLD. *and* LORD D. No, no!
  It needn't be a hymn one!

ALL (*dancing*). Oh, sweet surprise and dear delight
  To find it undisputed quite—
  All musty-fusty rules despite—
  That Art is wrong and Nature right!
      [*Dance and off.*

Enter LADY SOPHY.

RECIT.—LADY SOPHY.

Oh, would some demon power the gift impart
To quell my over-conscientious heart—
Unspeak the oaths that never had been spoken,
And break the vows that never shall be broken!

SONG.—LADY SOPHY.

When but a maid of fifteen year,
 Unsought—unplighted—
Short petticoated—and, I fear,
 Still shorter-sighted—

50

I made a vow, one early spring,
That only to some spotless king
Who proof of blameless life could bring,
    I'd be united.
For I had read, not long before,
Of blameless kings in fairy lore,
And thought the race still flourished here—
    Well, well—
I was a maid of fifteen year!

The KING *enters and overhears this verse.*   16

Each morning I pursued my game
    (An early riser);
For spotless monarchs I became
    An advertiser!
But all in vain I searched each land,
So, kingless, to my native strand
Returned, a little older, and
    A good deal wiser!
I learnt that spotless King and Prince
Have disappeared some ages since—
Even Paramount's angelic grace
    Ah, me!
Is but a mask on Nature's face!
    But so bad are the best
    That absurd is my quest
    If so stringent a test
       They are tried by—
    And I find, with remorse,
    I've adopted a course
    Which, though vain, I perforce
       Must abide by!
Too late! Too late
    To break the vow I swore!
Too late! Too late!
    It binds we evermore!
Though the terms of my vow
Were absurd—anyhow
To those terms I must bow
    And abide by!

               (KING *comes forward.*)

RECIT.

KING.   Ah, Lady Sophy—then you love me!
               For so you sing—
LADY S.   No, by the stars that shine above me,
(indignant and surprised)   Degraded King!
(Producing "Palace Peeper.")
       For while these rumours, through the city bruited,
       Remain uncontradicted, unrefuted,

---

16. A stanza omitted here appeared in Gilbert's manuscript copy. See Appendix, no. 16.

51

The object thou of my aversion rooted,
      Repulsive thing!

KING.   Be just—the time is now at hand
            When truth may published be,
         These paragraphs were written and
            Contributed by me!

LADY S.   By you?   No, no!

KING.   Yes, yes, I swear, by me!
         I, caught in Scaphio's ruthless toil,
            Contributed the lot!

LADY S.   And *that* is why you did not boil
            The author on the spot!

KING.   And *that* is why I did not boil
            The author on the spot!

BOTH. {   I *couldn't* think why you did not boil
           She *couldn't* think why I did not boil
            The author on the spot!

DUET.—LADY SOPHY *and* KING.

LADY S.   Oh rapture unrestrained
            Of a candid retractation!
         For my sovereign has deigned
            A convincing explanation—
         And the clouds that gathered o'er,
            All have vanished in the distance,
         And of Kings of fairy lore
            One, at least, is in existence!

KING.   Oh, the skies are blue above,
            And the earth is red and rosal,
         Now the lady of my love
            Has accepted my proposal!
         For that *asinorum pons*
            I have crossed without assistance,
         And of prudish paragons
            One, at least, is in existence!

(KING *and* LADY SOPHY *dance gracefully, and exeunt together.*)   17

[*Enter excitedly* TARARA, *meeting* SCAPHIO *and* PHANTIS.   *

SCA.   Well—how works the plot?   Have you done our bidding?
Have you explained to the happy and contented populace the nature
of their wrongs, and the desperate consequences that must ensue if
they are not rectified?

TAR.   I have explained nothing.   I have done better—I have
made an affidavit that what they supposed to be happiness was really
unspeakable misery—and they are furious!   You know you can't
help believing an affidavit.

17. The stage direction in Gilbert's manuscript copy, which was followed in performance, was more complete. See Appendix, no. 17.
      *These three lines were deleted after the opening.

5²

Sca. Of course—an admirable thought! Ha! they come!]

*Enter all the male Chorus, in great excitement, from various
entrances, followed by the female chorus.*

CHORUS.

Upon our sea-girt land
At our enforced command
Reform has laid her hand
　　　Like some remorseless ogress—
And make us darkly rue
The deeds she dared to do—
And all is owing to
　　　Those hated Flowers of Progress.

All (*drawing swords*). 　So down with them!
　　　　　　　　　So down with them!
　　　　　Reform's a hated ogress.
　　　　　　　　　So down with them!
　　　　　　　　　So down with them!
　　　Down with the Flowers of Progress!

(*Flourish. Enter* King, *his three daughters,* Lady Sophy,
and the Flowers of Progress.)

King. 　What means this most unmannerly irruption?
Is this your gratitude for boons conferred?

Sca. 　Boons? Bah! A fico for such boons, say we!
These boons have brought Utopia to a standstill!
Our pride and boast—the Army and the Navy—
Have both been re-constructed and re-modelled
Upon so irresistible a basis
That all the neighbouring nations have disarmed—
And War's impossible! Your County Councillor
Has passed such drastic Sanitary laws
That all the doctors dwindle, starve, and die!
[Commerce is stagnant. Every man is now　　　　　　　*
A Company Limited, and when he's dunned,
Winds himself up, and then begins afresh!]
The laws, remodelled by Sir Bailey Barre,
Have quite extinguished crime and litigation:
The lawyers starve, and all the jails are let
As model lodgings for the working-classes!
In short—
Utopia, swamped by dull Prosperity,
[Stifled with benefits, all English born,]　　　　　　　†
Demands that these detested Flowers of Progress
Be sent about their business, and affairs
Restored to their original complexion!

---

*These three lines, 'Commerce is stagnant . . .' to '. . . then begins afresh!' were deleted
before the opening.

　†This single line was deleted after the opening.

53

KING (*to people*).   Is this your will?

ALL.   It is—it is.   Down with the Flowers of Progress!

KING (*to* ZARA).   My daughter, this is a very unpleasant state of things.   What is to be done?

ZARA.   I don't know—there's something wrong.   I don't understand it.

[KING.   Is everything at a standstill in England?   Is there no   *
litigation there? no bankruptcy? no poverty? no squalor? no crime? no sickness?

ZARA.   Plenty; it's the most prosperous country in the world!]
We must have omitted something.

KING.   Omitted something?   Yes, that's all very well, but—

(SIR BAILEY BARRE *whispers to* ZARA.)

ZARA (*suddenly*).   Of course!   Now I remember!   Why, I had forgotten the most important, the most vital, the most essential element of all!

KING.   And that is?—

ZARA.   Government by Party!   Introduce that great and glorious element—at once the bulwark and foundation of England's greatness —and all will be well!   No political measures will endure, because one Party will assuredly undo all that the other Party has done; [in-   †
experienced civilians will govern your Army and your Navy; no social reforms will be attempted, because out of vice, squalor, and drunkenness no political capital is to be made;] and while grouse is to be shot, and foxes worried to death, the legislative action of the country will be at a standstill.   Then there will be sickness in plenty, endless lawsuits, crowded jails, interminable confusion in the Army and Navy, and, in short, general and unexampled prosperity!

ALL.   Hurrah! hurrah!

PHAN. (*aside*).   Baffled!

SCA.   But an hour *will* come!

KING.   Your hour has come already—away with them, and let them wait my will!   (SCAPHIO *and* PHANTIS *are handcuffed*.) [Tarara,   ‡
you deserve some compensation in exchange for the privilege of blowing us up, and succeeding to the throne, so we appoint you Perpetual Chief Inspector of Explosives, under 38 and 39 Vic., cap. 17, s. 62.   (TARARA *immediately pulls out a cracker, and putting on his spectacles, proceeds to inspect it*)] From this moment Government by Party is adopted, with all its attendant blessings; and henceforward Utopia will no longer be a Monarchy (Limited), but, what is a great deal better, a Limited Monarchy!

*This speech and the first line of the following were deleted after the opening.
†The lines from 'inexperienced civilians . . .' to '. . . no political capital is to be made' were deleted after the opening.
‡The lines about Tarara's appointment were deleted before the opening.

54

FINALE.   18

ZARA.

There's a little group of isles beyond the wave,
  So tiny you might almost wonder where it is;
That nation is the bravest of the brave,
  And cowards are the rarest of all rarities:
The proudest nations kneel at her command;
  She terrifies all foreign-born rapscallions,
And holds the peace of Europe in her hand,
  With half a score invincible battalions.
    Such at least is the tale
    Which is borne on the gale
      From the island that dwells in the sea—
    Let us hope for her sake
    That we make no mistake,
      That she's all we believe her to be!

KING.

Oh, may we copy all her methods wise,
  And imitate her virtues and her charities,
And may we by degrees acclimatize
  Her Parliamentary peculiarities!
By doing so we shall, in course of time,
  Regenerate completely our entire land;
Great Britain is that monarchy sublime,
  To which some add (but others do not) Ireland.
    Such at least is our view,
    If it prove to be true
      We shall rise to the top of the tree—
    But supposing instead
    That we've all been misled,
      What a kettle of fish there will be!

CURTAIN.

18. There were three Finales to *Utopia, Limited*. See Appendix, no. 18.

Nancy McIntosh as Princess Zara.

Appendix

Utopia, Limited

THE major variant passages which were included in Gilbert's manuscript copy of *Utopia, Limited* (British Library) or in the set of lyrics which were sent to Sullivan (Pierpont Morgan Library) are published here for the first time. Numbers 4, 6, 7 and the first versions of the Finale (18) are from Sullivan's set of lyrics; the rest are all from Gilbert's manuscript copy.

The numbers by which the excerpts are listed correspond to footnotes in the preceding libretto indicating the points in the opera at which the cancelled passages originally appeared.

1   The opening stage direction in Gilbert's manuscript copy ran as follows:

ACT I. Scene. *Garden of* KING PARAMOUNT's *Palace, showing a picturesque and luxuriant Tropical landscape with the Sea in the distance. Maidens discovered lying about lazily, some in hammocks, and some lying on the ground reading, some eating grapes, some fanning each other. All thoroughly enjoying themselves in lotus-eating fashion.*

2   King Paramount had two entrance stanzas which were cancelled.

SONG. – KING.

Why should Royalty be stately?
  King and people widely parted?
Why should I, jocose innately,
  Seem reserved and strong hearted?

Life is what you please to make it.
  Happy all who best employ it.
Sad are those who wisely take it –
  Let's be foolish and enjoy it!

3   The following verses were intended to precede Zara's entrance.

CHORUS.

After Exile home returning,
Crammed with first-class English learning,
Our Princess is doubtless yearning
   To complete our Education.
Lamp of Wisdom burning brightly,
For your coming – daily, nightly –
We've been waiting all politely,
   So indeed has all the nation.

4   King Paramount's song about the origin of his Anglomania was
actually sent to Sullivan to be set. Like so many cancelled lyrics from
this opera, it is superior to a lot that were kept. The last four lines of
each stanza could be sung *either* by the King or the Chorus.

SONG. – KING (& FULL CHORUS).

From yacht that lay in yonder bay
   Ten years ago, or more,
A stranger, clad in shepherd's plaid,
   Was deftly rowed ashore.
We wished politely to salute
That stranger in the tourist suit,
So spread a meal of bread and fruit,
   And fired of guns a score.
For him we killed the fatted calf,
And gave him rather more than half.
Besides, as I remarked before
We fired of guns at least a score –

CHORUS.   Besides as he remarked before etc.

He looked around and sternly frowned
   At all our poor display –
Our simple food he quite pooh-poohed,
   To our complete dismay.
At all our ways he sneered aloud.
For O that tourist youth was proud,
And we were all completely cowed
   And didn't know what to say.
We looked to right – we looked to left –
Like creatures quite of sense bereft –
We tried our best the host to play
And didn't know what the deuce to say!

CHORUS.   We tried in vain etc.

> Then up spoke he as trembled we
>   Beneath his lordly, ban,
> 'To show respect, it's quite correct
>   To do the best you can.
> But your cuisine is coarse and crude –
> Your welcome rough – your language rude –
> From which remarks you will conclude
>   I am an Englishman' –
> And when he said we ought to be
> Extremely proud that such as he
> Had honoured thus our island clan –
> We said, 'He's the typical Englishman.'

CHORUS.   We said, directly he began
          'This is the Typical Englishman.'

> Profoundly stirred by what we heard
>   On that eventful day,
> 'My Lord,' said we, 'we'll guided be
>   By all you please to say.'
> For England rules from East to West
> And when she lifts her warlike crest
> (In greeting our distinguished guest)
>   There'll be the deuce to pay.
> Let's set to work without relapse;
> Who knows but, some fine day perhaps –
> When we *our* warlike crest display
> There'll also be the deuce to pay!

CHORUS.   Let's set to work etc.

(March – exeunt all except Scaphio & Phantis)
Dialogue scene.

5   Gilbert's original version of the duet for Zara and Fitzbattleaxe was very short. It was expanded, no doubt, for the benefit of Nancy McIntosh. The shorter version runs as follows:

> Oh fortunate invention!
>   Oh brilliant inspiration!
> Oh well-devised intention!
>   Oh bright equivocation!
> Your ⎱
> My ⎰ love they would have wedded
>   But those who worship beauty,

When old and hoary headed
Should read 'De Senectute.'

Exit Fitzbattleaxe.

6   These lines originally provided the cue for the beginning of the
First Act Finale. A British vessel, the HMS *Victoria*, had recently
been sunk during manœuvres off Tripoli. The lines were cut for
obvious political reasons.

KING.   My dear Zara, how can I thank you! I will consent to anything that will
release me from the abominable tyranny of these two men. (*Calling*) What ho!
Without there! (*Enter an attendant.*) Summon my *court* without an instant's
delay! (*Exit attendant.*) Six did you say?

ZARA.   Yes. I had intended to bring a seventh – a British Admiral in his own
iron-clad – typical of England's naval supremacy – but unhappily he ran his
ship aground at the Mouth of the Thauser and I was obliged to leave him there.

KING.   Bless my heart that's very unlucky! I should like to have seen a British
Admiral in his own iron-clad.

7   During the spring of 1893 Gilbert sent Sullivan an eleven-page
version of the Act I Finale. Sullivan objected to the introduction of all
six Flowers of Progress at the same time. In Gilbert's first draft, many
of the verses of introduction were in the same metre. Gilbert appreciated Sullivan's problem, and while he still wanted to bring in all six
Ministers together, he offered to write a song for Zara in which she
would introduce the first three Flowers of Progress, and allow the
last three to introduce themselves. At the same time, Gilbert suggested further changes.

I may mention that I have suppressed the Butler and the Policeman and sub-
stituted for them a Captain in the Navy and an Attorney General – a change
which will, I hope, meet with your approval . . . I think I should make the
Captain in the Navy prominent in Act II instead of the Company promoter – he
would be a more picturesque and popular figure as a lover of one of the two girls. *

These suggestions were made on 20 June. The first version of the
Finale follows. It was found among Sullivan's papers. Several verses
which were patently offensive Gilbert later saw fit to alter.

* Letter at the Pierpont Morgan Library.

FINALE.

March. Enter all the Court, with Scaphio, Phantis, Lady Sophy, Nekaya, Kalyba, Tarara, Calynx and others. (King and Zara already onstage.)

CHORUS.

Although your Royal summons to appear
From courtesy was singularly free,
Obedient to that summons we are here –
What would your Majesty?

RECIT. – KING.

My worthy people, my beloved daughter
Most thoughtfully has brought with her from England
The types of all the causes that have made
That great and glorious country what it is.

CHOR. Oh joy unbounded!

SCA., PHAN., TARARA (*aside*). Why what *does* this mean? What does it mean? What does it mean? What does it mean? What does it mean?

ZARA. Let them advance and introduce themselves.

March. Enter Fitzbattleaxe, Police Constable Bulstrode, Lord Dramaleigh, Mr Alderman Blushington, Mr Goldbury and Mr Vimpany. They march round stage.

CHORUS.

(During which Sca., Phan., and Tarara growl pp. to each other, 'What does it mean?')

Hail, types of great Britannia's power –
Hail emblematic band –
We bless the day, we bless the hour
That brought you to our land!

SOLO. – FITZBATTLEAXE.

When Britain sounds the mighty trump of War
 (And Europe trembles)
The army of that doughty conqueror
 In serried ranks assembles.
Each man indulges in a glorious dream
 Of vivisection –
I represent our military scheme
 In its perfection!

CHORUS.

Oh warrior bold, oh warrior true,
With glad acclaim we welcome you.
You bring the Horse Guards to our doors –
So welcome to Utopian shores!
    Ulahlica! Ulahlica –

KING (*explaining*).   Utopian for Hip, hip hurrah!
CHORUS.   Ulahlica! Ulahlica! Ulahlica!

SOLO. – P. C. BULSTRODE.

When Crime malignant desecrates the night,
    And through the darkness rings the victim's wail,
The bold detective's zeal is all alight –
    He follows (more or less) upon the trail.
      His pockets stored
        With wig and whisker,
    (A large reward
        To make him brisker)
    His watch he'll keep
      As tinker, stoker,
    Archbishop, sweep,
      Or smart Stockbroker!
    (His bold assumptions rarely fail.)
He follows (more or less) upon the trail!

CHORUS.

Detective bold, detective true,
With glad acclaim we welcome you.
No work so difficult as yours –
So welcome to Utopian shores.

SOLO. – MR VIMPANY.

Though solemn and majestic,
    A simple butler I:
Felicity domestic
    I humbly typify.
A mind than others subtler
    Has spread this truth afar:
'Oh let me see your butler
    And I'll tell you what you are.'

189

CHORUS.

Oh butler bold, oh butler true,
With glad acclaim we welcome you.
Your lack of rank our hearts ignore –
So welcome to Utopian shore!
    Ulahlica, etc.!

SOLO. – LORD DRAMALEIGH.

Behold in one Lord Chamberlain,
    Of purity the gauge –
I purge the Court of moral stain
    And purify the Stage.
Court reputations I revise
And presentations scrutinize;
New plays I read with jealous eyes,
    And purify the Stage.

SOLO. – MR ALDERMAN BLUSHINGTON.

As County-Councillor, right through
    From gallery to stalls
I rule the theatres and I pu-
    Rify the Music Halls.
In town I make improvements great
(Which go to swell the County Rate).
I dwelling houses sanitate,
    And purify the Halls.

CHORUS.

Lord Chamberlain with Garter blue,
With loud acclaim we welcome you.
Though County Councillors are bores –
Yet welcome to Utopian shores!

SOLO. – MR GOLDBURY.

A Company Promoter I, with special education
That teaches what Contango means, and also Backwardation –
To speculators I supply a grand financial leaven,
Time was when two were Company – but now it must be seven.
    Stupendous loans to foreign thrones
      I've largely advocated;
    In ginger pops and peppermint drops
      I've freely speculated;

Then mines of gold, of wealth untold,
    Successfully I've floated,
And sudden falls in Apple Stalls
    Occasionally quoted.
Then soon or late,
    I always call
        For Stock Exchange quotation –
No schemes too great
    And none too small,
        For Companification.

CHORUS.

Promoter bold, promoter true,
With glad acclaim we welcome you!
He'll float Cooperative Stores,
So welcome to Utopian shores!

RECIT. – KING.

Ye Flowers of Progress, you must understand
    That though an Autocratic Despot we,
The Constitution of this favoured land
    Is not exactly what it ought to be.
If from your vast experience you will
    Some European remedy suggest,
With gratitude eternal you will fill
    The heart that beats within this manly breast!

TRIO. – SCAPHIO, PHANTIS and TARARA (*aside*).

What does he mean? What does he mean? Give us a kind of clue!
What does he mean? What does he mean? What is he going to do?

The manuscript breaks off at this point. It probably continued through to the end of the act (from Fitzbattleaxe's line, 'Increase your army!') exactly as it is performed today.

8   Gilbert's final stage direction for Act I read as follows:

Wild dance. Tarara, Scaphio and Phantis working together at one side of the stage. Lady Sophy, Nekaya, Kalyba (the two girls with their eyes bandaged) dancing primly together on the opposite side.
                    Curtain.

9   Gilbert's original draft of the duet 'Sweet and Low' ran as follows. It makes more sense this way.

DUET. – FITZBATTLEAXE & ZARA.

ZARA.

Words of love too loudly spoken
　Ring their own untimely knell;
Noisy vows are rudely broken,
　Soft the song of Philomel!
Tis a truth needs no refutal,
　Always whisper when you woo.
Sweet and low the ringdoves tootle;
　Sweetly let us tootle too.

BOTH.

Sweet and low, etc.

FITZ.

Let the conqueror, flushed with glory,
　Bid his noisy clarion bray!
Lovers tell their artless story
　In a whispered roundelay.
Let him shout his paean brutal
　Who proclaims a conquest new.
Sweet and low the ringdoves tootle;
　Sweetly let us tootle too.

BOTH.

Sweet and low, etc.

10　This is the original 'Minstrel Scene' which Gilbert planned to include in King Paramount's Cabinet Council Meeting. The dialogue is one of the earliest passages that Gilbert ever wrote, for it appears in his sketch plot for the opera. Sullivan objected to the 'Fire-flies' lyric, and on 7 August, Gilbert wrote him from Hamburg, 'Of course the Septette No. 14 could be omitted and I propose to omit the Nigger dialogue.'

(*Capt. Fitzbattleaxe has his banjo. Mr Blushington takes a set of bones out of his pocket. Mr Goldbury finds a tambourine on his chair.*)

CHORUS.

When the fire-flies dance in the dark,
　And the white moon sails in the sky,
And hushed is the song of the blithe little lark
　(Having warbled his own lullaby)
　　To our bowers we steal
　　For to ponder awhile
　All our plans for the weal
　　of this lone little isle –
Of this lone little, lone little isle!
For at night time we may remark,

That hushed is the song of the lark
Oh hushed is the song of the blithe little lark
Having warbled his own lullaby!

MR B.   I say, Bister King!

KING.   Well, Mr Bones?

MR B.   Do you keep a carriage?

KING.   Oh yes, I keep a very nice carriage.

MR B.   And horses?

KING.   Most assuredly. What would be the use of a carriage without horses?

MR B.   Well it might have been a pre-ambulator.

KING.   Very true: that consideration had not occurred to me. No, I have, alas! no occasion for a perambulator.

MR B.   Well now, what do you call your horses?

KING.   What do I call my horses? Oh they have very pretty names. I call one 'Beauty' and the other 'Prince.'

MR B.   Ah, I don't think much of them names.

KING.   (*mildly surprised*) You don't think much of those names, Mr Bones?

MR B.   No. Now *I've* got a pair of horses.

KING.   Indeed Mr Bones? You must be prospering in the world.

MR B.   Oh yaas – getting on nicely. Well now, what d'ye think *I* call *them*?

KING.   Really the question is so wide, it opens out such a vast field of speculation that really I –

MR B.   I call one 'Bryant' and the other 'May.'

KING.   (*mildly surprised*) You call one Bryant and the other May?

MR B.   Yaas. Because they're such a good match!*

KING.   Oh let us kiss him for his mother!

Symphony – banjo, bones and tambourine.

11   Gilbert altered the fourth line in this chorus.

It really is surprising
What a thorough Anglicizing
We have brought about – Utopia's quite another land.
In her great progressive movements
She is England – with improvements
Which we dutifully offer to our mother-land!

12   Gilbert's original stage direction for the 'Drawing Room' appears below. It follows the King's patter song and omits all dialogue, as well as the chorus 'Eagle High'. This scene, as finally staged, was far less elaborate, probably due to considerations of the set. But

---

* When Gilbert moved to Grim's Dyke he named two of his horses 'Bryant' and 'May'!

Gilbert's original plan shows how his writing was often guided by his abilities as a master stage director.

At the end all rise and replace their chairs. The King and the Flowers of Progress thus mount the dias. Zara and the two young Princesses and Lady Sophy enter from the back and join them. (Lord Chamberlain on R. of the line.) Then enter (1st E.R.) the ladies of the Court, in Court Costume – with occasionally a gentleman in uniform – as at a Drawing Room. The ladies are presented to various members of the Royal Family. They then retire down L. and go off 1st E.L. While 'off' they get rid of their trains, re-enter behind curtains at back when the presentations are finished, all the curtains are raised, discovering moonlit sea, and the ladies ranged upstage C. They descend. The Gentlemen join them from R. and L. – then
   Minuet

Then exeunt all.

Enter Scaphio and Phantis . . .

13   Gilbert's original layout for the 'Furious Trio' was slightly different.

FURIOUS TRIO. – sca., phan., and king.

PHAN.

> If you think that when banded in unity
> We may both be defied with impunity
>   You are sadly misled of a verity !
> If you value repose and tranquillity
> You'll revert to a state of docility
>   Or prepare to regret your temerity !

SCA.

> We'll apply, without quibble or quiddity,
> Such a powerful dose of acidity
>   It will act on your comfort corrosively.
> We need only denounce your morality
> And then, in some public locality
>   Your reign will be finished explosively !

BOTH (*dancing*).

> As we've a dance for every mood,
> With *pas de deux* we now conclude.
> What it implies now try to guess ?

(*King considers the question as they continue dancing, then gives it up.*)

> It typifies remorselessness !

ALL THREE
(*dancing melo-
dramatically*).

> Remorselessness, remorselessness !
> Of course it does, remorselessness !
> Its meaning $\left\{ \begin{array}{c} \text{I} \\ \text{you} \end{array} \right\}$ would never guess;
> It typifies remorselessness !

194

KING.   A plea I would offer correctively,
Which, if I present it effectively,
     Will probably check your vivacity.
Deprived of in*div*iduality,
I am here, by a funny fatality,
     In a corporate kind of capacity.

If my speech is unduly refractory
You will find it a course satisfactory
     At an early Board meeting to show it up.
Though if proper excuse you can trump any,
You may *wind* up a Limited Company,
     You cannot conveniently *blow* it up!

(*Scaphio and Phantis thoroughly baffled.*)

KING (*dancing*   Whene'er I chance to baffle you
  quietly).   I also, dance a step or two.
                Of this now guess the hidden sense:

(*Scaphio and Phantis consider the question as King continues dancing quietly – then give it up.*)

                It means complete indifference!

ALL THREE   Indifference, indifference,
  (*dancing*   Of course it does, indifference!
  quietly). $\left\{\begin{array}{l}\text{You}\\ \text{We}\end{array}\right\}$ might have guessed its hidden sense.

                It means complete indifference!

KING (*dancing*
  quietly),
  SCA. and PHAN.
  (*dancing*
  furiously).   As we've a dance for every mood
                With *pas de trois* we will conclude.
                What this may mean you all may guess:
$\left\{\begin{array}{l}\text{SCA. and PHAN.}\\ \text{KING.}\end{array}\right\}$ $\left\{\begin{array}{l}\text{It typifies remorselessness!}\\ \text{It means unruffled cheerfulness!}\end{array}\right\}$

(*King dances off placidly. Scaphio and Phantis dance furiously then sink exhausted on chairs on each side of stage.*)

14 The following sequence was intended to follow the trio, 'A Capital Plot'. It looks backward to the suicide scene in *Cox and Box* and forward to the mad scene in *The Grand Duke*. It was eliminated prior to rehearsals.

SCA.   That being settled, there is only one thing left to consider. Six months ago we entrusted Zara to Capt. Fitzbattleaxe as stakeholder until we shall have decided which of us is to survive the other. That delicate question is still unsettled.

PHAN.   Not in my mind. I particularly wish to survive you. I have special reasons for wishing it.

SCA.   In truth if one of us is to die, it would seem that I am he. Everything points to me. I am much older than you and I will not conceal from you that I attach but little value to existence. But the girl, Phantis, we must consider the girl. She has a vested interest in two eligible suitors. Have we the right to deprive her of one half of her admirers for our own selfish convenience? I think not. While we wear these wigs, Phantis, we must be just. It is not the broken old man who speaks. It is the upright and impartial judge.

(Enter Fitzbattleaxe and Zara)

PHAN.   It may be that you are right, Scaphio. But as Capt. Fitzbattleaxe has had six months' experience of Zara's character and disposition, we may as well receive his half-yearly report.

ZARA   *(aside to Fitzbattleaxe)*. Oh Arthur, you are not going to give me a good character?

FITZBATTLEAXE   *(aside to Zara)*. The best in the world.
ZARA.   But —
FITZBATTLEAXE.   Leave it in my hands and take your cue from me.

FITZ.   For Zara is very warm-hearted.
SCA. and PHAN.   That news is exceedingly pleasant!
FITZ.   You haven't a notion
                     Of Zara's devotion.
                She dotes upon me, just at present.

                From my arms she will scarcely be parted.
SCA. and PHAN.   But that is extremely annoying!
                    She's eternally doing
                    Her billing and cooing.
                Now and then it's a little bit cloying!

(Zara acts up to this, showing overwhelming affection for Fitzbattleaxe.)

SCA. and PHAN.   I like a warmhearted young girl.
  (aside to each   Her love has the genuine spark;
  other).   But when it's devoted
                        To Captains red-coated,
                    It seems to be missing the mark!

(They retire up, discussing the matter with each other.)

FITZ. and ZARA (*aside*).	Oh little heart
	That plays a part
	   To further our design
	Take up the cue
	In earnest time,
	   And be my very mine!

FITZ.	Her spirits are high and undaunted.
SCA. and PHAN. (*pleased*).	High spirits give spice to existence!
FITZ.	When she lets herself go It's a word and a blow; It's judicious to keep at a distance
	For her play with the poker she's vaunted.
SCA. and PHAN.	But the poker's an unpleasant frightful!
FITZ.	Then the crockery flies At your ears and your eyes! Her spirits are really delightful.

(*Zara acts up to this, seizing a stick and breaking vases, etc.*)

SCA. and PHAN. (*aside, watching her*).	High spirits are all very well,
	But play with the poker I bar,
	   When spirit in mockery
	   Smashes the crockery,
	Spirit is carried too far!

(*They retire up conversing, as before.*)

FITZ.	She is jealous – not much, but a little.
SCA. and PHAN.	I'm glad there's some jealousy in her.
FITZ.	Then, without affectation, My congratulation To him who is destined to win her.
	If she thinks that of cause she's a tittle –

SCA. and PHAN.	But my wife in such things must be lenient,
	   With a shriek in falsetto
	   She'll use her stiletto
	If no prussic acid's convenient!

(*Zara acts up to this – drawing a stiletto and stabbing about melodramatically.*)

SCA. and PHAN. (*aside, watching her*).	Now jealousy's all very well.
	To my wife it is sure to belong,
	   But poison and dagger
	   Our confidence stagger.
	That's coming it rather too strong!

(*They retire up, conversing as before.*)

FITZ. and ZARA (*aside*).	The fiction works!
	These two old Turks
	From hand will soon resign.
	Such jealous fire
	They don't admire.
	My love will soon be mine!
SCA. and PHAN. (*coming down*).	We think, on the whole,
	That a girl who displays
	Such extravagant soul,
	Such intemperate ways,
	So vindictive's a clutch,
	Has of frenzy a touch
	She's a little too much
	For a councillor wise.
	Then the tang of her tongue
	Is exceedingly free
	For we are not as young
	As we used for to be;
	And without diatribe,
	The displays you describe
	Need a heavier bribe
	Than mere beauty supplies.

So take her pray, and make the best of her,
Her spirits high and all the rest of her.
No fear that we shall come in quest of her;
So take her pray, and make the best of her.

ENSEMBLE

SCA. and PHAN.	FITZ.	ZARA
So take her pray, etc.	I'll take the maid, etc.	So take her pray, etc.

Exeunt Scaphio and Phantis

FITZ. There! have I not managed it cleverly? They had no idea what a terrible little Tartar they were contending for!

ZARA. Poor old gentlemen! I'm really very sorry for them! They have been so injudicious.

FITZ. Sorry, Zara? Surely it cannot be that you feel any regret, any compunction for what you have done?

ZARA. No, dear. I am very happy! But what a pity it is that when a man has lived a certain number of years, he loses all charm in a woman's eyes! Ah, if we could only make up our minds to invest our stock of youth on commercial principles, old age would be as extinct as the dodo!

SONG.–ZARA.

Youth is a gift of worth
        To one and all allowed
With which all men, at birth,
        Are equally endowed.
But Man's a prodigal
        Who madly lives upon
His little capital
        Till every penny's gone.

And finds himself, at life's concluding stage
With no youth left to comfort his old age!

ENSEMBLE

Alas, alas,
He finds himself, etc.

ZARA (*coming forward*)

Ah dame, all wrinklefaced,
        If you, in very sooth
In infancy had placed
        Your capital of Youth
At four or five percent
        Prepared, within your breast,
To rub along content
        Upon the interest,

You might be still in girlhood's mid-career,
A merry mad-cap maid of four score year!

ENSEMBLE

Alas, alas,
You might be still, etc.

Exeunt together.

15   Sullivan wanted to cut the entire preceding sequence. Gilbert was not altogether happy with the material, but he wanted to retain as much of it as possible, presumably because it centred about Nancy McIntosh. On 8 August he wrote to Sullivan with the following suggestion:

. . . immediately after 'Capital Plot' – enter Zara. She moralizes about youth etc. Then her song 'Youth is a gift of worth.' Then enter Fitz – to tell her that he has interviewed Sca and Ph – and as neither will consent to slay the other (for absurd reasons to be invented) she is practically his forever. Then a duet for Fitz and Zara . . . I suppose the duet needn't be a mere love duet – it ought to be bright, joyous and with a good deal of acting in it – so at least it seems to me. Perhaps I can hit upon a good quaint acting idea which is nevertheless capable of effective musical treatment.

In accordance with this outline he sent Sullivan the following sequence a short time later. It would appear that Gilbert had his 'quaint acting idea' well in mind when he wrote Sullivan the above letter.

The 'duet' appears to be a rewrite of an earlier poem which consisted only of the stanzas here assigned to Fitzbattleaxe. The lyric is better without the Zara verses.

Enter Fitzbattleaxe – in great excitement

FITZ. Victory! Victory! Not complete or decisive, but invaluable as far as it goes!

ZARA. Then has neither old gentleman determined which is to survive the other?

FITZ. No – not yet. Each is so extremely fond of the other that he can't make up his mind to part with him, so I persuaded them to renew my guardianship, and for another six months you are safe.

ZARA. My clever, but not intellectual darling! You seem to be able to twist them round your fingers.

FITZ. Mere diplomacy – nothing more. The tongue, properly considered, is the most powerful instrument in the world. You know the story of the man to whom Jove granted three wishes?

ZARA. No – it's not in *my* Lamprière (*producing a very small thin book*).

FITZ. (*looking at it*). Oh, I see – the Expurgated Edition.

ZARA. Of course.

FITZ. Well it *is* in mine and I'll tell it to you – with judicious reservations.

ZARA. If you please.

DUET. – FITZBATTLEAXE & ZARA.

FITZ.

Once, Love – on gallantry intent –
    Too near the wind was sailing,
And risked discovery – which meant
    Acute Jovonic railing:
A mortal, in resources quick,
Came forward in the very nick,
And saved his godship by a trick –
    Which will not bear detailing.

ZARA.

    Then nothing say
      of this affair –
    My expurga-
      Ted Lamprière
(The only one we ever quote)

200

Contains no reference remote
To any kind of anecdote
 Which will not bear detailing.

FITZ.

The god, escaped from social ban
 (So strict in this austere age)
Resolved to recompense the man
 And pay off all arrearage:
So offered to endow the boor
With wealth to make a Rothschild poor,
Complete success in each amour,
 Or, a Gladstonian peerage.

ZARA.

  Now there you twist
   And torture fact:
  Do, I insist
   Be more exact
You ought to know Gladstonian peers
Are luxuries of later years –
In classic times one never hears
 Of *any* kind of peerage.

FITZ.

'Nay, nay' exclaimed the lucky loon
 (And scratched his auburn tresses)
'Reward me with another boon
 Which all the three expresses.
Give me the power, if so inclined,
To coax and wheedle woman-kind
For he who weedles well, I find
 All other gifts possesses!'

ZARA.

  You're quite aware
   That that's untrue
  And Lamprière
   Must know it too.
For everything depends, you see,
On who the wheedle-or may be –
And who, my love, the wheedle-ee
 Who favours his addresses.

16 The following stanza came after the first half of Lady Sophy's song in Gilbert's manuscript copy.

  But so bad are the best
  That absurd is my quest
  If so stringent a test
   They are tried by –
  And I find, with remorse

201

I've adopted a course
Which, though vain, I perforce
　　Must abide by!
Too late! Too late
　　Another line to choose!
Too late! Too late
　　To modify my views!
And I find with remorse
I've adopted a course
Which, though vain, I perforce
　　Must abide by!

17   This stage direction originally followed the duet for Lady Sophy and the King. Most of the choreography was eliminated and then re-instated.

King and Sophy dance gracefully – during this Lord Dramaleigh enters with Nekaya and Mr Goldbury with Kalyba from opposite entrances. They are much amused and join, unobserved, in the dance. Then Zara and Capt. Fitzbattleaxe enter C. and join, also unobserved. The King and Lady Sophy are suddenly aware of the presence of the others. They are taken aback for the moment – then, throwing off all reserve, they join in a Tarantella and all go off in couples at different entrances.

18   The Finale printed in the text, minus the last six lines, was the version that was published in the vocal score, and the one that was ultimately adopted in performance. Gilbert's original draft (printed below) was somewhat longer.

There's a little group of isles beyond the wave
　　So tiny you might almost wonder where it is;
Where people are the bravest of the brave,
　　And cowards are the rarest of all rarities.
Her people all so prosperous have grown
　　The poorest, if they wished it might acquire land –
Great Britain is the name by which it's known –
　　To which some add (but others do not) Ireland.
　　　　Such at least is the tale
　　　　Which is borne on the gale
　　　　　From the island that dwells in the sea.
　　　　Let us hope for her sake
　　　　That she makes no mistake
　　　　　That she's all we believe her to be.

Her constitution's envied near and far –
　　Her Parliament's a model of sincerity;

Her simpleminded Politicians are
    The source of her remarkable prosperity.
The proudest nations kneel at her command –
    She terrifies all foreign born rapscallions –
And holds the fate of Europe in her hand
    With half a score invincible battalions.
                Such at least, etc.

O may we copy all their methods wise,
    And intimate their virtues and their charities,
And may we, by degrees, acclimatize
    Her Parliamentary peculiarities!
By doing it we shall, in course of time,
    Regenerate completely our entire land –
Great Britain is that monarchy sublime,
    To which some conscientous folk add – Ireland
            Such at least is our view,
            If it prove to be true
                We shall rise to the top of the tree.
            But supposing instead
            That we've all been misled –
                What a kettle of fish there will be!

Gilbert was fond of this Finale. Sullivan was not. In the script conference at Grim's Dyke on 27 May, Sullivan apparently raised objection to it, for on 22 June Gilbert wrote, 'I have altered the finale in a manner which I hope you will like,'* and sent him the two stanza version which is printed in the text. Sullivan was still not satisfied. He held his ground past the middle of the rehearsal period. Finally Gilbert agreed to write a new set of lyrics for the Finale, and to ensure that they would not be rejected, he secured Sullivan's agreement to compose the music *first* – the only time in the entire Gilbert and Sullivan collaboration that this was done!

On 26 September, eleven days before the opera opened, Gilbert sent a highly unsatisfactory new Finale to Sullivan with the following letter.

Dear S.

I got up at seven this morning and polished off the new finale before breakfast – Here it is. It is mere doggerel – but words written to an existing tune are nearly sure to be that. I'm sorry to lose the other finale but I quite see your difficulty and that it can't be helped . . .

* All correspondence quoted on the Finale is from the Pierpont Morgan Library.

Sullivan's difficulty was probably Gilbert's metre, which was a bit too ponderous to set as an up tempo chorus. Gilbert's willingness to write a new Finale was an example of the very good co-operation which existed between the partners at the time.

ZARA.

> There's an isle beyond the wave,
>> Held by a blameless race –
> Where all are great and good and brave
>> And godlike in their grace.
> To whose resplendent King (or Queen)
>> All nations bend the knee –
> Where everyone and everything
>> Are all they ought to be

CHORUS.

>> Yes! Yes! Yes!

ZARA (or CHORUS).

> At least that is the tone they take
> Let's hope for everybody's sake
> That in our view there's no mistake –
>> They're all they claim to be!

KING.

> May we adopt her methods wise
>> And stifle discontent
> And may we soon acclimatize
>> Her acts of Parliament.
> All her peculiarities
>> We'll copy day by day.
> For from all minor Monarchies
>> She bears the bell away.

CHORUS.

>> Yes! Yes! Yes!

KING (or CHORUS).

> At least that is their island view
> If it should prove to be untrue
> There'll surely be (twixt me and you)
>> The deuce and all to pay!

Gilbert's letter continued:

You can chop this about just as you please. A verse to Zara and a verse to the King – or the first half of each verse to Zara and the last half to the King – or the first half of the first verse to Zara – and the first half of the second verse to Fitz – giving the King the end of each verse – which perhaps is the arrangement that will suit you most.

No arrangement however was found to be satisfactory and on 6 October the reviewer who covered the public dress rehearsal of

Utopia, Limited for the *Westminister Gazette* reported the following conversation as taking place at about 5.30 in the afternoon:

... 'You can't sing the finale to-day,' said Sir Arthur, 'for a new one is to be written. When can we rehearse again, Mr Harris?'

'In twenty-four hours,' answered Mr Harris, 'at the least.'

'The floor is being parqueted for the Drawing Room scene,' answered Mr Gilbert.

The fact that the first performance was then less than twenty-eight hours away, and the stage would not be available for further rehearsing for at least twenty-four hours, did not discourage Gilbert and Sullivan from putting a new Finale into the opera in the very limited time available. The critic who reviewed the first performance of *Utopia, Limited* for the *Sunday Times* said:

And with a return to a military chorus that had welcomed the appearance of the First Life Guards, the curtain falls for the second and last time.

This description fits the Finale printed in the official 'First Edition' of the libretto, the one on sale in the lobby of the theatre on the evening of the first performance. The last two quatrains of the lyric here re-printed begin a reprise of the First Act scena 'Oh Gallant Soldier Brave and True' which finishes with the 'military chorus' referred to in the *Sunday Times* review.

FINALE

KING.
> When Monarch of barbaric land,
>   For self-improvement burning,
> Foregathers with a glorious band
>   Of sweetness, light and learning –
> A group incalculably wise –
>   Unequalled in their beauty –
> Their customs to acclimatize
>   Becomes a moral duty.

ZARA (*to Fitzbattleaxe*).
> Oh gallant soldier brave and true
> In tented field and tourney,
> I trust you'll ne'er regret that you
>   Embarked upon this journey.

FITZ.
> To Warriors all it may befall
>   To gain so pure a beauty,
> When they obey the trumpet call
>   Of Regimental Duty!

These lyrics presumably led into the triple ensemble, 'Knightsbridge Nursemaids Serving Fairies' which closed the opera. This chorus was musically the most complex number in the opera.

The above lyric was reprinted from the first edition of the *Utopia, Limited* libretto. It was apparently written, composed, orchestrated, rehearsed, memorized and staged during the twenty-four hours directly prior to the first performance. Not only that, but the band parts were copied out and the text was set in type, printed, and bound up with the first issue of the libretto, all of which were ready by 8 p.m. on the following day!

In spite of this tremendous effort, however, this Finale too failed to satisfy.

The finale is short and even insignificant.

Daily Graphic

The day after the opera opened Gilbert expressed himself similarly in a letter to Sullivan:

The present musical finale is not to the point – and, magnificent as a musical number, is surely not bright enough to finish the piece with.

Sullivan had been wanting Gilbert to make some cuts in the opera's closing dialogue. Sullivan had also wanted the chorus 'Down with the Flowers of Progress' to follow directly after the Tarantella, eliminating a few lines of dialogue. In the same letter, Gilbert offered Sullivan a deal:

I propose to cut out Barrington's last speech – finishing with 'general and un-exampled prosperity –' and going at once to the Finale – and I do most earnestly hope that you will see your way to setting the words I originally wrote – 'There's a (something) little isle beyond the wave' . . . If you will do this, I will endeavour to carry out your suggestions as to dialogue – even if I don't agree with them.

Sullivan accepted. Gilbert did not make the dialogue changes exactly as outlined in this letter (see p. 182), but he did make them to Sullivan's satisfaction, and on Monday the 9th, the composer finally set Gilbert's first (and last) Finale to *Utopia, Limited*. When it was finished, the music was sent over to Chappell's to go into the vocal score, the issuing of which had been delayed.

The new Finale went into the opera by the end of the first week, and was *still* not satisfactory. Gilbert wrote to Sullivan shortly thereafter.

I don't know how you feel about the finale – it seems to me to be too *andante* in character for the end of the piece – I fancy it wants something more vigorous and decided.

Sullivan may have anticipated Gilbert's reaction when he declined to set the lyrics originally. But by the time this last Finale was set, the opera was open and running. Gilbert and Sullivan had tried three different ways of ending *Utopia, Limited* and finally, having come full circle, they made no further attempts to improve their opera.

Sullivan set Zara's song, 'Youth is a Boon Avowed', as well as the alternative Finales, but no copies of this music are known to exist. In all probability it will not be known whether this music, or the music to any of the other cancelled lyrics, survives until Sullivan's autograph score to *Utopia, Limited* turns up. In April 1915 Herbert Sullivan, who had inherited the autograph score, donated it to a Red Cross Sale at Christie's, where it was sold for 50 guineas to one Mr Hudson. It has not been heard of since.

The Grand Duke, *Act I, a rare full stage photograph of W. Hereford's set. (Bridget D'Oyly Carte.)*

THE GRAND DUKE

THE libretto reprinted here follows the text of the copy in the Library of Congress. It appears to conform to the 'Advance proof' issue which Sullivan cut up and pasted into his autograph score. This is almost certainly the version with which the Savoy Company began rehearsals. It is the earliest known edition of the text. No manuscript copy in Gilbert's hand is known to survive.

This version includes the lyrics to several songs which have never been published before – a quartet for Julia, the Baroness, Ludwig and Lisa (referred to throughout as Elsa) (p. 259), a duet for the Prince and Princess of Monte Carlo (p. 274), and a quintet for Julia, the Baroness, Lisa, the Prince of Monte Carlo, and Ludwig (p. 275).

The three songs which Gilbert deleted after the opera opened are included here as well: 'The Drinking Song' (p. 263), 'The Roulette Song' (p. 272), and the Grand Duke's patter song (p. 277). *

This edition also includes additional verses to many songs, as well as occasional passages of dialogue that were deleted or changed before the first night. The original anti-German lyrics to the Chamberlains' Chorus appear on p. 232, and an unusual early draft of the Grand Duke's First Act solo appears on p. 239.

Wherever the text was changed significantly before or after the opera's opening, the libretto has been footnoted, and the variant version printed in the Appendix. Minor variations in the dialogue and versification have not been collated.

---

* These songs were printed in the vocal score. Their orchestrations, however, survive in Sullivan's manuscript score. A few bars of the quartet (p. 259) also survive in Sullivan's manuscript but serve to establish no more than the fact that he actually set it, and that it was not in 6/8 time. As no music for any of the other cancelled lyrics survives in Sullivan's score, it is not possible to determine if they were set to music or not.

AN ORIGINAL COMIC OPERA

IN TWO ACTS

ENTITLED

THE GRAND DUKE

OR

THE STATUTORY DUEL

WRITTEN BY

W. S. GILBERT

COMPOSED BY

ARTHUR SULLIVAN

LONDON: CHAPPELL & CO., 50 New Bond Street, W
BOSTON: WALTER H. BAKER & CO., 23 Winter Street

BOSTON
GEO. H. ELLIS, PRINTER, 141 FRANKLIN STREET
1896

ACT I.

SCENE.—*Market Place of Speisesaal, in the Grand Duchy of Hesse Halbpfennig. A well, with decorated iron-work, up* L.C.   *
GRETCHEN, BERTHA, OLGA, *and other members of* ERNEST DUMM-
KOPF'S *theatrical company are discovered, seated at several small
tables, enjoying a repast in honour of the nuptials of* LUDWIG, *his*   †
leading comedian, and ELSA, *his soubrette.*

CHORUS.

Won't it be a pretty wedding?
    Doesn't Elsa look delightful?
Smiles and tears in plenty shedding —
    Which in brides of course is rightful.
    One might say, if one were spiteful,
Contradiction little dreading,
    Her bouquet is simply frightful —
Still, it is a pretty wedding!
Oh, it is a pretty wedding!
    Such a pretty, pretty wedding!

GRET.   If her dress *is* badly fitting,
        Theirs the fault who made her *trousseau.*

BERTHA.   If her gloves *are* always splitting,
        Cheap kid gloves, we know, will do so.

OLGA.   If her wreath *is* all lop-sided,
        That's a thing one's always dreading.

GRET.   If her hair *is* all untidied,
        Still, it is a pretty wedding!

CHORUS.   Oh, it is a pretty wedding!
        Such a pretty, pretty wedding!

CHORUS.

Here they come, the couple plighted —
    On life's journey gaily start them.
Soon to be for age united,
    Till divorce or death shall part them.

(LUDWIG *and* ELSA *come forward.*)

DUET.— LUDWIG *and* ELSA.

LUD.   Pretty Elsa, fair and tasty,
        Tell me now, before we're wedded,
    Haven't you been rather hasty?
        Just a little feather-headed?

---

*Hesse Halbpfennig is used in place of Pfennig Halbpfennig throughout.
†Elsa is used in place of Lisa throughout.

2

Am I quite the dashing *sposo*
That your fancy could depict you?
Perhaps you think I'm only so-so?
(*She expresses admiration.*)
Well, I will not contradict you!

CHORUS. No, he will not contradict you!

ELSA. Who am I to raise objection?
I'm a child, untaught and homely —
When you tell me you're perfection,
Tender, truthful, true, and comely —
That in quarrel no one's bolder,
Though dissensions always grieve you —
Why, my love, you're so much older
That, of course, I must believe you!

CHORUS. Yes, of course, she must believe you!

CHORUS.

If he ever acts unkindly,
Shut your eyes and love him blindly —
Should he call you names uncomely,
Shut your mouth and love him dumbly —
Should he rate you, rightly — leftly —
Shut your ears and love him deafly.
Ha! ha! ha! ha! ha! ha! ha!
Thus and thus and thus alone
Ludwig's wife may hold her own!
(LUDWIG *and* ELSA *retire up.*)

Enter NOTARY TANNHÄUSER.

NOT. Hallo! Surely I'm not late?

(*All chatter unintelligibly in reply.*)

NOT. But, dear me, you're all at breakfast! Has the wedding taken place?

(*All chatter unintelligibly in reply.*)

NOT. My good girls, one at a time, I beg. Let me understand the situation. As solicitor to the conspiracy to dethrone the Grand Duke — a conspiracy in which the members of this company are deeply involved — I am invited to the marriage of two of its members. I present myself in due course, and I find, not only that the ceremony has taken place — which is not of the least consequence — but the wedding breakfast is half eaten — which is a consideration of the most serious importance.

(LUDWIG *and* ELSA *come down.*)

LUD. But the ceremony has *not* taken place. We can't get a parson!

NOT. Can't get a parson? Why, how's that?

LUD. Oh, it's the old story — the Grand Duke!

ALL. Ugh!

214

3

LUD. It seems that the little imp has selected this, our wedding day, for a convocation of all the clergy in the town to settle the details of his approaching marriage with the enormously wealthy Baroness von Krakenfeldt, and there won't be a parson to be had for love or money until six o'clock this evening!

ELSA. And as we produce our magnificent classical revival of *Troilus and Cressida* to-night at seven, we have no alternative but to eat our wedding-breakfast before we've earned it. So sit down, and make the best of it.

GRET. Oh, I should like to pull his Grand Ducal ears for him, that I should! He's the meanest, the cruellest, the most spiteful little ape in Christendom!

OLGA. Well, we shall soon be freed from his tyranny. To-morrow the Despot is to be dethroned!

LUD. Hush, rash girl! You know not what you say.

OLGA. Don't be absurd! We're all in it — we're all tiled, here.

LUD. That has nothing to do with it. Know ye not that in alluding to our conspiracy without having first given and received the secret sign, you are violating a fundamental principle of our Association?

SONG.— LUDWIG.

By the mystic regulation
Of our dark Association,
Ere you open conversation
    With another kindred soul,
    You must eat a sausage-roll! (*Producing one.*)

ALL.   You must eat a sausage-roll!

LUD.   If, in turn, he eats another,
That's a sign that he's a brother —
Each may fully trust the other.
    It is quaint and it is droll,
    But it's bilious on the whole.

ALL.   Very bilious on the whole.

LUD.   It's a greasy kind of pasty,
Which, perhaps, a judgment hasty
Might consider rather tasty:
    Once (to speak without disguise)
    It found favour in our eyes.

ALL.   It found favour in our eyes.

LUD.   But when you've been six months feeding
(As we have) on this exceeding
Bilious food, it's no ill-breeding
    If at these repulsive pies
    Our offended gorges rise!

ALL.   Our offended gorges rise!

GRET. Oh, bother the secret sign! I've eaten it until I'm

Rutland Barrington as Ludwig, Act I.

4

quite uncomfortable! I've given it six times already to-day — and (*whimpering*) I can't eat any breakfast!

BERTHA. And it's so unwholesome. Why, we should all be as yellow as frogs if it wasn't for the make-up!

LUD. All this is rank treason to the cause. I suffer as much as any of you. I loathe the repulsive thing — I can't contemplate it without a shudder — but I'm a conscientious conspirator, and if you won't give the sign I will. (*Eats sausage roll with an effort.*)

ELSA. Poor martyr! He's always at it, and it's a wonder where he puts it!

NOT. Well, now, about *Troilus and Cressida*. What do *you* play?

LUD. (*struggling with his feelings*). If you'll be so obliging as to wait until I've got rid of this feeling of warm oil at the bottom of my throat, I'll tell you all about it. (ELSA *gives him some brandy.*) Thank you, my love; it's gone. Well, the piece will be produced upon a scale of unexampled magnificence. It is confidently predicted that my appearance as King Agamemnon, in a Louis Quatorze wig, will mark an epoch in the theatrical annals of Hesse Halbpfennig. I endeavoured to persuade Ernest Dummkopf, our manager, to lend us the classical dresses for our marriage. Think of the effect of a real Athenian wedding procession cavorting through the streets of Speisesaal! Torches burning — cymbals banging — flutes tootling — cithera twanging — and a throng of fifty lovely Spartan virgins capering before us, all down the High Street! It would have been tremendous!

NOT. And he declined?

LUD. He did, on the prosaic ground that it might rain, and the ancient Greeks didn't carry umbrellas! If, as is confidently expected, Ernest Dummkopf is elected to succeed the dethroned one, mark my words, he will make a mess of it.

OLGA. He's sure to be elected. His entire company has promised to plump for him on the understanding that all the places about the Court are filled by members of his troupe, according to professional precedence.

GRET. I'm sure he'll make a lovely Grand Duke. How he will   *
stage-manage the processions!

BERTHA. And won't it make Julia Jellicoe, the English actress, furious! She has always rejected his advances, hitherto — but now I fancy the tables will be turned and he'll reject hers. The pretentious little London cockney — there's nobody good enough for her!

LUD. Bah! — Ernest's a stick — a very stick! And what a part it is! What a chance for an actor who is really a master of stage resource! Why, a Grand Duke of Hesse Halbpfennig might have a different make-up for every day in the week! Monday, touch-and-go light comedy in lavender trousers and a flaxen wig. Tuesday, irritable old uncle from India. Wednesday, heavy philan-

*The following three lines were deleted shortly after the opening.

Charles Kenningham as Ernest Dummkopf.

5

thropist with benevolent "bald." Thursday, incisive baronet with diamond ring and cigarette to show it off. Friday, slimy solicitor with club foot and spectacles. Saturday, escaped convict with one eye and a gulp! It's one of those parts that really give a man a chance!

(*He strolls up and off with* ELSA *as* ERNEST *enters in great excitement.*)

NOT. Well — what's the news? How is the election going?

ERN. Oh, it's a certainty — a practical certainty! Two of the candidates have been arrested for debt, and the third is a baby in arms — so, if you keep your promises, and vote solid, I'm cocksure of election!

GRET. Trust to us. But you remember the conditions?

ERN. Yes — all of you shall be provided for, for life. Every man shall be ennobled — every lady shall have unlimited credit at the Court Milliner's, and all salaries shall be paid weekly in advance!

BERTHA. Oh, it's quite clear he knows how to rule a Grand Duchy!

ERN. Rule a Grand Duchy? Why, my good girl, for ten years past I've ruled a theatrical company! A man who can do that can rule anything!

SONG.— ERNEST.

Were I a king in very truth,
And had a son — a guileless youth —
    In probable succession ;
To teach him patience, teach him tact,
How promptly in a fix to act,
He should adopt, in point of fact,
    A manager's profession.
To that condition he should stoop
    (Despite a too fond mother),
With eight or ten "stars" in his troupe,
    All jealous of each other !
Oh, the man who can rule a theatrical crew,
Each member a genius (and some of them two),
And manage to humour them, little and great,
    Can govern this tuppenny State !

ALL. Oh, the man, &c.

Both A and B rehearsal slight —
They say they'll be "all right at night"
    (They've both to go to school yet) ;
C in each act *must* change her dress,
D *will* attempt to "square the press" ;
E won't play Romeo unless
    His grandmother plays Juliet ;
F claims all hoydens as her rights
    (She's played them thirty seasons) ;

The Strollers' life is freedom true — ~~all the truth~~ *a fact he now attesting*
The Actor's life is gay all through — a merry a real one:
The King, well he's an Actor too — ~~maybe a prisoner bad one~~ *hardworked & never resting.*
From eight to ten ~~Comedians~~ *your strollers play — say twelve, to be within time —*
The King plays fifty parts a day, from dawn to turning-in time.
The King dies once & dies outright, then flies to regions upper.
The ~~Actor~~ Stroller *he dies every night & toddles home to supper.*
With dangers dark & dangers drear your modern Monarch grapples —
The deadliest missile ~~Actors~~ Strollers *fear are oranges & apples.*

> *On kingly crimes falls vengeance dread*
> *A king may sometimes lose his head:*
> *If fairly clean (though men say)*
> *An Actor never loses his.*

The Monarch who resentment shows — his country always blames him.
The ~~Actor~~ Stroller *stabs a dozen foes & no policeman claims him.*
When Kings disburse their subjects' gold, they rouse the papers weekly —
When ~~Actors~~ Strollers *give "a sum twice-told", the country hears it meekly.*
The King from Royalty deposed finds life a dull Chimera —
The Actor when his theatre's closed turns lightly to the "Era"
In short, to sum in brief degree my argument precedent,
A king must always Kingly be — a light Comedian needn't.

> *On dead ... a Monarch's crown*
> *To bed of rose or bed of down —*
> *Condemned to State as Monarchs are,*
> *A stroller's fate is fairer far!*

Original manuscript in Gilbert's hand of the 'Stroller's Song'. This lyric was found among Gilbert's papers. (British Library.)

6

> And G must show herself in tights
> For two convincing reasons —
> Two very well-shaped reasons!
> Oh, the man who can drive a theatrical team,
> With wheelers and leaders in order supreme,
> Can govern and rule, with a wave of his fin,
> All Europe — with Ireland thrown in!

ALL.   Oh, the man, &c.

(Exeunt all but ERNEST.)

ERN.   Elected by my fellow-conspirators to be Grand Duke of Hesse Halbpfennig as soon as the contemptible little occupant of that historical throne is deposed — here is promotion indeed! Why instead of playing Troilus of Troy for a month, I shall play Grand Duke of Hesse Halbpfennig for a lifetime! Yet am I happy? No — far from happy! The lovely English *comédienne* — the beautiful Julia, whose dramatic ability is so overwhelming that our audiences forgive even her strong English accent — that rare and radiant being treats my respectful advances with disdain unutterable! And yet, who knows? She is haughty and ambitious, and it may be that the splendid change in my fortunes may work a corresponding change in her feelings towards me! If so — ah, she is here!

Enter JULIA JELLICOE.

JULIA.   Herr Ernest, a word with you, if you please.

ERN.   Beautiful English maiden —

JULIA.   No compliments, I beg. I desire to speak with you on a strictly professional matter, so we will, if you please, dispense with allusions to my personal appearance, which can only tend to widen the breach which already exists between us.

ERN. *(aside).*   My only hope shattered! The haughty Londoner still despises me! *(Aloud.)* It shall be as you will.

JULIA.   I understand that the conspiracy in which we are all involved is to develop to-morrow, and that the company is likely to elect you to the throne on the understanding that the posts about the court are to be filled by members of your theatrical troupe, according to their professional importance.

ERN.   That is so.

JULIA.   Then all I can say is that it places me in an extremely awkward position.

ERN. *(very depressed).*   I don't see how it concerns you.

JULIA.   Why, bless my heart, don't you see that, as your leading lady, I am bound under a serious penalty to play the principal part in all your productions?

ERN.   Well?

JULIA.   Why, of course, the principal part in this production will be the Grand Duchess!

ERN.   My wife?

221

Mme Ilka von Palmay, Act I.   *Mme Palmay, Act II.*

Note the sharp contrast in her two costumes.

222

7

JULIA. That is another way of expressing the same idea.

ERN. (*aside — delighted*). I scarcely dared even to hope for this!

JULIA. Of course, as your leading lady, you'll be mean enough to hold me to the terms of my agreement. Oh, that's so like a man! Well, I suppose there's no help for it — I shall have to do it!

ERN. (*aside*). She's mine! (*Aloud.*) But — do you really think you would care to play that part? (*Taking her hand.*)

JULIA (*withdrawing it*). Care to play it? Certainly not — but what am I to do? Business is business, and I am bound by the terms of my contract.

ERN. It's for a long run, mind — a run that may last many, many years — and once embarked upon there's no throwing it up.

JULIA. Oh, we're used to these long runs in England : they are the curse of the stage — but, you see, I've no option.

ERN. You think the part of Grand Duchess will be good enough for you?

JULIA. Oh, I think so. It's a very good part in Gerolstein, and oughtn't to be a bad one in Hesse Halbpfennig. Why, what did you suppose I was going to play?

ERN. (*keeping up a show of reluctance*). But, considering your strong personal dislike to me and your persistent rejection of my repeated offers, won't you find it difficult to throw yourself into the part with all the impassioned enthusiasm that the character seems to demand? Remember, it's a strongly emotional part, involving long and repeated scenes of rapture, tenderness, adoration, devotion — all in luxuriant excess, and all of the most demonstrative description.

JULIA. My good sir, throughout my career I have made it a rule never to allow private feeling to interfere with my professional duties. You may be quite sure that (however distasteful the part may be) if I undertake it, I shall consider myself professionally bound to throw myself into it with all the ardour at my command.

ERN. (*aside — with effusion*). I'm the happiest fellow alive! (*Aloud.*) Now — would you have any objection — to — to give me some idea — if it's only a mere sketch — as to how you would play it? It would be really interesting — to me — to know your concep-tion of — of — my wife.

JULIA. How would I play it? Now, let me see — let me see. (*Considering.*) Ah, I have it!

BALLAD.— JULIA.

How would I play this part —
  The Grand Duke's Bride?
All rancour in my heart
  I'd duly hide —
  I'd drive it from my recollection

8

And 'whelm you with a mock affection,
Well calculated to defy detection —
That's how I'd play this part —
　　The Grand Duke's Bride.

With many a winsome smile
　　I'd witch and woo ;
With gay and girlish guile
　　I'd frenzy you —
　I'd madden you with my caressing,
　Like turtle, her first love confessing —
　That it was "mock," no mortal would be guessing,
With so much winsome wile
　　I'd witch and woo !

Did any other maid
　　With you succeed,
I'd pinch the forward jade —
　　· I would indeed !
　With jealous frenzy agitated
　(Which would, of course, be simulated),
　I'd make her wish she'd never been created —
Did any other maid
　　With you succeed !

And should there come to me,
　　Some summers hence,
In all the childish glee
　　Of innocence,
　Fair babes, aglow with beauty vernal,
　My heart would bound with joy diurnal !
　This sweet display of sympathy maternal,
Well, that would also be
　　A mere pretence !

My histrionic art,
　　Though you deride,
That's how I'd play that part —
　　The Grand Duke's Bride !

ENSEMBLE.

ERNEST.	JULIA.
Oh joy ! when two glowing young hearts,	My boy, when two glowing young hearts,
From the rise of the curtain,	From the rise of the curtain,
Thus throw themselves into their parts,	Thus throw themselves into their parts,
Success is most certain !	Success is most certain !
If the *rôle* you're prepared to endow	The *rôle* I'm prepared to endow
With such delicate touches,	With most delicate touches,
By the heaven above us, I vow	By the heavens above us, I vow
You shall be my Grand Duchess !	I will be your Grand Duchess !

　　　　　　　　　　　　　　　　(*Dance.*)

Enter all the Chorus with LUDWIG, NOTARY, *and* ELSA — *all
greatly agitated.*

EXCITED CHORUS.

My goodness me! what shall we do? Why, what a dreadful
 situation!
(*to* Lud.) It's all your fault, you booby you — you lump of in-
 discrimination!
I'm sure I don't know where to go — it's put me into such
 a tetter —
But this at all events I know — the sooner we are off, the
 better!

Ern.   What means this *agitato?* What d'ye seek?
    As your Grand Duke elect I bid you speak!

SONG.— Ludwig.

Ten minutes since I met a chap
 Who bowed an easy salutation —
Thinks I, "This gentleman, mayhap,
 Belongs to our Association."
  But, on the whole,
   Uncertain yet,
  A sausage-roll
   I took and eat —
That chap replied (I don't embellish)
By eating *three* with obvious relish.

Chorus (*angrily*). Why, gracious powers,
    No chum of ours
  Could eat three sausage-rolls with relish!

Lud.   Quite reassured, I let him know
    Our plot — each incident explaining;
  That stranger chuckled much, as though
   He thought me highly entertaining.
    I told him all,
     Both bad and good;
    I bade him call —
     He said he would:
  I added much — the more I muckled,
  The more that chuckling chummy chuckled!

All (*angrily*). A bat could see
    He couldn't be
  A chum of ours if he chuckled!

Lud.   Well, as I bowed to his applause,
    Down dropped he with hysteric bellow —
  And *that* seemed right enough, because
   I *am* a devilish funny fellow.
    Then suddenly,
     As still he squealed,
    It flashed on me
     That I'd revealed
  Our plot, with all details effective,
  To Grand Duke Wilhelm's own detective!

10

ALL.   What folly fell,
                   To go and tell
          Our plot to any one's detective!

CHORUS.

(*Attacking* LUDWIG.) You booby dense —
                   You oaf in mense,
                   With no pretence
                   To common sense!
                   A stupid muff
                   Who's made of stuff
                   Not worth a puff
                   Of candle-snuff!
Pack up at once and off we go, unless we're anxious to exhibit
Our fairy forms all in a row, strung up upon the Castle
          gibbet!

[*Exeunt Chorus.   Manent* LUDWIG, ELSA, ERNEST, JULIA, *and*
     NOTARY.

JUL. Well, a pretty mess you've got us into! There's an end
of our precious plot! All up — pop — fizzle — bang — done for!

LUD. Yes, but — ha! ha! — fancy my choosing the Grand
Duke's private detective, of all men, to make a confidant of!
When you come to think of it, it's really devilish funny!

ERN. (*angrily*). When you come to think of it, it's extremely
injudicious to admit into a conspiracy every pudding-headed baboon who presents himself!

LUD. Yes — I should never do that. If I were chairman of
this gang, I should hesitate to enrol *any* baboon who couldn't produce satisfactory credentials from his last Zoölogical Gardens.

ELSA. Ludwig is far from being a baboon. Poor boy, he could
not help giving us away — it's his trusting nature — he was deceived.

JULIA (*furiously*). His trusting nature! (*To* LUDWIG.) Oh, I
should like to talk to you in my own language for ten minutes —
only ten minutes! I know some good, strong, energetic English
remarks that would shrivel your trusting nature into raisins — only
you wouldn't understand them!

LUD. Here we perceive one of the disadvantages of a
neglected education!

ERN. (*to* JULIA). And I suppose you'll never be my Grand
Duchess, now!

JULIA. Grand Duchess? My good friend, if you don't produce
the piece how can I play the part?

ERN. True. (*To* LUDWIG.) You see what you've done.

LUD. But, my dear sir, you don't seem to understand that the
man eat three sausage-rolls. Keep that fact steadily before you.
Three large sausage-rolls.

226

JULIA. Bah!—Plenty of people eat sausage-rolls who are not conspirators.

LUD. Then they shouldn't. It's bad form. It's not the game. When one of the Human Family proposes to eat a sausage-roll, it is his duty to ask himself, "Am I a conspirator?" And if, on examination, he finds that he is *not* a conspirator, he is bound in honour to select some other form of refreshment.

ELSA. Of course he is. One should always play the game. (*To* NOTARY, *who has been smiling placidly through this.*) What are you grinning at?

NOT. Nothing—don't mind me. It is always amusing to the legal mind to see a parcel of laymen bothering themselves about a matter which to a trained lawyer presents no difficulty whatever.

ALL. No difficulty!

NOT. None whatever! The way out of it is quite simple.

ALL. Simple?

NOT. Certainly! Now attend. In the first place, you two men fight a Statutory Duel.

ERN. A Statutory Duel?

JULIA. A Stat-tat-tatutory Duel! Ach! what a crack-jaw language this German is!

LUD. Never heard of such a thing.

NOT. It is true that the practice has fallen into abeyance through disuse. But all the laws of Hesse Halbpfennig (which are framed upon those of Solon, the Athenian law-giver) run for a hundred years, when (again like the laws of Solon) they die a natural death, unless, in the meantime, they have been revived for another century. The Act that institutes the Statutory Duel was passed a hundred years ago, and as it has never been revived, it expires to-morrow. So you're just in time.

JULIA. But what is the use of talking to us about Statutory Duels when we none of us know what a Statutory Duel is?

NOT. Don't you? Then I'll explain.

SONG.—NOTARY.

About a century since,
   The code of the duello
     To sudden death
     For want of breath
Sent many a strapping fellow.
The then presiding Prince
   (Who useless bloodshed hated),
     He passed an Act,
     Short and compact,
Which may be briefly stated:
Unlike the complicated laws
A Parliamentary draughtsman draws,
     It may be briefly stated.

Scott Russell as Dr Tanhauser, the Notary.

12

ALL.	We know that complicated laws, Such as a legal draughtsman draws, Cannot be briefly stated.
NOT.	By this ingenious law, If any two shall quarrel, They may not fight With falchions bright (Which seemed to him immoral) ; But each a card shall draw, And he who draws the lowest Shall (so 'twas said) Be thenceforth dead — In fact, a legal "ghoest" (When exigence of rhyme compels, Orthography foregoes her spells, And "ghost" is written "ghoest.")
ALL (*aside*).	With what an emphasis he dwells Upon "orthography" and "spells"! That kind of fun's the lowest.
NOT.	When off the loser's popped (By pleasing legal fiction), And friend and foe Have wept their woe In counterfeit affliction, The winner must adopt The loser's poor relations — Discharge his debts, Pay all his bets, And take his obligations. In short, to briefly sum the case, The winner takes the loser's place, With all its obligations.
ALL.	How neatly lawyers state a case! The winner takes the loser's place, With all its obligations!

LUD. I see. The man who draws the lowest card —

NOT. Dies, *ipso facto*, a social death. He loses all his civil rights —his identity disappears—the Revising Barrister expunges his name from the list of voters, and the winner takes his place, whatever it may be, discharges all his functions and adopts all his responsibilities.

ERN. This is all very well, as far as it goes, but it only protects one of us. What's to become of the survivor?

LUD. Yes, that's an interesting point, because *I* might be the survivor.

NOT. The survivor goes at once to the Grand Duke, and, in a burst of remorse, denounces the dead man as the moving spirit of the plot. He is accepted as King's evidence, and, as a matter of

13

course, receives a free pardon. To-morrow, when the law expires, the dead man will, *ipso facto*, come to life again — the Revising Barrister will restore his name to the list of voters, and he will resume all his obligations as though nothing unusual had happened.

JULIA. When he will be at once arrested, tried, and executed on the evidence of the informer! Candidly, my friend, I don't think much of your plot!

NOT. Dear, dear, dear, the ignorance of the laity! My good young lady, it is a beautiful maxim of our glorious Constitution that a man can only die once. Death expunges crime, and when he comes to life again, it will be with a clean slate.

ERN. It's really very ingenious.

LUD. (*to* NOTARY). My dear sir, we owe you our lives!

ELSA (*aside to* LUDWIG). May I kiss him?

LUD. Certainly not: you're a big girl now. (*To* ERNEST.) Well, miscreant, are you prepared to meet me on the field of honour?

ERN. At once. By Jove, what a couple of fire-eaters we are!

ELSA Ludwig doesn't know what fear is.

LUD. Oh, I don't mind this sort of duel!

ERN. It's not like a duel with swords. I hate a duel with swords. It's not the blade I mind — it's the blood.

LUD. And I hate a duel with pistols. It's not the ball I mind — it's the bang.

NOT. Altogether it is a great improvement on the old method of giving satisfaction.

QUINTETTE.

LUDWIG, ELSA, NOTARY, ERNEST, JULIA.

Strange the views some people hold!
Two young fellows quarrel —
Then they fight, for both are bold —
Rage of both is uncontrolled —
Both are stretched out, stark and cold!
Prithee where's the moral?
Ding dong! Ding dong!
There's an end to further action,
And this barbarous transaction
Is described as "satisfaction"!
Ha! ha! ha! ha! satisfaction!
Ding dong!
Each is laid in churchyard mould —
Strange the views some people hold!

Better than the method old,
Which was coarse and cruel,
Is the plan that we've extolled.
Sing thy virtues manifold

14

(Better than refinèd gold),
    Statutory Duel!
        Sing song! Sing song!
Sword or pistol neither uses —
Playing card he lightly chooses,
And the loser simply loses!
      Ha! ha! ha! ha! simply loses.
        Sing song! Sing song!
Some prefer the churchyard mould!
Strange the views some people hold!

NOT. (*offering a card*   Now take a card and gaily sing
  to ERNEST).   How little you care for Fortune's rubs —

ERN. (*drawing a card*).   Hurrah, hurrah! — I've drawn a King!

ALL.   He's drawn a King!
                 He's drawn a King!   [Clubs!
       Sing Hearts and Diamonds, Spades and

ALL (*dancing*). He's drawn a King!
          How strange a thing!
An excellent card — his chance it aids —
Sing Hearts and Diamonds, Spades and Clubs —
Sing Diamonds, Hearts and Clubs and Spades!

NOT. (*to* LUDWIG). Now take a card with heart of grace —
        (Whatever our fate, let's play our parts).

LUD. (*drawing card*). Hurrah, hurrah! — I've drawn an Ace!

ALL.   He's drawn an Ace!
                He's drawn an Ace!   [Hearts!
       Sing Clubs and Diamonds, Spades and

ALL (*dancing*). He's drawn an Ace!
          Observe his face —
Such very good fortune falls to few —
Sing Clubs and Diamonds, Spades and Hearts —
Sing Clubs, Spades, Hearts and Diamonds too!

NOT.   That both these maids may keep their troth,
          And never misfortune them befall,
      I'll hold 'em as trustee for both —

ALL.   He'll hold 'em both!
                He'll hold 'em both!   [and all!
       Sing Hearts, Clubs, Diamonds, Spades

ALL (*dancing*). By joint decree
      As $\left\{ \begin{array}{c} \text{our} \\ \text{your} \end{array} \right\}$ trustee

   This Notary $\left\{ \begin{array}{c} \text{we} \\ \text{you} \end{array} \right\}$ will now instal —

  In custody let him keep $\left\{ \begin{array}{c} \text{their} \\ \text{our} \end{array} \right\}$ hearts,

  Sing Hearts, Clubs, Diamonds, Spades and all!

(*Dance and Exeunt — *LUDWIG* R., *ERNEST* L., *and* NOTARY
    off* C. *with the two girls*.)

251

15

March. Enter the seven Chamberlains of the GRAND DUKE *
WILHELM.*

CHORUS OF CHAMBERLAINS.

The good Grand Duke of Hesse Halbpfennig,   1
Though he may be of German Royalty a sprig,
In point of fact he's nothing but a miserable pig,
Is the good Grand Duke of Hesse Halbpfennig!

Though quite contemptible, as every one agrees,
We must dissemble if we want our bread and cheese,
So hail him in a chorus, with enthusiasm big,
The good Grand Duke of Hesse Halbpfennig!

Enter the GRAND DUKE WILHELM. *He is meanly and miserably
dressed in old and patched clothes, but blazes with a profusion
of orders and decorations. He is very weak and ill, from
low living.*

SONG. — WILHELM.

A pattern to professors of monarchial autonomy,
I don't indulge in levity or compromising *bonhomie,*
But dignified formality, consistent with economy,
          Above all other virtues I particularly prize.
I never join in merriment — I don't see joke or jape any —
I never tolerate familiarity in shape any —
This, joined with an extravagant respect for tuppence ha'penny,
          A keynote to my character sufficiently supplies.

(*Speaking.*) Observe. (*To Chamberlains.*) My snuff-box!

(*The snuff-box is passed with much ceremony from the Junior
      Chamberlain, through all the others, until it is presented by
      the Senior Chamberlain to* WILHELM, *who uses it. It is
      returned by a reversal of this course.*)

          That incident a keynote to my character supplies.

ALL.   That incident, &c.

WIL. I weigh out tea and sugar with precision mathematical —
Instead of beer, a penny each — my orders are emphatical —
(Extravagance unpardonable, any more than that I call),
          But, on the other hand, my Ducal dignity to keep —
All Courtly ceremonial — to put it comprehensively —
I rigidly insist upon (but not, I hope, offensively)
Whenever ceremonial can be practised inexpensively —
          And, when you come to think of it, it's really very cheap!

(*Speaking.*) Observe. (*To Chamberlains.*) My handkerchief!

(*Handkerchief is handed by Junior Chamberlain to the next in
      order, and so on until it reaches* WILHELM, *who is much
      inconvenienced by the delay. He uses it and returns it.*)

          It's stately and impressive — and it's really very cheap!

ALL.   It's stately and impressive, &c.

*Grand Duke Wilhelm is used for Grand Duke Rudolph throughout.
  1. This is the offensive chorus which was changed before the opening. See Appendix,
no. 1.

Walter Passmore as Grand Duke Rudolph. (British Library.)

Rosina Brandram as Baroness von Krakenfeldt, Act I.

WIL. My Lord Chamberlain, as you are aware, my marriage with the wealthy Baroness von Krakenfeldt will take place to-morrow, and you will be good enough to see that the rejoicings are on a scale of unusual liberality. Pass that on. (*Chamberlain whispers to Vice-Chamberlain, who whispers to the next, and so on.*) The sports will begin with a Wedding Breakfast Bee. The leading pastrycooks of the town will be invited to compete, and the winner will not only enjoy the satisfaction of seeing his breakfast devoured by the Grand Ducal pair, but he will also be entitled to have the Royal Arms of Hesse Halbpfennig tattoo'd between his shoulder-blades. The Chamberlain will see to this. All the public fountains of Speisesaal will run with Gingerbierheim and Currant-weinmilch at the public expense. The Assistant Vice-Chamberlain will see to this. At night, everybody will illuminate; and as I have no desire to tax the public funds unduly, this will be done at the inhabitants' private expense. The Deputy Assistant Vice-Chamberlain will see to this. All my Grand Ducal subjects will wear new clothes, and the Sub-Deputy Assistant Vice-Chamberlain will collect the usual commission on all sales. Wedding presents (which, on this occasion, should be on a scale of extraordinary magnificence) will be received at the Palace at any hour of the twenty-four, and the Temporary Sub-Deputy Assistant Vice-Chamberlain will sit up all night for this purpose. The entire population will be commanded to enjoy themselves, and with this view the Acting-Temporary Sub-Deputy Assistant Vice-Chamberlain will sing comic songs in the Market Place from noon to nightfall. Finally, we have composed a Wedding Anthem, with which the entire population are required to provide themselves. It can be obtained from our Grand Ducal publishers at the usual discount price, and all the Chamberlains will be expected to push the sale. (*Chamberlains bow and exeunt.*) I don't feel at all comfortable. I hope I'm not doing a foolish thing in getting married. After all, it's a poor heart that never rejoices, and this wedding of mine is the first little treat I've allowed myself since my christening. Besides, Caroline's income is very considerable, and as her ideas of economy are quite on a par with mine, it ought to turn out well. Bless her tough old heart, she's a mean little darling! Oh, here she is, punctual to her appointment!

Enter BARONESS VON KRAKENFELDT.

BAR. Wilhelm! Why, what's the matter?

WIL. Why, I'm not quite myself, my pet. I'm a little worried and upset. I want a tonic. It's the low diet, I think. I am afraid, after all, I shall have to take the bull by the horns and have an egg with my breakfast.

BAR. I shouldn't do anything rash, dear. (*He sits by her and tries to put his arm round her waist.*) Wilhelm, don't! What in the world are you thinking of?

WIL. I was thinking of embracing you, my sugarplum. Just as a little cheap treat.

BAR. What, here? In public? Really you appear to have no sense of delicacy.

WIL. No sense of delicacy, Bon-bon!

BAR. No. I can't make you out. When you courted me, all your courting was done publicly in the Market Place. When you proposed to me, you proposed in the Market Place. And now that we're engaged you seem to desire that our first *tête-à-tête* shall occur in the Market Place! Surely you've a room in your Palace — with blinds — that would do?

WIL. But, my own, I can't help myself. I'm bound by my own decree.

BAR. Your own decree?

WIL. Yes. You see, all the houses that give on the Market Place belong to me, but the drains (which date back to the reign of Charlemagne) want attending to, and the houses wouldn't let — so, with a view of increasing the value of the property, I decreed that all love-episodes between affectionate couples should take place, in public, on this spot, every Monday, Wednesday, and Friday, when the band doesn't play.

BAR. Bless me, what a happy idea! So moral too! And have you found it answer?

WIL. Answer? The rents have gone up fifty per cent., and the sale of opera glasses (which is a Grand Ducal monopoly) has received an extraordinary stimulus! So, under the circumstances, *would* you allow me to put my arm round your waist? As a source of income. Just once!

BAR. But it's so very embarrassing. Think of the opera glasses!

WIL. My good girl, that's just what I *am* thinking of. Hang it all, we must give them *something* for their money! What's that?

BAR. (*unfolding paper, which contains a large letter, which she hands to him*). It's a letter which your detective asked me to hand to you. I wrapped it up in yesterday's paper to keep it clean.

WIL. Oh, it's only his report! That'll keep. But, I say, you've never been and bought a newspaper?

BAR. My dear Wilhelm, do you think I'm mad? It came wrapped round my breakfast.

WIL. (*relieved*). I thought you were not the sort of girl to go and buy a newspaper! Well, as we've got it, we may as well read it. What does it say?

BAR. Why — dear me — here's your biography! "Our Detested Despot!"

WIL. Yes — I fancy that refers to me.

BAR. And it says — Oh it can't be!

WIL. What can't be?

BAR. Why, it says that although you're going to marry me to-morrow, you were betrothed in infancy to the Princess of Monte Carlo!

WIL. Oh yes — that's quite right. Didn't I mention it?

BAR. Mention it! You never said a word about it!

WIL. Well, it doesn't matter, because, you see, it's practically off.

BAR. Practically off?

WIL. Yes. By the terms of the contract the betrothal is void unless the Princess marries before she is of age. Now, her father, the Prince, is stony-broke, and hasn't left his house for years for fear of arrest. Over and over again he has implored me to come to him to be married — but in vain. Over and over again he has implored me to advance him the money to enable the Princess to come to me — but in vain. I am very young, but not as young as that; and as the Princess comes of age at twelve to-morrow, why at twelve to-morrow I'm a free man, so I appointed that hour for our wedding, as I shall like to have as much marriage as I can get for my money.

BAR. I see. Of course, if the married state is a happy state, it's a pity to waste any of it.

WIL. Why, every hour we delayed I should lose a lot of you and you'd lose a lot of me!

BAR. My thoughtful darling! Oh, Wilhelm, we ought to be very happy!

WIL. If I'm not, it'll be my first bad investment. Still there *is* such a thing as a slump even in Matrimonials.

BAR. I often picture us in the long, cold, dark December evenings, sitting close to each other for warmth — thinking of all the lovely things we could afford to buy if we chose, and, at the same time, planning out our lives in a spirit of the most rigid and exacting economy!

WIL. It's a most beautiful and touching picture of connubial bliss in its highest and most rarified development!

DUET.— BARONESS *and* WILHELM.

BAR.   As o'er our penny roll we sing,
        It is not reprehensive
    To think what joys our wealth would bring
    Were we disposed to do the thing
        Upon a scale extensive.
    There's rich mock-turtle — thick and clear —

WIL. (*confidentially*). Perhaps we'll have it once a year!

BAR. (*delighted*). You *are* an open-handed dear!

WIL.   Though, mind you, it's expensive.

BAR.   No doubt it *is* expensive.

BOTH.   How fleeting are the glutton's joys!
    With fish and fowl he lightly toys,

WIL.   And pays for such expensive tricks
    Sometimes as much as two-and-six!

19

BAR. (*surprised*).   As two-and-six?

WIL.   As two-and-six.

BOTH.   Sometimes as much as two-and-six!
It gives him no advantage, mind —
For you and he have only dined.

BAR.   And you remain, when once it's down,
A better man by half-a-crown!

WIL. (*doubtfully*).   By half-a-crown?

BAR. (*decisively*).   By half-a-crown.

BOTH.   Yes, two-and-six is half-a-crown.
(*Dancing*). Then let us be modestly merry,
And rejoice with a derry down derry,
For to laugh and to sing
No extravagance bring —
It's a joy economical, very!

BAR.   Although, as you're of course aware   *
(I never tried to hide it),
I moisten my insipid fare
With water — which I can't abear —

WIL.   Nor I — I can't abide it.

BAR.   This pleasing fact our souls will cheer,
With fifty thousand pounds a year
We *could* indulge in table beer!

WIL. (*incredulously*). Get out!

BAR.   We could — I've tried it!

BOTH.   Oh, he who has an income clear
Of fifty thousand pounds a year
Can purchase all his fancy loves —

BAR.   Conspicuous hats —

WIL.   Two-shilling gloves —

BAR. (*doubtfully*).   Two-shilling gloves?

WIL. (*positively*).   Two-shilling gloves —

BOTH. .   Cheap shoes and ties of gaudy hue,
And Waterbury watches, too —
And think that he could buy the lot
Were he a donkey —

WIL.   Which he's *not!*

BAR.   Oh no, he's *not!*

WIL.   Oh no, he's *not!*

BOTH.   That kind of donkey he's *not!*
(*Dancing*.)   Then let us be modestly merry,
And rejoice with a derry down derry.
For to laugh and to sing

*This second verse was deleted from the second edition of the libretto, and presumably from performance as well.

20

Is a rational thing —
It's a joy economical, very!

[*Exit* BARONESS.

WIL. Oh, now for my detective's report. (*Opens letter.*) What's this! Another conspiracy! A conspiracy to depose *me!* And my private detective was so convulsed with laughter at the notion of a conspirator selecting him for a confidant that he was physically unable to arrest the malefactor! Why, it'll come off! This comes of engaging a detective with a keen sense of the ridiculous! And the plot is to explode to-morrow! My wedding day! Oh, Caroline, Caroline! (*Weeps.*) This is perfectly frightful! What's to be done? I don't know! I ought to keep cool and think, but you *can't* think when your veins are full of hot soda water, and your brain's fizzing like a firework, and all your faculties are jumbled in a perfect whirlpool of tumblication! And I'm going to be ill! I know I am! I've been living too low, and I'm going to be very ill indeed!

SONG.— WILHELM.   2

When your clothes, from your hat to your socks,
   Have tickled and scrubbed you all day —
When your brain is a musical box
   With a barrel that turns the wrong way —
When you find you're too small for your coat,
   And a great deal too big for your vest —
With a pint of warm oil in your throat,
   And a pound of tin tacks in your chest —
When you've got a beehive in your head,
   And a sewing machine in each ear,
And you feel that you've eaten your bed,
   And you've got a bad headache *down here* —
When your lips are like underdone paste,
   And your highly gamboge in the gill,
And your mouth has a coppery taste
   As if you'd just bitten a pill —
When everything spins like a top,
   When your stock of endurance gives out —
When some miscreant proposes a chop,
   (Mutton chop with potatoes and stout) —
When your mouth is of flannel like mine,
   And your teeth not on terms with their stumps,
And spiders crawl over your spine,
   And your muscles have all got the mumps —
When you're bad with the creeps and the crawls,
   And the shivers and shudders and shakes,
And the pattern that covers your walls
   Is alive with black beetles and snakes —
When you doubt if your head is your own,
   And you jump when an open door slams,
Then you've got to a state which is known
   To the medical world as "jim-jams."

2. Gilbert originally wrote this lyric for *The Mountebanks*. Before the *Grand Duke* opening, he rewrote it. See Appendix, no. 2.

> If such symptoms you find
> In your body or head,
> They're not easy to quell —
> You may make up your mind
> You are better in bed,
> For you're not at all well!

(Sinks exhausted and weeping at foot of well.)

Enter LUDWIG.

LUD. They told me the Grand Duke was dancing duets in the Market Place, but I don't see him. I must find him and peach upon Ernest before the detective peaches on me. (*Sees* WILHELM.) Hallo! Who's this? (*Aside.*) Why, it *is* the Grand Duke!

WIL. (*sobbing*). Who are you, sir, who presume to address me in person? If you've anything to communicate, you must fling yourself at the feet of my Acting Temporary Sub-Deputy Assistant Vice-Chamberlain, who will fling himself at the feet of his immediate superior, and so on, with successive foot-flingings through the various grades — your communication will, in course of time, come to my august knowledge.

LUD. But when I inform your Highness that in me you see the most unhappy, the most unfortunate, the most completely miserable man in your whole dominion —

WIL. (*still sobbing*). *You* the most miserable man in my whole dominion? How can you have the face to stand there and say such a thing? Why, look at me! Look at me! (*Bursts into tears.*)

LUD. Well, I wouldn't be a cry-baby.

WIL. A cry-baby? If you had just been told that you were going to be deposed to-morrow, and perhaps blown up with dynamite for all I know, wouldn't *you* be a cry-baby? I do declare if I could only hit upon some cheap and painless method of putting an end to an existence which has become insupportable, I would unhesitatingly adopt it!

LUD. You would? (*Aside.*) I see a magnificent way out of this! By Jupiter, I'll try it! (*Aloud.*) Are you, by any chance, in earnest?

WIL. In earnest? Why, look at me!

LUD. If you are really in earnest — if you really desire to escape scot free from this impending — this unspeakably horrible catastrophe — without trouble, danger, pain, or expense — why not resort to a Statutory Duel?

WIL. A Statutory Duel?

LUD. Yes. The Act is still in force, but it will expire to-morrow afternoon. You fight — you lose — you are dead for a day. To-morrow, when the Act expires, you will come to life again and resume your Grand Duchy as though nothing had happened. In the meantime, the explosion will have taken place and the survivor will have had to bear the brunt of it.

WIL. Yes, that's all very well, but who'll be fool enough to *be* the survivor?

LUD. (*kneeling*). Actuated by an overwhelming sense of attachment to your Grand Ducal person, I unhesitatingly offer myself as the victim of your subjects' fury.

WIL. You do? Well, really that's very handsome. I daresay being blown up is not nearly as unpleasant as one would think. But suppose I were to lose?

LUD. Oh, that's easily arranged. (*Producing a pack of cards.*) I'll put a Three up my sleeve — you'll put a Two up yours. When the drawing takes place, I shall seem to draw the higher card and you the lower. And there you are!

WIL. But that's cheating.

LUD. So it is. I never thought of that.

WIL. (*hastily*). Not that I mind. But I say — you won't take an unfair advantage of your day of office? You won't go tipping people, or squandering my little savings in fireworks, or any nonsense of that sort?

LUD. I am hurt — really hurt — by the suggestion.

WIL. You — you wouldn't like to run down a deposit, perhaps?

LUD. No. I don't think I should like to run down a deposit.

WIL. Or give a guarantee?

LUD. A guarantee would be equally open to objection.

WIL. It would be more regular. Very well, I suppose you must have your own way.

LUD. Good. I say — we must have a devil of a quarrel!

WIL. Oh, a devil of a quarrel!

LUD. Just to give colour to the thing. Shall I give you a sound thrashing before all the people? Say the word — it's no trouble.

WIL. No, I think not, though it would be very convincing and it's extremely good and thoughtful of you to suggest it. Still, a devil of a quarrel!

LUD. Oh, a devil of a quarrel!

WIL. No half measures. Big words — strong language — rude remarks. Oh, a devil of a quarrel!

LUD. Now the question is, how shall we summon the people?

WIL. Oh, there's no difficulty about that. Bless your heart, they've been staring at us through those windows for the last half hour!

23

FINALE.

WIL.   Come hither, all you people —
        When you hear the fearful news,
    All the pretty women weep'll,
        Men will shiver in their shoes.
    And they'll all cry, " Lord, defend us ! "
    When they learn the fact tremendous
        That to give this man his gruel
        In a Statutory Duel —
        This plebeian man of shoddy —
        This contemptible nobody —
        Your Grand Duke does not refuse !

(*During this, Chorus of men and women have entered — all trembling with apprehension.*)

CHORUS.

    With faltering feet,
        And our muscles in a quiver,
    Our fate we meet
        With our feelings all unstrung !
    If our plot complete
        He has managed to diskiver,
    There is no retreat —
        We shall certainly be hung !

WIL. (*aside to* LUDWIG).
    Now *you* begin and pitch it strong — walk into me abusively —

LUD. (*aside to* WILHELM).
    I've several epithets that I've reserved for you exclusively.
    A choice selection I have here when you are ready *to* begin.

WIL.   Now *you* begin —

LUD.   No, *you* begin —

WIL.   No, *you* begin —

LUD.   No, *you* begin !

CHORUS (*trembling.*) Has it happed as we expected?
        Is our little plot detected?
        Or are they proceeding to
        Doughty deeds of derring do?

DUET.— WILHELM *and* LUDWIG.

WIL. (*furiously*).
    Big bombs, small bombs, great guns and little ones !
        Put him in a pillory !
        Rack him with artillery !

LUD. (*furiously*).
    Long swords, short swords, tough swords and brittle ones !
        Fright him into fits !
        Blow him into bits !

WIL.   You muff, sir !
        You lout, sir !

24

LUD.	Enough, sir!
	Get out, sir! (*Pushes him.*)
WIL.	A hit, sir?
	Take that, sir! (*Slaps him.*)

LUD. (*slapping* WILHELM).
> It's tit, sir,
> For tat, sir!

CHORUS (*appalled*).
> When two doughty heroes thunder,
> All the world is lost in wonder;
> When such men their temper lose,
> Awful are the words they use!

LUD.   Tall snobs, small snobs, rich snobs and needy ones!

WIL. (*jostling him*).   Whom are you alluding to?

LUD. (*jostling him*).   Where are you intruding to?

WIL.   Fat snobs, thin snobs, swell snobs and seedy ones!

LUD.
> I rather think you err.
> To whom do you refer?

WIL.   To you, sir!

LUD.   To me, sir?

WIL.   I do, sir!

LUD.   We'll see, sir!

WIL.   I jeer, sir!

(*makes a face at* LUDWIG).   Grimace, sir!

LUD.   Look here, sir—

(*makes a face at* WILHELM).   A face, sir!

CHORUS (*appalled*).
> When two heroes, once pacific,
> Quarrel, the effect's terrific!
> What a horrible grimace!
> What a paralyzing face!

ALL.   Big bombs, small bombs, &c.

LUD. *and* WIL. (*recit.*).
> He has insulted me, and, in a breath,
> This day we fight a duel to the death!
> (*Drawing swords.*)

NOT. (*checking them*).   You mean, of course, by duel (*verbum sat.*),
> A Statutory Duel.

ALL.   Why, what's that?

NOT.
> According to established legal uses,
> A card a piece each bold disputant chooses —
> Dead as a doornail is the dog who loses —
> The winner steps into the dead man's shoeses!

ALL.   The winner steps into the dead man's shoeses!

WIL. *and* LUD.   Agreed! Agreed!

243

WIL.   Come, come — the pack !

NOT. (*producing one*).   Behold it here !

WIL.   I'm on the rack !

LUD.   I quake with fear !

(NOTARY *offers card to* LUDWIG.)

LUD.   First draw to me !

WIL.   First draw to you !

LUD. (*taking card from his sleeves*).

          Behold the Three !

WIL. (*ditto*).   Behold the Two !

CHORUS.   Hurrah, hurrah ! Our Ludwig's won,
          And wicked Wilhelm's course is run —
          So Ludwig will as Grand Duke reign
          Till Wilhelm comes to life again —

WIL.   Which will occur to-morrow !

ALL.   Yes, yes.
          That will occur to-morrow !

JULIA (*with mocking curtsy*).
          My Lord Grand Duke, farewell !
              A pleasant journey, very,
          To your convenient cell
              In yonder cemetery !

ELSA (*curtsying*). Though malcontents abuse you,
              We're much distressed to lose you !

OLGA.   You were, when you were living,
          So liberal, so forgiving !

BERTHA.   So merciful, so gentle !
          So highly ornamental !

GRET.   And now that you've departed,
          You leave us broken-hearted !

ALL FOUR. Yes, truly, truly, truly, truly —
          Truly broken-hearted !

ALL (*pretending to weep*). Yes, truly, truly, truly, truly —
              Truly broken-hearted !
          Ha ! ha ! ha ! ha ! ha ! ha ! (*Mocking him.*)

WIL. (*furious*). Rapscallions, in penitential fires,
              You'll rue the ribaldry that from you falls !
          To-morrow afternoon the law expires,
              And then — look out for squalls !

          [*Exit* WILHELM, *amid general ridicule.*

CHORUS (*to*   You've done it neatly ! Pity that your powers   3
LUDWIG).   Are limited to four-and-twenty hours !

LUD.   No matter, though the time will quickly run,
          In hours twenty-four much may be done !

3. A short chorus was inserted after the Grand Duke's exit. See Appendix, no. 3.

SONG.— Ludwig.

Oh, a monarch who boasts intellectual graces
  Can do, if he likes, a good deal in a day —
He can put all his friends in conspicuous places,
  With plenty to eat and with nothing to pay !
You'll tell me, no doubt, with unpleasant grimaces,
To-morrow, deprived of your ribbons and laces,
You'll get your dismissal — with very long faces —
  But wait ! on that topic I've something to say !
(*Dancing.*) I've something to say — I've something to say — I've
    something to say !
  Oh, our rule shall be merry — I'm not an ascetic —
   And while the sun shines we will get up our hay —
  By a pushing young Monarch, of turn energetic,
   A very great deal may be done in a day !

Chorus.   Oh, his rule will be merry, &c.

  (*During this*, Ludwig *whispers to* Notary, *who writes.*)

For instance, this measure (his ancestor drew it),
       (*alluding to* Notary)
  This law against duels — to-morrow will die —
The Duke will revive, and you'll certainly rue it —
  He'll give you " what for " and he'll let you know why !
But in twenty-four hours there's time to renew it —
With a century's life I've the right to imbue it —
It's easy to do — and, by Jingo, I'll do it !
(*Signing paper which* Notary *presents.*)
  It's done ! Till I perish your Monarch am I !
Your Monarch am I — your Monarch am I — your Monarch
  am I !
  Though I do not pretend to be very prophetic,
   I fancy I know what you're going to say —
  By a pushing young Monarch, of turn energetic,
   A very great deal may be done in a day !

All (*astonished*). Oh, it's simply uncanny, his power prophetic —
   It's perfectly right — we *were* going to say.
   By a pushing, &c.

Lud. (*recit.*). This very afternoon — at two (about) —
   The Court appointments will be given out.
   To each and all (for that was the condition)
   According to professional position !

All.   Hurrah !

Julia According to professional position ?

Lud. According to professional position !

Julia. Then, horror !

All. Why, what's the matter ? What's the matter ? What's
   the matter ?

SONG. — JULIA. (ELSA *clinging to her*.)

Ah, pity me, my comrades true,
Who love, as well I know you do,
    This gentle child,
        To me so fondly dear!

ALL.   Why, what's the matter?

JULIA.   Our sister love so true and deep
           From many an eye unused to weep
              Hath oft beguiled
                  The coy, reluctant tear!

ALL   Why, what's the matter?

JULIA.   Each sympathetic heart 'twill bruise
           When you have learnt the frightful news
              (O will it not?)
                  That I must now impart!

ALL.   Why, what's the matter?

JULIA.   Her love for him is all in all!
           Ah, cursed fate! that it should fall
              Unto *my* lot
                  To break my darling's heart!

ALL.   Oh, *that's* the matter!

LUD.   What means our Julia by those fateful looks?
           Please do not keep us all on tenter-hooks —
                Now, what's the matter?

JULIA.   Our duty, if we're wise,
              We never shun.
           This Spartan rule applies
              To every one.
           In theatres, as in life,
              Each has her line —
           This part — the Grand Duke's wife
              (Oh agony!) is mine!
           A maxim new I do not start —
           The canons of dramatic art
           Decree that this repulsive part
              (The Grand Duke's wife)
                Is mine!

ELSA (*appalled, to* LUDWIG).   Can that be so?

LUD.   I do not know —
           But time will show
           If that be so.

CHORUS.   Can that be so? &c.

ELSA (*recit.*).   Be merciful!

28

DUET. — Elsa *and* Julia.

ELSA. Oh, listen to me, dear —
  I love him only, darling!
   Remember, oh, my pet,
   On him my heart is set!
 This kindness do me, dear —
  Nor leave me lonely, darling!
   Be merciful, my pet,
   Our love do not forget!

JULIA. Now don't be foolish, dear —
  You couldn't play it, darling!
   It's "leading business," pet,
   And you're but a soubrette.
 So don't be mulish, dear —
  Although I say it, darling,
   It's not your line, my pet —
   I play that part, you bet!
   I play that part —
   I play that part; you bet!
     (ELSA *overwhelmed with grief.*)

CHORUS.   Can this be so?
    I do not know,
    But time will show
    If this be so.

NOT. The lady's right. Though Julia's engagement
    Was for the stage meant —
 It certainly frees Ludwig from his
    Connubial promise.
 Though marriage contracts — or whate'er you call 'em —
    Are very solemn,
 Dramatic contracts (which you all adore so)
    Are even more so!

ALL.   That's very true!
 Though marriage contracts, &c.
     (ELSA *is prostrate, weeping.*) 4

LUD. (*recit.*). Poor child, where will she go? What will she do?

JULIA. *That* isn't in your part, you know.

LUD. (*sighing*).   Quite true!
(*With an effort*) Depressing topics we'll not touch upon —
   Let us begin as we are going on!
 For this will be a jolly Court, for little and for big!

ALL. Sing hey, the jolly jinks of Hesse Halbpfennig!

LUD. From morn to night our lives shall be as merry as a grig!

ALL. Sing hey, the jolly jinks of Hesse Halbpfennig!

LUD. All state and ceremony we'll eternally abolish —
 We don't mean to insist upon unnecessary polish —
 And, on the whole, I rather think you'll find our rule tol-
  lolish!

4. Elsa [Lisa] was given a short solo prior to her exit. See Appendix, no. 4.

29

ALL.   Sing hey, the jolly jinks of Hesse Halbpfennig!

LUD.   The costumes of our Court   5
              (Which should be new completely),
                  The dresses gay
                  Of our new play
              Will furnish very neatly.
        In clothes of common sort
              Let mere mechanics grovel —
                  For our *noblesse*
                  A classic dress
              Will be both quaint and novel!

ALL.   Agreed! Agreed!
        For this will be a jolly Court for little and for big! &c.
                  Wild Dance.

              ACT DROP.

─────────────

ACT II.

(THE NEXT MORNING.)

SCENE.   *Entrance Hall of the Grand Ducal Palace.   Wreaths of bay and ivy decorate the entrance.   Braziers of lighted fires are burning.*

Enter a procession of the members of the theatrical company (now dressed in the costumes of Troilus and Cressida), carrying garlands, playing on pipes, citharæ and tabors, and heralding the return of LUDWIG *and* JULIA *from the marriage ceremony, which has just taken place.*

CHORUS.

As before you we defile,
        Eloia! Eloia!
Pray you, gentles, do not smile
If we shout, in classic style,
        Eloia!
Ludwig and his Julia true
Wedded are each other to —
So we sing, till all is blue,
        Eloia! Eloia!
        Opoponax! Eloia!

Wreaths of bay and ivy twine,
        Eloia! Eloia!
Fill the bowl with Lesbian wine,
And to revelry incline —
        Eloia!
For as gaily we pass on
Probably we shall, anon,
Sing a Diergeticon —   •
        Eloia! Eloia!
        Opoponax! Eloia!

5. These lyrics were slightly extended before the opening. See Appendix, no. 5.

Florence Perry as Lisa, Act I.   Florence Perry as Lisa, Act II.

Note the strong visual contrast in costumes.

Rutland Barrington in his 'Troilus and Cressida' costume, Act II. Gilbert made his part too long by writing him a Greek patter song.

30

RECIT.— Ludwig.

Your loyalty our Ducal heartstrings touches :
Allow me to present your new Grand Duchess.
Should she offend, you'll graciously excuse her —
And kindly recollect *I* didn't choose her !

ALL.
     Eloia ! Eloia !
     Opoponax ! Eloia !

SONG.— Ludwig.

At the outset I may mention it's my sovereign intention
 To revive the classic memories of Athens at its best,
For the company possesses all the necessary dresses
 And a course of quiet cramming will supply us with the rest.
We've a choir hyporchematic (that is, ballet-operatic)
 Who respond to the *choreutæ* of that cultivated age,
And our clever chorus-master, all but captious criticaster,
 Would accept as the *choregus* of the early Attic stage.
This return to classic ages is considered in their wages,
 Which are always calculated by the day or by the week —
And I'll pay 'em (if they'll back me) all in *oboloi* and *drachmæ*,
 Which they'll get (if they prefer it) at the Kalends that are Greek !

 (*Confidentially to audience.*)

   At this juncture I may mention
    That this erudition sham
   Is but classical pretension,
    The result of steady "cram." ;
   Periphrastic methods spurning,
   To this audience discerning
   I admit this show of learning
    Is the fruit of steady "cram." !

CHORUS.   Periphrastic methods, &c.

In the period Socratic every dining-room was Attic
 (Which suggests an architecture of a topsy-turvy kind),
There they'd satisfy their thirst on a recherché cold ἄριστον,
 Which is what they call their lunch — and so may you, if you're
  inclined.
As they gradually got on, they'd τρέπεσθαι πρὸς τὸν πότον
 (Which is Attic for a steady and a conscientious drink).
But they mixed their wine with water — which I'm sure they didn't
  oughter —
 And we modern Saxons know a trick worth two of that, I think !
Then came rather risky dances (under certain circumstances)
 Which would shock that worthy gentleman, the Licenser of Plays,
Corybantian mani*ac* kick — Dionysiac or Bacchic —
 And the Dithryambic revels of those undecorous days.

 (*Confidentially to audience.*)

   And perhaps I'd better mention,
    Lest alarming you I am,

31

That it isn't our intention
To perform a Dithryamb —
It displays a lot of stocking,
Which is always very shocking,
And of course I'm only mocking
At the prevalence of "cram."

CHORUS. It displays a lot, &c.

Yes, on reconsideration, there are customs of that nation
Which are not in strict accordance with the habits of our day,
And when I come to codify, their rules I mean to modify,
Or Mrs. Grundy, p'r'aps, may have a word or two to say.
For they hadn't macintoshes or umbrellas or goloshes —
And a shower with their dresses must have played the very deuce,
And it must have been unpleasing when they caught a fit of sneezing,
For, it seems, of pocket handkerchiefs they didn't know the use.
They wore little underclothing — scarcely anything — or no-thing —
And their dress of Coan silk was quite transparent in design —
Well, in fact, in summer weather, something like the "altogether."
And it's *there*, I rather fancy, I shall have to draw the line !

(*Confidentially to audience.*)

And again I wish to mention
That this erudition sham
Is but classical pretension,
The result of steady "cram."
Yet my classic love aggressive
(If you'll pardon the possessive)
Is exceedingly impressive
When you're passing an exam.

CHORUS. Yet his classic love, &c.

[*Exeunt Chorus.*

Manent LUDWIG, JULIA, *and* ELSA.

LUD. (*recit.*). Yes, Ludwig and his Julia are mated !
For when an obscure comedian, whom the law backs,
To sovereign rank is promptly elevated,
He takes it with its incidental drawbacks !
So Julia and I are duly mated !

JULIA (*to* ELSA, *who is weeping*). *
Resign yourself to circumstances, do, dear :
Remember, he will have my sole affection —
With me he will be happier than with you, dear —
And you may soothe yourself with that reflection.

ELSA (*weeping*). Oh, Julia, see how his bright eyes glisten !
He loved me from the moment that he met me !
Be good to him — and, if you'll kindly listen,
I'll teach you how to make my love forget me !

*These two quatrains were eliminated in rehearsal.

32

SONG. — ELSA.

Take care of him — he's much too good to live
       With him you must be very gentle;
Poor fellow, he's so highly sensitive,
       And O so sentimental!
Be sure you never let him sit up late
       In chilly open air conversing —
Poor darling, he's extremely delicate,
       And wants a deal of nursing!

LUD.   I want a deal of nursing!

ELSA.   And O, remember this —
       When he is cross with pain
       A flower and a kiss —
       A simple flower — a tender kiss
       Will bring him round again!

His moods you must assiduously watch:
       When he succumbs to sorrow tragic,
Some hardbake or a bit of butter-scotch
       Will work on him like magic.
To contradict a character so rich
       In trusting love were simple blindness —
He's one of those exalted natures which
       Will only yield to kindness!

LUD.   I only yield to kindness!

ELSA.   And O, the byegone bliss!
       And O, the present pain!
       That flower and that kiss —
       That simple flower — that tender kiss
       I ne'er shall give again!

                          [*Exit, weeping.*

JULIA. And now that everybody has gone, and we're happily and comfortably married, I want to have a few words with my new-born husband.

LUD. (*aside*). Yes, I expect you'll often have a few words with your new-born husband! (*Aloud.*) Well, what is it?

JULIA. Why, I've been thinking that as you and I have to play our parts for life, it is most essential that we should come to a definite understanding as to how they shall be rendered. Now, I've been considering how I can make the most of the Grand Duchess.

LUD. Have you? Well, if you'll take my advice, I should make a very fine part of it.

JULIA. How very odd! — that's quite *my* idea.

LUD. I shouldn't make it one of your hoity-toity vixenish viragos.

JULIA. You think not?

LUD. Oh, I'm quite clear about that. I should make her a tender, gentle, submissive, affectionate (but not too affectionate) child-wife — timidly anxious to coil herself into her husband's heart, but kept in check by an awestruck reverence for his exalted intellectual qualities and his majestic personal appearance.

JULIA.   Oh, that is your idea of a good part?

LUD.   Yes — a wife who regards her husband's slightest wish as an inflexible law, and who ventures but rarely into his august presence, unless (which would happen seldom) he should summon her to appear before him.   A crushed, despairing violet, whose blighted existence would culminate (all too soon) in a lonely and pathetic death-scene!   A fine part, my dear.

JULIA.   Yes.   There's a good deal to be said for your view of it.   Now there are some actresses whom it would fit like a glove.

LUD. (*aside*).   I wish I'd married one of 'em!

JULIA.   But, you see I *must* consider my temperament.   For instance, my temperament would demand some strong scenes of justifiable jealousy.

LUD.   Oh, there's no difficulty about that.   You shall have *them*.

JULIA.   With a lovely but detested rival —

LUD.   Oh, *I'll* provide the rival.

JULIA.   Whom I should stab — stab — stab!

LUD.   Oh, I wouldn't stab her.   I should treat her with a silent and contemptuous disdain, and delicately withdraw from a position which, to one of your sensitive nature, would be absolutely untenable.   Dear me, I can see you delicately withdrawing, up centre and off!

JULIA.   *Can* you?

LUD.   Yes.   It's a fine situation — and in your hands, full of quiet pathos!

DUET.— LUDWIG *and* JULIA.

LUD.   Now Julia, come,
            Consider it from
                    This dainty point of view —
            A timid tender
            Feminine gender,
                    Prompt to coyly coo —
            Yet silence seeking,
            Seldom speaking
                    Till she's spoken to —
            A comfy, cosy,
            Rosy-posy
                    Innocent *ingenoo!*
                        The part you're suited to —
                        (To give the deuce her due)
                    A sweet (O, jiminy!)
                    Miminy-piminy,
                        Innocent ingen*oo!*

34

ENSEMBLE.

LUD.	JULIA.
The part you're suited to —	I'm much obliged to you,
(To give the duce her due)	I don't think that would do —
A sweet (O, jimini!)	To play (O, jimini!)
Miminy-piminy,	Miminy-piminy,
Innocent inge*noo!*	Innocent inge*noo!*

JULIA.   You forget my special magic
           (In a high dramatic sense)
        Lies in situations tragic —
           Undeniably intense.
        As I've justified promotion
           In the histrionic art,
        I'll submit to you my notion
           Of a first-rate part.

LUD.   Well, let us see your notion
           Of a first-rate part.

JULIA (*dramatically*).
        I have a rival! Frenzy thrilled
           I find you both together!
        My heart stands still — with horror chilled —
           Hard as the millstone nether!
        Then softly, slyly, snaily, snaky —
        Crawly, creepy, quaily, quaky —
           I track her on her homeward way,
           As panther tracks her fated prey!

(*Furiously.*)   I fly at her soft white throat —
           The lily-white laughing leman!
        On her agonized gaze I gloat
           With the glee of a dancing demon!
        My rival she — I have no doubt of her —
        So I hold on — till the breath is out of her!
           — till the breath is out of her!

        And then — Remorse! Remorse!
        O cold unpleasant corse,
           Avaunt! Avaunt!
           That lifeless form
             I gaze upon —
           That face, still warm
             But weirdly wan —
           Those eyes of glass
             I contemplate —
        And then, alas,
           Too late — too late!
        I find she is — your Aunt!
           Remorse! Remorse!

(*Shuddering.*)
        Then, mad — mad — mad!
           With fancies wild — chimerical —
         Now sorrowful — silent — sad —
           Now, hullaballoo hysterical!

(*Tears some straw out of a cushion and sticks it in her hair.*)

255

35

Ha! ha! ha! ha!
But whether I'm sad or whether I'm glad,
Mad! mad! mad! mad!

This calls for the resources of a high-class art,
And satisfies my notion of a first-rate part!

Enter all the Court, hurriedly, and in great excitement.

CHORUS.

Your Highness, there's a party at the door —
Your Highness, at the door there is a party —
She says that we expect her,
But we do not recollect her,
For we never saw her countenance before!

With rage and indignation she is rife,
Because our welcome wasn't very hearty —
She's as sulky as a super,
And she's swearing like a trooper,
O, you never heard such language in your life!

Enter BARONESS VON KRAKENFELDT, *in a fury.*

BAR. With fury indescribable I burn!
With rage I'm nearly ready to explode!
There'll be grief and tribulation when I learn
To whom this slight unbearable is owed!
For whatever may be due I'll pay it double —
There'll be terror indescribable and trouble!
With a hurly-burly and a hubble-bubble
I'll pay you for this pretty episode!

ALL. Oh, whatever may be due she'll pay it double! —
It's very good of her to take the trouble —
But we don't know what she means by "hubble-
bubble" —
No doubt it's an expression *à la mode.*

BAR. (*to* LUDWIG).
Do you know who I am?

LUD. (*examining her*).   I don't;
Your countenance I can't fix, my dear.

BAR.   This proves I'm not a sham.
(*Showing pocket-handkerchief.*)

LUD. (*examining it.*)   It won't;
It only says " Krakenfeldt, Six," my dear.

BAR.   Express your grief profound!

LUD.   I sha'n't!
This tone I never allow, my love.

BAR.   Wilhelm at once produce!

LUD.   I can't;
He isn't at home just now, my love.

Bar. (*astonished*). He isn't at home just now!

All. He isn't at home just now,
(*dancing derisively*) He has an appointment particular, very —
You'll find him, I think, in the town cemetery;
And that's how we come to be making so merry,
For he isn't at home just now!

Bar. But bless my heart and soul alive, it's impudence person-
ified!
I've come here to be matrimonially matrimonified!

Lud. For any disappointment I am sorry unaffectedly,
But yesterday that nobleman expired unexpectedly —

All (*sobbing*). Tol the riddle lol!
Tol the riddle lol!
Tol the riddle lol the riddle, lol lol lay!
(*Then laughing wildly*) Tol the riddle lol the riddle, lol lol lay!

Bar. But this is most unexpected. He was well enough at
half-past eleven yesterday.

Lud. Yes. He died at a quarter to twelve.

Bar. Bless me, how very sudden!

Lud. It *was* sudden.

All. Boo-hoo, boo-hoo! (*Pretending to weep.*)

Bar. But what in the world am I to do? I was to have been
married to him to-day!

All (*singing and dancing.*)
For any disappointment we are sorry unaffectedly,
But yesterday that nobleman expired unexpectedly —
Tol the riddle lol!

Bar. Is this Court Mourning or a Fancy Ball?

Lud. Well, it's a delicate combination of both effects. It is
intended to express inconsolable grief for the decease of the late
Duke and ebullient joy at the accession of his successor. *I* am his
successor. Permit me to present you to my Grand Duchess. (*Indicating* Julia.)

Bar. Your Grand Duchess? Oh, your Highness! (*Curtsying
profoundly.*)

Julia (*sneering at her*). Old frump!

Bar. Humph! A recent creation, probably?

Elsa. They were married only half-an-hour ago.

Bar. Exactly. I thought she seemed new to the position.

Julia. Ma'am, I don't know who you are, but I flatter myself
I can do justice to *any* part on the very shortest notice.

Bar. My dear, under the circumstances you are doing admirably
— and you'll improve with practice. It's so difficult to be a lady
when one isn't born to it.

JULIA (*in a rage to* LUDWIG). Am I to stand this? Am I not to be allowed to pull her to pieces?

LUD. (*aside to* JULIA). No, no — it isn't Greek. Be a violet, I beg.

BAR. And now tell me all about this distressing circumstance. How did the Grand Duke die?

LUD. He perished nobly — in a Statutory Duel.

BAR. In a Statutory Duel? But that's only a civil death! With whom did he fight?

LUD. With me. It was a combat of giants. We drew — he died. Thereupon, as in duty bound, I took his place with all its overwhelming responsibilities.

BAR. But the Act expires to-night, and then he will come to life again!

LUD. Well, no. Anxious to inaugurate my reign by conferring some inestimable boon on my people, I signalized this occasion by reviving the law for another hundred years.

BAR. (*aside*). Hah!

LUD. If you will call again this day century, I've no doubt you'll find him ready, and indeed eager, to fulfil the terms of his engagement.

BAR. (*with sudden tenderness*). But why should I wait so long — dear one?

LUD. (*startled*). Eh!

JULIA *and* ELSA. What does she mean?

BAR. Set the merry joy-bells ringing! Let festive epithalamia resound through these ancient halls! Cut the satisfying sandwich — broach the exhilarating Marsala — and let us rejoice to-day, if we never rejoice again!

LUD. But I don't think I quite understand. We have already rejoiced a good deal.

ELSA. Quite as much as is good for us.

BAR. Happy man, you little reck of the extent of the good things you are in for. When you killed Wilhelm you adopted all his overwhelming responsibilities. Know then that I, Caroline von Krakenfeldt, am the most overwhelming of them all!

LUD. But stop, stop — I've just been married to some one else!

BAR. A fig for some one else!

JULIA. What!

LUD. (*aside to* JULIA). Be a violet — a crushed, despairing violet.

BAR. Was this young woman engaged to Wilhelm?

LUD. Certainly not. Never saw him.

BAR. Then the marriage is void. You can't marry any one

38

Wilhelm wasn't engaged to, and he was to have been married to me to-day. It's indisputable. I am here — you are here — he is dead — you are he — and I am yours! (JULIA *has been expressing impatience and indignation through this.*) Do keep that young woman quiet — she fidgets me.

JULIA. Fidgets you? Do you suppose I intend to give up such a magnificent part as the Grand Duchess of Hesse Halbpfennig without a struggle?

LUD. My good girl, she has the law on her side. Let us both bear this calamity with resignation. If you must struggle, go away and struggle in the seclusion of your chamber.

QUARTETTE.   *

JULIA, BARONESS, ELSA, LUDWIG, *and* CHORUS.

JULIA. But half an hour ago
I was a Ducal bride —
Extremely fair,
With nose in air,
To indicate my pride :
And now it seems before you all
I sing extremely small !

CHORUS (*dancing*). Now here we have a terrible fall !
The stoutest heart it might appal —
Though lately she despised us all,
She sings extremely small !

BAR. Though he gave you his hand,
It wasn't his own to give —
Your marriage rite
In legal sight
Was quite inopera*tive.*
All Wilhelm's bonds he's taken to,
And Wilhelm wasn't engaged to you.

CHORUS (*dancing*). Now here we have a pretty to-do —
That logic nobody can pooh-pooh —
He's been and married a bride brand-new,
He wasn't contracted to !

ELSA. Alas, poor Ludwig's fate !
Although I was his flame,
He put me by
With scarce a sigh
To yield to Julia's claim.
Now he'll fall victim, I'm afraid,
To this old lady's rhodomontade !

CHORUS (*dancing*). Now here we have a pretty young maid
Despised — deceived — cast off — betrayed —
We'd say much more, but we're afraid
To rouse her rhodomontade !

*Although Sullivan set this quartet it was never performed.

LUD. This complication great —
It is my fault, because
I'm not, mayhap,
As clever a chap
As I supposed I was ;
But nobody is, it seems to me,
As clever as he's supposed to be !

CHORUS (*dancing*). Now here we have, I'm glad to see,
A fact on which we all agree —
Nor we, nor he, nor she, nor ye
Are clever as we should be !

BARONESS. Now away to the wedding we go,
So summon the charioteers —
No kind of reluctance we show
To embark on our married careers.
Though Julia's emotion may flow
For the rest of her maidenly years,
To the wedding we eagerly go,
So summon the charioteers !

CHORUS. Now away, &c.

(*All dance off to wedding except* JULIA.)

RECIT.— JULIA.

So ends my dream — so fades my vision fair !
Of hope no gleam — distraction and despair !
My cherished dreams, the Ducal throne to share,
That aim supreme has vanished into air !

SONG.— JULIA.

Broken every promise plighted —
All is darksome — all is dreary.
Every new-born hope is blighted !
Sad and sorry — weak and weary !
Death the Friend or Death the Foe,
Shall I call upon thee? No !
I will go on living, though
Sad and sorry — weak and weary !
No, no ! Let the bygone go by !
No good ever came of repining :
If to-day there are clouds o'er the sky,
To-morrow the sun may be shining !
To-morrow, be kind,
To-morrow, to me !
With loyalty blind
I curtsy to thee !
To-day is a day of illusion and sorrow,
So *viva* To-morrow, To-morrow, To-morrow !

God save you, To-morrow!
Your servant, To-morrow!
God save you, To-morrow, To-morrow, To-morrow!

[*Exit* JULIA.

Enter ERNEST.

ERN. It's of no use — I can't wait any longer. At any risk I must gratify my urgent desire to know what is going on. (*Looking off.*) Why, what's that? Surely I see a procession winding down the hill, dressed in my Troilus and Cressida costumes! That's Ludwig's doing! I see how it is — he found the time hang heavy on his hands, and is amusing himself by getting married to Elsa. No — it can't be to Elsa, for here she is!

Enter ELSA.

ELSA (*not seeing him*). I really cannot stand seeing my Ludwig married twice in one day to somebody else!

ERN. Elsa!

(ELSA *sees him, and stands as if transfixed with horror.*)

ERN. Come here — don't be a little fool — I want you.

(ELSA *suddenly turns and bolts off.*)

ERN. Why, what's the matter with the little donkey? One would think she saw a ghost! But if he's not marrying Elsa, whom *is* he marrying? (*Suddenly.*) Julia! (*Much overcome.*) I see it all! The scoundrel! He had to adopt all my responsibilities, and he's shabbily taken advantage of the situation to marry the girl I'm engaged to! But no, it can't be Julia, for here *she* is!

(*Enter* JULIA.)

JULIA (*not seeing him*). I've made up my mind. I won't stand it! I'll send in my notice at once!

ERN. Julia! Oh, what a relief!

(JULIA *gazes at him as if transfixed.*)

ERN. Then you've not married Ludwig? You are still true to me?

JULIA *turns and bolts in grotesque horror.* ERNEST *follows and stops her.*)

ERN. Don't run away! Listen to me. Are you all crazy?

JULIA (*in affected terror*). What would you with me, spectre? Oh, ain't his eyes sepulchral! And ain't his voice hollow! What are you doing out of your tomb at this time of day — apparition?

ERN. I do wish I could make you girls understand that I'm only technically dead, and that physically I'm as much alive as ever I was in my life!

JULIA. Oh, but it's an awful thing to be haunted by a technical bogie!

ERN. You won't be haunted much longer. The law must be on its last legs, and in a few hours I shall come to life again — resume all my social and civil functions, and claim my darling as my blushing bride!

JULIA. Oh — then you haven't heard?

ERN. My love, I've heard nothing. How could I? There are no daily papers where I come from.

JULIA. Why, Ludwig challenged Wilhelm and won, and now *he's* Grand Duke, and he's revived the law for another century!

ERN. What! But you're not serious — you're only joking!

JULIA. My good sir, I'm a light-hearted girl, but I don't chaff bogies.

ERN. Well, that's the meanest trick I ever heard of!

JULIA. Shabby trick, *I* call it.

ERN. But you don't mean to say that you're going to cry off!

JULIA. I really can't afford to wait until your time is up. You know, I've always set my face against long engagements.

ERN. Then defy the law and marry me now. We will fly to your native country, and I'll play broken-English in London as you play broken-German here!

JULIA. No. These legal technicalities cannot be defied. Situated as you are, you have no power to make me your wife. At best you could only make me your widow.

ERN. Then be my widow — my little, dainty, winning, winsome widow!

JULIA. Now what would be the good of that? Why, you goose. I should marry again within a month!

DUET. — ERNEST *and* JULIA.

ERN.

> If the light of love's lingering ember
>   Has faded in gloom,
> You cannot neglect, O remember,
>   A voice from the tomb!
> That stern supernatural diction
> Should act as a solemn restriction,
> Although by a mere legal fiction
>   A voice from the tomb!

JULIA (*in affected terror*).

> I own that that utterance chills me —
>   It withers my bloom!
> With awful emotion it thrills me —
>   That voice from the tomb!
> Oh, spectre, won't anything lay thee?
> Though pained to deny or gainsay thee,
> In this case I cannot obey thee,
>   Thou voice from the tomb!

42

Because, you see, I shouldn't be your wife in stern reality —. *

ERN.   Some truth in that lies hid, O !
         Some truth in that lies hid, O !

JULIA. A spectre don't indulge in matrimonial conjugality —

ERN.   I never said he did, O !
         I never said he did, O !

JULIA. To use a common form of speech, a well-worn technicality —
         On you has dropped the *rideau* —
         On you has dropped the *rideau* —
         And at the best I should become that emblem of mortality
         A broken-hearted widow —
         A broken-hearted widow !
(*dancing*).   So, spectre appalling,
             I bid you good-day —
         Perhaps you'll be calling
             When passing this way.
         Your bogydom scorning,
         And all your love-lorning,
         I bid you good-morning,
             I bid you good-day.

ERN. (*furious*).   My offer recalling,
                 Your words I obey —
             Your fate is appalling,
                 And full of dismay.
             To pay for this scorning
             I give you fair warning
             I'll haunt you each morning,
                 Each night, and each day !

(*Repeat Ensemble, and exeunt in opposite directions.*)

Re-enter the Wedding Procession of LUDWIG *and* BARONESS,
dancing.

CHORUS,

Now bridegroom and bride let us toast
    In a magnum of merry champagne —
Let us make of this moment the most,
    We may not be so lucky again.
So drink to our sovereign host
    And his highly intelligent reign —
His health and his bride's let us toast
    In a magnum of merry champagne !

BRINDISI.— BARONESS.   †

Come, bumpers — aye, ever-so-many —
    And then, if you will, many more !
This wine doesn't cost us a penny,
    Though its Pommery, Seventy-four !

*These twelve lines in the middle of this duet were never performed.
†The 'Drinking Song' was cut shortly after the opening. The music was printed in the vocal score.

Old wine is a true panacea
    For every conceivable ill,
When you cherish the soothing idea
    That somebody else pays the bill!
Old wine is a pleasure that's hollow
    When at your own table you sit,
For you're thinking each mouthful you swallow
    Has cost you a threepenny bit!

CHORUS.   So bumpers — aye, ever-so-many —
        And then, if you will, many more!
    This wine doesn't cost us a penny,
        Though it's Pomméry, Seventy-four!

I once gave an evening party
    (A sandwich and cut-orange ball),
But my guests had such appetites hearty,
    That I couldn't enjoy it at all!
I made a heroic endeavour
    To look unconcerned, but in vain,
And I vowed that I never — oh never —
    Would ask anybody again!
But there s a distinction decided —
    A difference truly immense —
When the wine that you drink is provided
    At somebody else's expense.

CHORUS.   So bumpers — aye, ever-so-many —
        The cost we may safely ignore!
    For the wine doesn't cost us a penny,
        Though it's Pomméry, Seventy-four!

                    [*Exit* BARONESS.
        (*March heard.*)

LUD. (*recit.*).   Why, who is this approaching,
        Upon our joy encroaching?
        Some rascal come a-poaching
        Who's heard that wine we're broaching?

ALL.   Who may this be?
              Who may this be?
       Who is he? Who is he? Who is he?

        (*Enter* HERALD.)

HER.   The Prince of Monte Car*lo*,
        From Mediterranean water,
        Has come here to bestow
            On you his beautiful daughter.
        They've paid off all they owe,
            As every statesman oughter —
        That Prince of Monte Car*lo*
            And his be-eutiful daughter!

CHORUS.   The Prince of Monte Carlo, &c.

Jones Hewson as the Herald who woke up the audience on opening night with his unexpectedly successful song 'The Prince of Monte Carlo'. Note the playing-card motif in his costume.

Scott Fishe as The Prince of Monte Carlo.

44

HER.   The Prince of Monte Car*lo*,
              Who is so very partickler,
         Has heard that you're also
              For ceremony a stickler —
         Therefore he lets you know
              By word of mouth auric'lar —
         (That Prince of Monte Car*lo*
              Who is so very particklar) —

CHORUS.   The Prince of Monte Carlo, &c.

HER.   That Prince of Monte Car*lo*,
              From Mediterranean water,
         Has come here to bestow
              On you his be-eutiful daughter!

LUD. (*recit.*).   His Highness we know not — nor the locality
                    In which is situate his Principality;
                    But, as he guesses by some odd fatality,
                    This *is* the shop for cut and dried formality!
                         Let him appear —
                         He'll find that we're
                    Remarkable for cut and dried formality,

(*Reprise of March. Exit* HERALD.   LUDWIG *beckons his Court.*)

LUD.   I have a plan — I'll tell you all the plot of it —
         He wants formality — he shall have a lot of it!
                    (*Whispers to them through symphony.*)
         Conceal yourselves, and when I give the cue
         Spring out on him — you all know what to do!

(*All conceal themselves behind the draperies that enclose the stage.*)

   Pompous March. Enter the PRINCE *and* PRINCESS OF MONTE
      CARLO, *attended by six theatrical-looking nobles and the
      Court Costumier.*

               DUET.— PRINCE *and* PRINCESS.

PRINCE.   We're rigged out in magnificent array
               (Our own clothes are much gloomier)
          In costumes which we've hired by the day
               From a very well-known costumier.

COST. (*bowing*). *I* am the well-known costumier.

PRINCESS. With a brilliant staff a Prince should make a show
                (It's a rule that never varies),
           So we've engaged from the Theatre Monaco
                Six supernumeraries.

NOBLES (*bowing*). We're the supernumeraries.

ALL.   At a salary immense,
                     Quite regardless of expense,
                  Six supernumeraries!

PRINCE.   They do not speak, for they break our grammar's laws,
              And their language is lamentable —

45

And they never take off their gloves, because
Their nails are not presentable.

NOBLES. Our nails are not presentable!

PRINCESS. To account for these shortcomings manifest
We explain, in a whisper bated,
They are wealthy members of the brewing interest
To the Peerage elevated.

NOBLES. To the Peerage elevated.

ALL. $\begin{Bmatrix} \text{They're} \\ \text{We're} \end{Bmatrix}$ very, very rich
And accordingly, as sich,
To the Peerage elevated.

PRINCE. Well, my dear, here we are at last — just in time to compel Duke Wilhelm to fulfil the terms of his marriage contract. Another hour and we should have been too late.

PRINCESS. Yes, papa, and if you hadn't fortunately discovered a means of making an income by honest industry, we should never have got here at all.

PRINCE. Very true. Confined for the last two years within the precincts of my palace by an obdurate bootmaker who held a warrant for my arrest, I devoted my enforced leisure to a study of the doctrine of chances — mainly with the view of ascertaining whether there was the remotest chance of my ever going out for a walk again — and this led to the discovery of a singularly fascinating little round game which I have called Roulette, and by which, in one sitting, I won no less than five thousand francs! My first act was to pay my bootmaker — my second, to engage a good useful working set of second-hand nobles — and my third, to hurry you off to Hesse Halbpfennig as fast as a *train de luxe* could carry us!

PRINCESS. Yes, and a pretty job-lot of second-hand nobles you've scraped together!

PRINCE (*doubtfully*). Pretty, you think? Humph! I don't know. I should say tol-lol, my love — only fol-lol. They are not wholly satisfactory. There is a certain air of unreality about them — they are not convincing.

COST. But, my goot friend, vhat can you expect for eighteen-pence a day!

PRINCE. Now take this Peer, for instance. What the deuce do you call *him*?

COST. Him? Oh, he's a swell — he's the Duke of Riviera.

PRINCE. Oh, he's a Duke, is he? Well, that's no reason why he should look so confoundedly haughty. (*To Noble.*) Be affable, sir! (*Noble takes attitude of affability.*) That's better. Now (*passing to another*) here's a nobleman's coat all in holes!

COST. (*to Noble*). Vhat a careless chap you are! Vhy don't you take care of the clo's? These cost money, these do! D'ye think I stole 'em?

Charles H. Workman, who eventually played the Grossmith parts, in his Gilbert and Sullivan début in the small role of Ben Hashbaz.

46

PRINCE. It's not the poor devil's fault—it's yours. I don't wish you to end our House of Peers, but you might at least mend them. (*Passing to another.*) Now, who's this with his moustache coming off!

COST. Why, you're Viscount Mentone, ain't you?

NOBLE. Blest if I know. (*Turning up sword belt.*) It's wrote here—yes, Viscount Mentone.

COST. Then why don't you say so? 'Old yerself up—you ain't carryin' sandwich boards now. (*Adjusts his moustache and hat—a handkerchief falls out.*)

PRINCE. And we may be permitted to hint to the Noble Viscount, in the most delicate manner imaginable, that it is not the practice among the higher nobility to carry their handkerchiefs in their hats.

NOBLE. I ain't got no pockets.

PRINCE. Then tuck it in here. (*Sticks it in his breast.*) Now,   6 once for all, you Peers—don't allow your heads to be turned by family pride. Try to assume the gracious condescension of noblemen whose aristocratic position is so assured that they can afford so far to derogate from their dignity as to treat persons of the upper middle-classes with easy but exquisitely well-bred affability. Now, try that. (*All assume grotesque attitudes of affability.*) Not a bit like it! I give it up!

PRINCESS. But, papa, where in the world is the Grand Duke?

PRINCE. Well, my love, you must remember that we have taken Duke Wilhelm somewhat by surprise. These small German potentates are famous for their scrupulous adherence to ceremonial observances, and it may be that the etiquette of this Court demands that we should be received with a certain elaboration of processional pomp—which Wilhelm may, at this moment, be preparing.

PRINCESS. I can't help feeling that he wants to get out of it. First of all you implored him to come to Monte Carlo and marry me there, and he refused on account of the expense. Then you implored him to advance us the money to enable us to go to him—and again he refused, on account of the expense. He's a miserly little wretch—that's what he is.

PRINCE. Well, I shouldn't go so far as to say that. I should rather describe him as an enthusiastic collector of coins—of the realm—and we must not be too hard upon a numismatist if he feels a certain disinclination to part with some of his really very valuable specimens. It's a pretty hobby: I've often thought I should like to collect some coins myself.

PRINCESS. Oh, papa, I'm sure there's somebody behind that curtain. I saw it move!

PRINCE. Then no doubt they're coming. Now pray bear in mind that these insignificant Grand Dukes are tremendous sticklers for forms and ceremonies, so watch them very carefully, and take

6. Much of the dialogue on the balance of this page was 'pruned' after the opening. But this speech was deemed so offensive that it was emasculated *before* the opening. For the more gentle version, as rewritten by Gilbert, see Appendix, no. 6.

47

your cue from them. Do as they do, and you can't go wrong. And you nobles — confound you! — do try to be equal to the occasion. (*To* COSTUMIER.) Can't you stick that aristocrat's moustache on?

COST. (*to* NOBLE). Oh, you silly gommy! Vhere's your spirit gum? (*Sticks his moustache on.*)

PRINCE. Now mind — easy affability combined with a sense of what is due to your exalted ranks, or I'll fine you half a franc all round. That's better, but it's not right. Never mind. Now then. (*All take affable attitudes.*)

> *Gong. The curtains that enclose the stage are withdrawn, and* LUDWIG *and all his Court rush on with a wild "Halloo!" and dance around the* PRINCE *and* PRINCESS. *At first they are staggered by this reception, but eventually, supposing it to be a Court ceremonial, they and the Nobles lend themselves to the situation and join in the wild dance,* LUDWIG *and the* PRINCESS *being especially conspicuous.*

LUD. Now that that's over, perhaps you'll be good enough to tell me what you want with me. Who are these Twelfth Night Characters?   7

PRINCE. They represent the Chivalry of the Riviera. All that is best and bravest in that favoured region. They are, in short, my suite. But pardon me — am I addressing the Grand Duke?

LUD. You enjoy that distinction, sir!

PRINCE (*to* PRINCESS). This is he! The cynosure of our hopes! Bless my soul, how he has grown!

PRINCESS. Oh, papa, I'm all of a tetter!

PRINCE (*to* LUDWIG). Prepare for a delightful surprise! I am the Prince of Monte Carlo! (LUDWIG *looks puzzled.*) Doesn't that convey an idea to your mind?

LUD. Nothing definite.

PRINCE. Never mind — try again. This is my daughter, Jacintha. Do you take?

LUD. (*still puzzled*). No — not yet. Go on — don't give it up — I daresay it will come presently.

PRINCE. Very odd — never mind — try again. (*With sly significance.*) Twenty years ago! Little doddle doddle! *Two* little doddle doddles! Happy father — hers and yours. Proud mother — yours and hers! Hah! *Now* you take? I see you do! I see you do!

LUD. Nothing is more annoying than to feel that you're not equal to the intellectual pressure of the conversation. I wish he'd say something intelligible.

PRINCE. You didn't expect me?

LUD. (*jumping at it*). No, no. I grasp that — thank you very much. (*Shaking hands with him.*) No, I did *not* expect you!

7. This dialogue was considerably rewritten before the opening. See Appendix, no. 7.

48

PRINCE. I thought not. But ha! ha! at last I have escaped from my enforced restraint. (*General movement of alarm.*)

LUD. *That* I also grasp. That is self-evident. Come, we're getting on!

PRINCE (*to crowd who are stealing off in alarm*). No, no — you misunderstand me. I mean I've paid my debts! And how d'you think I did it? (*All try to guess.*) You'll never guess it. Through the medium of Roulette!

ALL. Roulette?

LUD. Now you're getting obscure again. The lucid interval has expired.

PRINCE. I'll explain. It's an invention of my own — the simplest thing in the world — and what is most remarkable, it comes just in time to supply a distinct and long-felt want! I'll tell you all about it.

(*Nobles bring forward a double roulette table, which they unfold.*)

SONG.— PRINCE.   *

> Take my advice — when deep in debt
> Set up a bank and play Roulette!
> At once distrust you surely lull,
> And rook the pigeon and the gull.
> The bird will stake his every franc
> In wild attempt to break the bank —
> But you may stake your life and limb
> The bank will end by breaking him!

(*All crowd round and eagerly stake gold on the board.*)

> *Allons, encore —*
>   *Garçons, fillettes —*
> *Vos louis d'or —*
>   *Vos roux d'charette!*
>   *Hola! hola!*
> *Mais faites vos jeux —*
>   *Allons, la classe —*
>   *Le temps se passe —*
>   *La banque se casse —*
> *Rien n'va plus! Rien n'va plus! Rien n'va plus!*
> *Le dix-sept noir, impair et manque!*
> *Hola! hola! vive la banque!*
> For every time the board you spin,
> Be sure the bank is bound to win!

CHORUS.   For every time, &c.

(*During Chorus, PRINCE rakes-in all the stakes.*)

PRINCE.   A cosmic game is this Roulette!
      The little ball's a true coquette —
      A maiden coy whom "numbers" woo —

*'The Roulette Song' was cut shortly after the opening. The music was printed in the vocal score.

49

Whom six-and-thirty suitors sue !
Of all complexions, too, good lack !
For some are red and some are black,
And some must be extremely green,
For half of them are not nineteen !

(*All stake again.*)

Allons, encore —
  Garçons, fillettes —
Vos louis d'or —
  Vos roux d'charette !
   Hola ! hola !
Mais faites vos jeux —
  Allons, la foule !
  Ca roule — ça roule —
  Le temps s'écoule —
Rien n'va plus ! Rien n'va plus ! Rien n'va plus !
Le trente-cinq rouge — impair et passe !
Très-bien, étudiants de la classe —
The moral's safe — when you begin
Be sure the bank is bound to win !

CHORUS.   The moral's safe, &c.

(PRINCE *rakes-in all the stakes.*)

PRINCE.   The little ball's a flirt inbred —
She flirts with black — she flirts with red ;
From this to that she hops about,
Then back to this as if in doubt.
To call her thoughtless were unkind —
The child is making up her mind,
For all the world like all the rest,
Which *prétendant* will pay the best !

  Allons, encore —
    Garçons, fillettes —
  Vos louis d'or —
    Vos roux d'charette !
     Hola ! hola !
  Mais faites vos jeux —
    Qui perte fit
    Au temps jadis
    Gagne aujourd'hui !
Rien n'va plus ! Rien n'va plus ! Rien n'va plus !
Tra, la, la, la ! le double zéro !
Vous perdez tout, mes nobles héros —
Where'er at last the ball pops in,
Be sure the bank is bound to win !

CHORUS.   *Tra, la, la, la ! le double zéro, &c.*

(*Prince gathers in the stakes. Nobles fold up table and take it
   away.*)

LUD.   Capital game.— Haven't a penny left !

50

PRINCE. Pretty toy, isn't it? Have another turn?

LUD. Thanks, no. I should only be robbing you.

PRINCESS (*affectionately*). Do, dearest Wilhelm — it's such fun!

LUD. Wilhelm? Go away — whisht! I'm not Wilhelm. I'm another guess sort of Grand Duke altogether!

PRINCE (*astonished*). Another guess sort of Grand Duke!

PRINCESS. This comes of not asking the way. We've mistaken the turning and got into the wrong Grand Duchy.

PRINCE. But — let us know where we are. Who the deuce is this gentleman?

ELSA. He's the gentleman I married yesterday —

JULIA. He's the gentleman I married this morning —

BARONESS. He's the gentleman I married this afternoon —

PRINCESS. Well, I'm sure! Papa, let's go away — this is not a respectable Court.

PRINCE. All these Grand Dukes have their little fancies, my love. This Potentate appears to be collecting wives. It's a pretty hobby — I should like to collect a few myself. This (*admiring* BARONESS) is a charming specimen — an antique, I should say — of the early Merovingian period, if I'm not mistaken. (*To* LUDWIG.) Have you such a thing as a catalogue of the Museum?

PRINCESS. But this is getting serious. If this is not Wilhelm, the question is, where in the world is he?

LUD. No — the question is, where *out* of the world is he? And *that's* a very curious question, too!

PRINCE *and* PRINCESS. What do you mean?

LUD. (*pretending to weep*). The Grand Duke Wilhelm — died yesterday!

PRINCE *and* PRINCESS. What!

LUD. Quite suddenly — of — of — a cardiac affection.

ALL (*dancing wildly*).

> He had an appointment particular, very —
> You'll find him, I think, in the town cemetery
> And this is Court mourning — hey derry, down derry—
> Tol the rol lol, the rol lol the rol lay!

DUET.— PRINCE *and* PRINCESS.   8

PRINCESS (*weeping*). He was my maiden heart's first Prince!

PRINCE (*consoling her*). He was — you were but one. Though not so cold
> As natives of more Northern climes, I'm told,
> We don't begin before we're one year old —

PRINCESS. And though I've tried a many since —

8. This duet was deleted before the opening. For the dialogue that replaced it, see Appendix, no. 8.

51

PRINCE.   You have; that sort of thing is always done.
            A maiden, influenced by a Southern sun,
            Tries ever so many ere she's twenty-one —

PRINCESS. My heart reverts to him once more —

PRINCE.   Well, with the others you could hardly link —
            A toreador, two croupiers and (I think)
            A gentleman who kept a skating rink —

PRINCESS. To find my loved one's course is o'er !

PRINCE.   Yes, and a pretty penny I've to pay !
            Besides our travelling "exes" either way,
            These dresses stand me thirty francs a day !

PRINCE *to* LUDWIG (*recit.*).   How came about this catastrophe
                                    cruel ?

LUD. (*irritated*).   Once more, he fought a Statutory Duel,
            And I took over, as you may surmise,
            The Potentate's responsibilities.

PRINCESS (*struck by an idea*).   That Potentate's responsibilities ?
                            (*Throwing her arms round* LUDWIG.)
            My loved one !   (*All start.*)

LUD.   Another bride !   By the infernal powers,
            This is the fourth in four-and-twenty-hours !

ALL.   Hurrah !

TRIO.— BARONESS, JULIA, ELSA.   *

        Is this the law !
            Alack and well-a-day !
        With this last straw
            Three camels' backs give way !

QUINTETTE.— JULIA, BARONESS, ELSA, PRINCESS, LUDWIG.

JULIA (*to* PRINCESS).   You forward minx !

ELSA (*to* PRINCESS).   You painted jade !

BAR. (*to* PRINCESS).   You foreign sphinx !

PRINCESS (*to* BAR.).   You plain old maid !

JULIA (*to* PRINCESS).   You make too free !

BAR.   His hand resign !
            My husband he —

PRINCESS.   He's not — he's mine !

(*To* LUDWIG).   Now aren't you mine ?

ELSA (*to* LUDWIG).   Now aren't you mine ?

JULIA (*to* LUDWIG).   Now aren't you mine ?

BAR. (*to* LUDWIG).   Now aren't you mine ?

*This short Trio, and the Quintet which followed, were both deleted before the opening.

52

LUD.	Oh, don't ask me to solve the doubt — Among yourselves please fight it out — There's lot of time — away you go! And when you've settled, let me know?
ALL.	*We'll* let you know!
JULIA (*to* PRINCESS).	*I'll* let you know!
ELSA (*to* PRINCESS).	*I'll* let you know!
BAR. (*to* PRINCESS).	*I'll* let you know!
PRINCESS (*to* BAR.).	I'll let *you* know!
JULIA.	You forward minx!
ELSA.	You painted jade!
BARONESS.	You foreign sphinx!
PRINCESS.	You plain old maid!
JULIA.	You make too free,
BARONESS.	His hand resign! My husband he —
PRINCESS.	Get out, he's mine!

(*During this they struggle for* LUDWIG. *Finally* PRINCESS *secures him.*)

Hurrah, he's mine!
Hurrah, he's mine!
Hurrah, he's mine!

ALL.   Hurrah!   Hurrah!   Hurrah!

ENSEMBLE.

PRINCESS *and* LUDWIG *and* CHORUS.	PRINCE.	BARONESS, JULIA, ELSA.
It is the law — This is {her/my} wedding day — Ye thence withdraw — To nuptial joys away!	It is the law — This is her wedding day As I foresaw — To nuptial joys away!	Is this the law? Alack and well-a-day! With this last straw The camel's back gives way.

They are about to dance off to marry LUDWIG *to* PRINCESS *when they are arrested by the sudden appearance of* WILHELM, ERNEST *and* NOTARY.

RECITATIVE.

WIL., ERN., *and* NOT.	Forbear! This may not be! Frustrated are your plans! With paramount decree The Law forbids the banns!
LUD.	Why, what is this and who are these Who thus intrude — these varlets seize! *

*The following eight lines of verse were deleted before the opening.

THE GRAND DUKE

53

WIL., ERN., *and* NOT.   The Law —
ALL.   Which we regard with awe —
WIL., ERN., *and* NOT.   Forbids —
ALL.   We're her obedient kids —
WIL., ERN., *and* NOT.   The banns!
ALL.   Then this frustrates our plans!

SONG.— WILHELM.   *

(*furiously*) Well, you're a pretty kind of fellow, thus my life to
          shatter, O!
My little store of gold and silver recklessly you scatter, O!
You guzzle and you gormandize all day with cup and platter, O!
And eat my food and drink my wine — especially the latter, O!

ALL.   The latter, O!
                  The latter, O!
          Especially the latter, O!

WIL.   But when compared with other crimes, for which your
          head I'll batter, O!
                  This flibberty gibberty
                  Kind of a liberty
          Scarcely seems to matter, O!

My dainty bride — my bride elect — you wheedle and you flatter, O!
With coarse and clumsy compliment her senses you bespatter, O!
You fascinate her tough old heart with vain and vulgar patter, O!
Although — the deuce confound you! — you're unworthy to look at
     her, O!

ALL.   Look at her, O!
                  Look at her, O!
          Unworthy to look at her, O!

WIL.   But even this, compared with deeds that drive me mad
          as hatter, O!
                  This flibberty gibberty
                  Kind of a liberty
          Scarcely seems to matter, O!

For O, you vulgar vagabond, you fount of idle chatter, O!
You've done a deed on which I vow you won't get any fatter, O!
You fancy you've revived the Law — mere empty brag and clatter, O!
You can't — you shan't — you don't — you won't — you thing of rag
     and tatter, O!

ALL.   Of tatter, O!
                  Of tatter, O!
          You thing of rag and tatter, O!

WIL.   For this you'll suffer agonies like rat in clutch of
          ratter, O!

*The Grand Duke's patter song was cut shortly after the opening. The music was printed
in the vocal score.

277

54

This flibberty gibberty
Kind of a liberty
's quite another matter, O!

ALL.   This flibberty gibberty
Kind of a liberty
's quite another matter, O!

(WILHELM *sinks exhausted into* NOTARY'S *arms.*)

LUD. My good sir, it's no use your saying that I can't revive the Law, in face of the fact that I *have* revived it.

WIL. You didn't revive it! You couldn't revive it! You — you are an impostor, sir — a tuppenny rogue, sir! You — you never were, and in all human probability never will be — Grand Duke of Hesse Anything!

ALL. What!!!

WIL. Never — never, never! (*Aside.*) Oh, my internal economy!

LUD. That's absurd, you know. I fought the Grand Duke. He drew a King, and I drew an Ace. He perished in inconceivable agonies on the spot. Now, as that's settled, we'll go on with the wedding.

WIL. It — it isn't settled. You — you can't. I — I (*to* NOTARY) Oh, tell him — tell him! I can't!

NOT. Well, the fact is, there's been a little mistake here. On reference to the Act that regulates Statutory Duels, I find it is expressly laid down that Ace shall count invariably as lowest.

ALL. As lowest!

WIL. (*breathlessly*). As lowest — lowest — lowest! So *you're* the ghoest — ghoest — ghoest! (*Aside.*) Oh, what *is* the matter with me inside here!

JULIA (*to* NOTARY). Well, you've made a nice mess of this!   *

LUD. I don't want to say anything actionable, but of all the muddle-headed solicitors —

NOT. Sir, I can't recognize you. You are defunct, and have no legal status. If you've anything to say, address me through your executors.

ERN. Well, Julia, as it seems that the law hasn't been revived — and as, consequently, I shall come to life in about three minutes — (*consulting his watch*) —

JULIA. My objection falls to the ground. (*Resignedly.*) Very †
well. But will you promise to give me some strong scenes of justifiable jealousy?

ERN. Justifiable jealousy! My love, I couldn't do it!

JULIA. Then I won't play.

ERN. Well, well, I'll do my best! · (*They retire up together.*)

*This and the next three lines were cut prior to opening.
†The reference to 'justifiable jealousy' and the next three lines were cut after the opening.

55

LUD. And am I to understand that, all this time, I've been a dead man without knowing it?

BAR. And that I married a dead man without knowing it?

PRINCESS. And that I was on the point of marrying a dead man without knowing it? (*To* WILHELM, *who revives.*) Oh, my love, what a narrow escape I've had!

WIL. Oh — you are the Princess of Monte Carlo. I should never have recognized you. Well, you're an attractive little girl, you know, but you're as poor as a rat!

PRINCE. Pardon me — there you mistake. Accept her dowry — with a father's blessing! (*Gives him a small Roulette board, then flirts with* BARONESS.)   *

WIL. Why, what do you call this?

PRINCESS. It's my little Wheel of Fortune. I'll tell you all about it. (*They retire up, conversing.*)

ELSA. That's all very well, but what is to become of *me?* (*To* LUDWIG.) If you're a dead man —

LUD. But I'm not. Time's up — the Act has expired — I've come to life — the parson is still in attendance, and we'll all be married directly.

ALL. Hurrah!

FINALE.   9

---

*The references to Roulette were eliminated after the opening when the 'Roulette Song' (p. 272) was cut.

9. The Finale was not printed in this version of the libretto because it was not written until late in the rehearsal period. The Finale which was adopted is printed in Appendix, no. 9.

Appendix

The Grand Duke

THE major passages which were altered in rehearsal are reproduced here in their *final* form. The numbers by which the passages are listed correspond to the footnotes in the preceding libretto, indicating the points in the opera at which the changes were made.

1   These stanzas replaced Gilbert's original 'offensive' entrance chorus for the Chamberlains.

CHORUS OF CHAMBERLAINS

The good Grand Duke of Pfennig Halbpfennig,
Though, in his own opinion, very very big,
In point of fact he's nothing but a miserable prig,
Is the good Grand Duke of Pfennig Halbpfennig.

Though quite contemptible, as everyone agrees,
We must dissemble if we want our bread and cheese,
So hail him in a chorus, with enthusiasm big,
The good Grand Duke of Pfennig Halbpfennig!

2   The final version of Rudolph's song is as follows:

SONG. – RUDOLPH.

When you find you're a broken down critter,
Who is all of a trimmle and twitter,
With your palate unpleasantly bitter,
    As if you'd just bitten a pill –
When you're legs are as thin as dividers
And you're plagued with unruly insiders,
And your spine is all creepy with spiders,
    And you're highly gamboge in the gill –

When you've got a beehive in your head,
  And a sewing machine in each ear,
And you feel that you've eaten your bed,
  And you've got a bad headache *down here* –
    When such facts are about,
      And these symptoms you find
        In your body or crown –
    Well you'd better look out,
      You may make up your mind
      You had better lie down!

When your lips are all smeary – like tallow,
And your tongue is decidedly yallow,
With a pint of warm oil in your sw*a*llow,
  And a pound of tin-tacks in your chest –
When you're down in the mouth with the vapours,
And all over your new Morris papers
Black-beetles are cutting their capers,
  And crawly things never at rest –
When you doubt if your head is your own,
  And you jump when an open door slams –
Then you've got to a state which is known
  To the medical world as 'jim-jams.'
    If such symptoms you find
      In your body or head,
        They're not easy to quell –
    You may make up your mind
    You are better in bed,
      For you're not at all well!

3   This chorus was written to follow the Grand Duke's exit.

CHORUS.   Give thanks, give thanks to wayward fate –
     By mystic fortune's sway,
   Our Ludwig guides the helm of State
     For one delightful day!

    We hail you, sir!
      We greet you, sir!
    Regale you, sir!
      We treat you, sir!
       Our ruler be
        By fate's decree
   For one delightful day!

4   This verse for Lisa was written prior to opening.

SONG. – LISA.

The die is cast,
My hope has perished!
Farewell, O past,
Too bright to last,
Yet fondly cherished!
My light has fled,
My hope is dead,
Its doom is spoken –
My day is night,
My wrong is right
In all men's sight –
My heart is broken!

5   Just before opening Gilbert put an extra verse about the Second Act costumes into the First Act Finale.

JULIA.   But stay – your new-made Court
Without a courtly coat is –
We shall require
Some court attire,
And at a moment's notice.
In clothes of common sort
Your courtiers must not grovel –
Your new *noblesse*
Should have a dress
Original and novel!

LUDWIG.   Old Athens we'll exhume!
The necessary dresses,
Correct and true
And all brand-new
The company possesses:
Henceforth our Court costume
Shall live in song and story,
For we'll upraise
The dead old days
Of Athens in her glory!

6   Gilbert toned down his speech about the aristocracy. The expurgated line reads as follows:

PRINCE.   Now, once and for all you Peers – when His Highness arrives, don't stand like sticks, but appear to take an intelligent and sympathetic interest in

282

what is going on. You needn't say anything, but let your gestures be in accordance with the spirit of the conversation. Now take the word from me. Affability! (*attitude*). Submission! (*attitude*). Surprise! (*attitude*). Shame! (*attitude*). Grief! (*attitude*). Joy! (*attitude*). That's better! You can do it if you like!

7　The dialogue following the Wild Dance for the Prince and Princess of Monte Carlo was replaced by the following lines prior to the opening:

LUDWIG.　There, what do you think of that? That's our official ceremonial for the reception of visitors of the very highest distinction.

PRINCE.　(*puzzled*). It's very quaint – very curious indeed. Prettily footed, too. Prettily footed.

LUDWIG.　Would you like to see how we say 'good-bye' to visitors of distinction? That ceremony is also performed with the foot.

PRINCE.　Really, this tone – oh, but perhaps you have not completely grasped the situation?

LUDWIG.　Not altogether.

PRINCE.　Ah, then I'll give you a lead over. (*Significantly*). I am the father of the Princess of Monte Carlo. Doesn't that convey any idea to the Grand Ducal mind?

LUDWIG.　(*stolidly*). Nothing definite.

PRINCE.　(*aside*). H'm – very odd! Never mind – try again! (*Aloud*). This is the daughter of the Prince of Monte Carlo. Do you take?

LUDWIG.　(*still puzzled*). No – not yet. Go on – don't give it up – I daresay it will come presently.

8　This is the dialogue which Gilbert wrote to replace 'He Was My Maiden Heart's First Prince' and 'You Forward Minx.' These lines now directly precede the entrance of Rudolph, Ernest and the Notary.

LUDWIG.　Rudolph? Get along with you, I'm not Rudolph! Rudolph died yesterday!

PRINCE and PRINCESS.　What!

LUDWIG.　Quite suddenly of – of – a cardiac affection.

PRINCE and PRINCESS.　Of a cardiac affection?

LUDWIG.　Yes, a pack-of-cardiac affection. He fought a Statutory Duel with me and lost, and I took over all his engagements – including this imperfectly preserved old lady, to whom he has been engaged for the last three weeks.

PRINCESS.　Three weeks! But I've been engaged to him for the last twenty years!

BARONESS, LISA and JULIA.　Twenty years!

PRINCE.　(*aside*). It's all right, my love – they can't get over that. (*Aloud*). He's yours – take him, and hold him as tight as you can!

PRINCESS.　My own! (*Embracing Ludwig*).

LUDWIG.   Here's another! – the fourth in four-and-twenty hours! Would any-body else like to marry me? You, ma'am – or you – anybody! I'm getting used to it!

BARONESS.   But let me tell you, ma'am –

JULIA.   Why, you impudent little hussy –

LISA.   Oh, here's another – here's another ! (*Weeping*).

PRINCESS.   Poor ladies, I'm very sorry for you all; but, you see, I've a prior claim. Come, away we go – there's not a moment to be lost.

CHORUS (*as they dance towards exit*).
Away to the wedding we'll go
To summon the charioteers
Though her rival's emotion may flow
In the form of impetuous tears –

9   The Finale of *The Grand Duke* is as follows:

FINALE

Happy couples, lightly treading,
    Castle chapel will be quite full!
Each shall have a pretty wedding,
    As, of course, is only rightful,
    Though the bride be fair or frightful.
Contradiction little dreading,
    This will be a day delightful –
Each shall have a pretty wedding!
    Such a pretty, pretty wedding!
    Such a pretty wedding!

(*All dance off to get married as the curtain falls.*)

Bibliography

In addition to the primary sources acknowledged at the front of the book, the following works have been consulted:

Allen, Reginald, *The First Night Gilbert and Sullivan*, The Heritage Press, New York, 1958

Baily, Leslie, *The Gilbert and Sullivan Book*, Cassell and Co., London, 1952

Barrington, Rutland, *Rutland Barrington by Himself*, Grant Richards, London, 1908

Bond, Jessie, *The Life and Reminiscences of Jessie Bond*, John Lane, London, 1930

Cellier, François and Bridgemen, Cunningham, *Gilbert, Sullivan, and D'Oyly Carte*, Sir Isaac Pitman and Sons, London, 1914

Dark, Sidney and Grey, Rowland, *W. S. Gilbert, His Life and Letters*, Methuen and Co., London, 1923

Fitzgerald, Percy, *The Savoy Opera and the Savoyards*, Chatto and Windus, London, 1894

Fitz-Gerald, S. J. Adair, *The Story of the Savoy Opera*, Stanley Paul, London, 1924

Goldberg, Isaac, *The Story of Gilbert and Sullivan*, Crown Publishers, New York, 1935

Pearson, Hesketh, *Gilbert, His Life and Strife*, Methuen and Co., London, 1957

Philadelphia Savoy Opera Company, programme of *The Grand Duke*, 1938

Rollins, Cyril and Witts, R. John, *The D'Oyly Carte Opera Co. In Gilbert and Sullivan Operas*, Michael Joseph, London, 1962

Searle, Townley, *Sir William Schwenck Gilbert, a topsy turvy Adventure*, Alexander-Ousley, London, 1931

Strachey, Giles Lytton, *Queen Victoria*, Chatto and Windus, London, 1921

Sullivan, Herbert and Flower, Newman, *Sir Arthur Sullivan, His Life, Letters and Diaries*, Cassell and Co., London, 1927

Index

Index to Songs

The Grand Duke

Utopia, Limited